THE FORCE OF LAW

THE FORCE OF LAW

Frederick Schauer

Harvard University Press

Cambridge, Massachusetts
London, England
2015

Library of Congress Cataloging-in-Publication Data

Schauer, Frederick F., author.
  The force of law / Frederick Schauer.
      pages cm
  Includes bibliographical references and index.
  ISBN 978-0-674-36821-7 (alk. paper)
  1. Duress (Law)   2. Coercion.   I. Title.
  K579.D8S33 2015
  340'.1—dc23

                                    2014016093

for
Bobbie and Nikki,
who make me better

CONTENTS

PREFACE

This book was conceived as an intervention in debates within analytic jurisprudence, but it has outgrown its origins. The initial plan was to challenge an idea, predominant since H. L. A. Hart published his profoundly important *The Concept of Law* in 1961, that the very nature of law lies elsewhere than in its coercive capacity. Hart's target was the account first offered in depth by Jeremy Bentham in 1793 and then developed influentially by Bentham's disciple John Austin in lectures subsequently published in 1832 as *The Province of Jurisprudence Determined*. According to this account, the characteristic feature of law is the way in which it tells us what to do and threatens us with unpleasant consequences if we do not obey. But law can exist without coercion, Hart argued, and can be found whenever officials *internalize* a set of rules. That those rules are ordinarily backed by force may be an important fact about how law typically operates, Hart claimed, but is nevertheless largely beside the point as a philosophical or conceptual matter. For Hart, and even more for those who succeeded him, it is the systematic and structured internalization of rules that makes for law, and not the fact that law frequently supports those rules with the threat of force.

For reasons that will be summarized in Chapter 1 and developed in Chapters 2, 3, and 4, I question Hart's view and question whether force and coercion are as irrelevant to explaining the nature of law as perhaps Hart and certainly his legions of followers have assumed. But it has become apparent to me that the role of force in law cannot simply be relegated to one side of the debates within philosophical jurisprudence. Rather, the topic of legal force has sociological, psychological, political, and economic dimensions that go well beyond the conceptual and the philosophical. Grappling with these empirical dimensions of the legal system's pervasive coerciveness can help us to understand what law is, how it operates, and the role it plays in organizing society.

Understanding law as typically coercive is hardly a revelation. But there are reasons why Hart and his followers have downplayed this seemingly obvious feature of law. In particular, it is often claimed that many people obey the law just because it is the law and not because of what the law can do to them if they disobey. If this is true, and thus if unforced legal guidance is widespread, then legal coercion is best understood as the state's efforts to control its minority of disobedient outliers rather than explaining what law means and does for the majority of the population. But the claim that there is widespread following of the law just because it is the law may well be false—false for ordinary citizens and, perhaps surprisingly, even more false for officials. Explaining and documenting these conclusions make up a large part of this book. For if neither citizens nor officials are much inclined to obey the law when what law commands clashes with what they would have done on law-independent grounds, the necessity of coercion becomes apparent. One way of understanding the motivation of this book, therefore, is as attempting to account for what seems to be an obviously important fact about the world: law is commonly and valuably coercive. We could say, with much of the contemporary jurisprudential community, that the pervasive fact of law's coerciveness is not really that important, or at least not that jurisprudentially important. Or we could, preferably in my view, try to explain why the face of law that seems so important to ordinary citizens, to officials, and to nonjurisprudential commentators has become and is so important. Taking on that latter task, in numerous dimensions and from numerous angles, is the principal goal of this book.

That a feature of law that is so important and salient to almost everyone except legal philosophers is so marginal to the jurisprudential enterprise says something about the enterprise of philosophy of law—jurisprudence—itself. And thus a running subtext of this book is a challenge to a prevalent mode of jurisprudential inquiry. For most contemporary practitioners of jurisprudence, the principal or even exclusive task of their enterprise is to identify the *essential* properties of law, the properties without which it would not be law, and the properties that define law in all possible legal systems in all possible worlds. But that understanding of the jurisprudential enterprise rests on what is at least a highly contested and quite possibly a mistaken view of the nature of our concepts and categories, and of the nature of many of the phenomena—

including law—to which those concepts and categories are connected. In stressing the importance of coercion to law as it exists and as it is experienced, while still not insisting that coercion is an essential feature of every law or even every imaginable legal system, I challenge the methods of modern jurisprudence as well as one of its important conclusions. The two goals are linked in this book, but the reader should keep in mind that these are two distinct goals and not one.

I labor under the disability of the old-fashioned view that books should be written as books and that most books that are collections of previously published articles read like collections of previously published articles. But although this book has been written as a book from beginning to end, I have benefited from the opportunity to speak and write about the coercive dimensions of law on numerous occasions, and thus to refine my ideas in response to oral and published criticism. So although some of the ideas I offer here have been the subject of earlier articles in the *Canadian Journal of Philosophy, Ratio Juris,* the *Canadian Journal of Law and Jurisprudence,* the *Yale Law Journal,* and *Archiv für Rechts- und Sozialphilosophie,* of two lectures to the Jurisprudence Discussion Group at the University of Oxford, and of four subsequently published named lectures—the MacCormick Lecture at the University of Arizona, the Sibley Lecture at the University of Georgia, the "Or" Emet Lecture at the Osgoode Hall Law School of York University, and the Julius Stone Lecture at the University of Sydney—there is no duplication of text or structure. In writing about this topic with different words and a different focus, I am comfortable in asserting that my thinking about legal coercion is now both substantially different from and more refined than it was on these earlier occasions. Whether the subsequent changes and refinements have been for the better is for the reader to decide.

Much of this book was completed while on sabbatical leave from the University of Virginia School of Law, an institution to which I am grateful not only for the leave but also, and more importantly, for many other forms of support, both tangible and intangible. The sabbatical year was spent at the Columbia Law School, whose faculty and staff were helpful in numerous ways. Larry Alexander, Charles Barzun, Brian Bix, Sarah Conly, Nicoletta Ladavac, Dan Ortiz, Veronica Rodriguez-Blanco, Kenneth Winston, and Adrian Vermeule provided detailed comments on the entire manuscript, and Kim Ferzan, John Gardner, Grant Lamond,

Margaret Martin, Rip Verkerke, and Sai Prakash on much of it, all taking valuable time from their own work to help me with mine. I am also grateful to audiences at Cornell University, the Hebrew University of Jerusalem, Melbourne University, the University of Oxford, the University of Toronto, Stockholm University, and the University of Virginia, each of which provided a valuable forum for honing the arguments in the final manuscript. And to the extent that this book has shorter sentences and longer references to empirical data than would otherwise have been the case, I am especially grateful to Bobbie Spellman, who read the entire manuscript with just the right mixture of appreciation and skepticism, and whose support in so many other ways cannot be thanked in any words that I have the ability to write.

A NOTE ABOUT THE NOTES

By the standards of contemporary jurisprudential writing, the notes that accompany the text are extensive. When H. L. A. Hart wrote *The Concept of Law,* jurisprudence was dominated by lengthy treatises providing exhaustive references and elaborate categorization but few aspirations to new insight. Hart consequently thought it useful to emphasize that he was not writing a book about other books. His references were sparse, and, unconventionally at the time for scholarly writing, tucked away at the back of the book. But whatever the merits or demerits of Hart's approach, it has been enthusiastically embraced by most of his successors, such that these days the typical book or article on legal philosophy contains a woefully small number of references to other works.

I reject this approach. Scholarship is a collective enterprise, and scholarly works with few references tend to exaggerate the novelty of the author's contributions, ignore the extent to which the work builds on what has been done by others, and provide scant assistance to the reader seeking informed guidance to other writings and the place of the instant work in the relevant scholarly environment. Accordingly, I believe it far better to provide too many references than too few. If these references can provide bibliographical assistance to the reader seeking pointers to other work, that will be a valuable service. If they can make clear that my contributions build on those of others and are situated within a larger community of scholarship and scholars, that will be more valuable still.

That said, I recognize that trying to read a book or article while constantly toggling between text and footnotes is a distracting annoyance. The text that follows thus uses endnotes rather than footnotes, but the text can be read with little loss without consulting the endnotes. And where the endnotes contain textual digressions and not simply references, the digressions are just that, with the reader being invited to read them apart from the text to determine whether what they say and where they say it might be of interest.

THE FORCE OF LAW

1

INTRODUCTION: THE FORCE OF LAW

1.1 The Ubiquity of Coercion

Law makes us do things we do not want to do. It has other functions as well, but perhaps the most visible aspect of law is its frequent insistence that we act in accordance with its wishes, our own personal interests or best judgment notwithstanding. The law demands that we pay taxes even when we have better uses for our money and think the taxes unwise. It requires us to obey traffic regulations even when the circumstances make them seem pointless. And at times the law conscripts us into military service, though we may believe the wars immoral, the dangers exaggerated, or the enemies imagined.

Law is hardly the only inhabitant of our normative universe. Morality makes demands upon our behavior as well, as do manners, etiquette, and countless social norms. But law, unlike morality and etiquette, possesses the resources to compel compliance in ways that other normative systems do not. It may be wrong to tell a lie or to clip one's fingernails in public, but disobeying these strictures often brings no sanctions whatsoever. And even when such behavior attracts the social penalties of disapproval, shaming, guilt, ostracism, and damage to reputation, the penalties are diffuse and unsystematic. By contrast, the law has sanctions at its disposal that are systematic, often severe, and highly salient. The legal system can put us in prison, take our money, and in some places even flog us and kill us. Moreover, when the law imposes such sanctions, it is commonly understood to be operating justifiably—that is, legitimately. Of course, the law is often subject to moral and political criticism when it imposes its sanctions unfairly, unwisely, imprudently, or immorally, but it remains widely accepted that law may ordinarily and legitimately use force to ensure compliance with its directives.[1]

1

That the law can force people to do things they do not want to do, and which are sometimes against their own interests or their own best (and not necessarily self-interested) judgment, might seem far too obvious to justify thinking or writing much about it. But here, as elsewhere, things are often not what they seem. For more than half a century, legal philosophers, drawing their inspiration from H. L. A. Hart,[2] have questioned whether force, coercion, and sanctions are as important to understanding the nature of law as the ordinary person—the man on the Clapham omnibus, as the English quaintly put it—believes. Leslie Green, for example, claims that a regime of "stark imperatives" that simply "bossed people around" or that employed a "price system" to "[structure] their incentives while leaving them free to act as they pleased" would not even count as a "system of law" at all.[3] Such efforts to marginalize the place of raw force in explaining what makes law distinctive follow on Hart's seemingly sound observation that law often empowers rather than coerces. It establishes the structures and even the very concepts by which people can create corporations, make wills, and, especially, form governments. Yet understanding law as being coercive when it operates in this manner seems odd. The law, after all, does not appear to care whether I make a will or not, and it certainly does not coerce me into making or not making one. But although the choice to make or not make a will is mine, it is the law that enables me to make a will in the first place. Without the law there simply would be no such thing as a will, just as without the rules and the institution of chess there would be no such thing as checkmate, or castling, and without the rules of bridge (or baseball) it would be conceptually impossible to bid, make, or hit a grand slam. Because some aspects of what clearly is law do not appear to be coercive in any straightforward sense of coercion, we can appreciate the distortion inherent in attempting to shoehorn all of law into the ideas of force or compulsion.

That law is often constitutive[4] and empowering rather than coercive is an important part of why Hart and his successors have denigrated an emphasis on coercion in attempting to understand the phenomenon of law. But even more important is the fact that it is possible, certainly in theory and occasionally in practice, to understand why people do things they do not want to do just because the law tells them they must do so but not because these commands come with a threat of force. People might, that is, follow the law just because it is the law but still without regard to what the law might do to them if they disobey. For example, in some countries—although decidedly not mine—pedestrians will stand obediently at "Don't Walk" signs even when there is nary a car or police officer in sight. In doing so, they appear to believe that the law should be followed even when it seems to direct unnecessary, unreasonable, or unwise behavior, and even when the law's sanctions are either absent or so deep in the background as to make their existence irrelevant. By the same token, governments and legal systems, which are themselves the source of the power to coerce citizens into lawful behavior, exist in the first place not because of force but because the governors have accepted—internalized—the rules establishing and circumscribing official power, and often appear to have done so independent of any fear of sanctions or other forms of coercion.

It thus appears that noncoercive law both can and does exist. But the question remains as to what we should make of this phenomenon. For some theorists, as exemplified by Green's quotation above, we should make a great deal of it. In the tradition that Hart is taken to have established, the fact of law's possible and occasional noncoerciveness is seen to be dispositive in characterizing the *nature* of law,[5] at least if we understand, as Hart's followers (but maybe not Hart himself[6]) have understood, the nature of something as involving its necessary or essential properties, the properties without which it would be something else.[7] So if the nature of law is the collection of law's essential properties in all possible legal systems in all possible worlds, and if there are things that are plainly law—like the law of wills and the obedient behavior of Finns when confronting a pointless command not to cross at a deserted intersection—but that appear not to be coercive, then coercion can no longer be considered essential to law. And if coercion is not essential to the very idea or concept of law, so the argument goes, then coercion loses its philosophical or theoretical interest in explaining the nature of law, regardless of coercion's obvious importance to sociologists, psychologists, and the man on the Clapham omnibus. Joseph Raz is clearest and bluntest on the point: "The sociology of law provides a wealth of detailed information and analysis of the functions of law in some particular societies. Legal philosophy has to be content with those few features which all legal systems necessarily possess."[8]

Yet there is a problem: the soundness of the foregoing conclusion depends on two premises whose own soundness is hardly self-evident. First, it assumes that the nature of something is best understood in terms of its necessary or essential features, or properties. But this is far from obvious.[9] The nature or essence of any concept or category might some-times, often, or always be a cluster of interrelated properties, none of which is individually necessary.[10] Or it may be that the concept, category, or institution of law, at least, has no essence, it being too diverse a collec-tion of phenomena to be captured or explained by one or more necessary properties. Yet even without attempting to resolve some of the deepest issues about language, concepts, and the categorial division of the world, it may still often be more valuable to focus on the typical rather than the necessary features or properties of some category or social phenomenon. Just as we can learn a great deal about birds from the typical but not necessary fact that birds fly and can understand important aspects of the history and chemistry of wine by focusing on the fact that wine is typi-cally but not necessarily made from grapes, so too might we learn a great deal about law in general, and not just the law in this or that legal system at this or that time, from law's typical but not necessary features.

Second, we should not too quickly accept that the domain of inquiry designated as "philosophical" should be limited to the search for essen-tial properties, even if all or some of our concepts do have such essential properties.[11] I have neither interest in nor standing to delineate or police the boundaries of the discipline we call "philosophy" or the subdiscipline designated as the "philosophy of law." Still, the various analytic and ar-gumentative tools of philosophy might well be deployed with profit to forms of understanding other than the largely nonempirical search for necessary (or, occasionally, necessary and sufficient) conditions that char-acterizes contemporary conceptual analysis. And in any event we ought not let the contingent and contested contemporary demarcations of the academic disciplines circumscribe the inquiry or get in the way of follow-ing that inquiry wherever it might lead.

Therefore, although the present examination of the role of coercion in explaining the character and distinctiveness of law will at times be phil-osophical or conceptual in style and method, it will, unashamedly, often break out of those boundaries defined by the discipline of philosophy or accepted, rather more narrowly, by many contemporary practitioners of the philosophy of law. Some of what follows will be sociological, in the broadest sense, and more than some will draw on experimental psycho-logical research. Some will draw on empirical and analytical conclusions from economics and political science. And none of what is to come will be a theory of law—or for that matter a theory of anything else. Oliver Wendell Holmes may have overstated the case against general theories when he said, "I care nothing for the systems—only the insights."[12] But at least in the case of law, we may historically, and especially recently, have lost too many insights by too insistent a pursuit of a single systematic unifying account—or theory, if you will. Law might simply be too diverse a social phenomenon to support a unifying theory with very much explanatory power. Or even if a theory of the essence of law, or only of its necessary properties, were possible, such theories might turn out to be so abstract as to leave too many interesting questions, including philosophical questions, about law, about laws, and about legal systems unanswered. This book is thus an exploration of various aspects of law's coercive dimension, pursued largely philosophically and analytically but with some empirical assistance. It is an account and not a theory. It is certainly not a system. But perhaps a mere account can have some value.

1.2 Obedience to Law

Telling people how to behave may not be all of law, but it seems at least a large part of it. And when law is in its commanding or prohibiting rather than empowering mode, it typically backs its commands and prohibitions with the credible threat of brute force or other sanctions in the event of noncompliance. The law tells us what to do, and it tells us that if we do not obey, then bad things will happen to us—perhaps jail, perhaps a monetary fine, perhaps something else unpleasant. The threat of painful or expensive sanctions in the event of disobedience appears to be a large part of how law operates and how it seeks to ensure compliance with its commands.

Lying behind the ubiquity of legal force is the assumption that without force, the law is often impotent. Compliance with the law may strike us as widespread when what the law commands happens to align with what people would do anyway, but when what law mandates diverges from what people would otherwise do or from what they otherwise believe to be right, the need for the threat of force becomes apparent. Perhaps if people always, or even usually, obeyed the law just because it was the law, their personal interests or not-necessarily-self-interested best judgment notwithstanding, law would have less need to use the raw power it commonly has at its disposal. But as we will explore below, especially in Chapters 5 and 6, that is not our world. In our world—and more in some parts of our world than in others—people generally do what they want to do or what they think it is right to do unless some external force makes them do otherwise. Law's coercive side thus emerges as a consequence of the less than perfect—just how much less remains to be seen—willingness of law's subjects to follow the law just because it is the law.

Framing the issue in terms of people's proclivities toward obedience to law exposes issues that are both conceptual and empirical. What exactly does it mean to follow or obey the law? Is following the law the same as obeying the law just because it is the law? Is every act that is in compliance with the law also an act of obedience to the law? Sorting out these matters is important, as it has been for generations. Indeed, if we look back to Socrates and his reasons for following a legal judgment to his own death even though he thought the judgment unjust, the issue has been with us even longer.[13] So we must engage in careful analysis, distinguishing obeying the law (or having a reason to obey the law) from acting consistently with or in compliance with the law and thus distinguishing having a reason to follow the law just because it is the law from engaging in the same behavior we would have engaged in even if no laws regulating it existed.[14] It is true, after all, that my practice of refraining from murder, rape, arson, and perhaps even insider trading puts me in compliance with the law, but the law is no part of my unwillingness to engage in these activities, and neither my behavior nor even any of my behavioral inclinations would change one whit were the laws prohibiting such acts to be repealed tomorrow.

Having delineated what it means to obey or follow the law, and thus for law to make a difference in our decisions and behavior, we will turn then to the empirical side, examining whether people really do obey the law just because it is the law. And if there are people who do so, how often do they do so, and under what circumstances? As we will see in later chapters, it is far from clear that sanction-independent obedience to law, whether on the part of officials or of ordinary citizens, is nearly as common as many theorists and others believe.[15] When we specify what it is to obey the law, and when we remove punishment and other coercive sanctions from the picture, it turns out that obeying the law just because it is the law, and not because of what will happen to us if we do not, is hardly widespread. Plainly this varies with the area of law, and even more with time, place, and legal culture, but the notion that law can do what it purports to do simply because of its own intrinsic moral or other power—its normativity, in the technical jurisprudential jargon[16]—appears to be substantially exaggerated.[17]

And thus force reenters the picture. If the mandates of law often conflict with the law-independent judgments of officials or citizens, and if on many of those occasions the law is right and what its subjects would otherwise do is mistaken, and if, further, the law's subjects typically follow their own judgment and not the law's on such occasions, then law's coercive power—its raw force, if you will—becomes necessary for law to do what it needs to do. Indeed, the pervasiveness of force and the threat of it may be what make law distinctive. Morality urges us to take some actions and refrain from others, and public officials and other advocates do much the same thing when they are operating in persuasive and not coercive mode. But there is a difference between the mandates of morality and those of law, and between the urgings of officials and the edicts of those officials when they are backed by sanctions. As we shall see, it may well be that sanctions and coercion—the force of law—are what distinguishes law from morality; from the suggestions, urgings, and importunings of public officials and countless others; and from the social norms that pervade our personal and professional lives.

1.3 The Dimensions of Force

But just what is it for law to exert force, and how does it do it? Most obvious, of course, is the simple threat of imprisonment (or worse) for disobedience. But the criminal law does not exhaust all of law, and incarceration and capital punishment do not exhaust the coercive devices at law's disposal. Fines and lawsuits are also coercive, even though they are threats to the disobedient's wallet and not his liberty. But there can be rewards as well as punishments, and law's coercive (or at least action-inducing) power often includes its ability to create positive as well as negative incentives.[18] Sometimes the law does this by granting immunity from otherwise applicable and legally enforced obligations, as when the tax laws give tax exemptions for donations to charity or when the conscription laws grant exemptions to schoolteachers. And sometimes law's rewards are even more direct. The law can simply prohibit people from driving unsafely, and of course it does that in many ways. But if instead of or in addition to the standard negative sanctions for unsafe driving, the law granted those with clean driving records the opportunity to renew their driver's licenses with less effort, at less cost, or less frequently, it would be attempting to achieve the same goals with positive rewards rather than negative punishment. Whether we want to call this latter approach "coercive" or even "law" is a difficult question, and one that will be addressed in Chapter 8, but for now we ought not to constrict the inquiry preliminarily by assuming at the outset that law's sanctions are only negative and that punishment is the only coercive or motivating implement at law's disposal. Chapters 8 and 9 explore in multiple directions the varieties of coercive powers that modern legal systems appear to have at their disposal.

Things are vastly more complicated than even this, however. Law may have the power to use force, but how and when it does so are complex matters involving overlapping psychological, sociological, political, economic, and moral considerations. The U.S. Internal Revenue Service, for example, conducts extensive audits of the tax returns of only a minuscule number of taxpayers, and it prosecutes genuine tax cheats even more rarely. But it publicizes the possibility of audits especially heavily shortly before the tax return deadline for most taxpayers, and it initiates visible tax fraud criminal prosecutions on much the same schedule, a strategy plainly designed to instill in taxpayers a subjective belief in the probability of an audit or prosecution that is considerably higher than the actual or objective probability of such an event.[19] Is this strategy illegitimate, or is it simply a more efficient way for the government to threaten legally available and legally legitimate punishment?

Or consider the possibility that the same sanctions are vastly more severe for some people than for others. If a fine of $500 for exceeding the speed limit by a given amount—say twenty miles per hour over the posted limit—is a week's wages for a poor laborer and mere pocket change for a wealthy investment banker, and if the likelihood (and consequences) of the two individuals engaging in the prohibited activity is the same, is it wrong for the penalty to be the same? Or is it wrong for the penalty *not* to be the same?

Thus, simply identifying coercion as the characteristic and arguably distinguishing feature of law is not nearly enough. Opening the door to a consideration of law's coercive character exposes a myriad of important conceptual complications and normative questions. Historically, law's coercive power was associated with the criminal law, and with the law's ability to threaten imprisonment or death for violating its prohibitions. But then the monetary fine was added to law's punitive arsenal, and things became more complicated. Is a $20 fine for overtime parking a penalty, or is it simply a tax, or perhaps merely a different way of expressing the price for parking? Is a $10,000 fine for operating an unsafe workplace a sanction, or is it only, as some employers undoubtedly see it, a cost of doing business? And is it possible that what the state sees as a penalty is perceived by the subjects as only a tax or price? Moreover, the varieties of law's coercive forces present additional complexity. Is there a difference, for example, between being liable for a $10,000 fine and being liable for an award for damages in a civil lawsuit of the same amount? Now that the law is so much more than the criminal law and the king's executioner, and includes civil penalties and the entire administrative apparatus, examining the complete arsenal of law's coercive options is an essential part of exploring the coercive dimensions of law.

Once we see that legal coercion is itself a diverse phenomenon, we are prompted to inquire into what, if anything, makes law distinctive. Is it some special connection with the nation-state, such that the idea of non-state law is an oxymoron? Is there an important difference between law and the numerous social norms that govern our behavior? It may seem silly to try to make too much of the difference between law and other normative systems, but in a world of lawyers, judges, law schools, bar examinations, and the like, all of them premised on a difference between law and other social institutions, ignoring the way in which law is at least somewhat distinctive is a mistake. Chapters 10 and 11 address the question of what differentiates law from other sources of guidance and command and the extent to which law's coercive power contributes to its differentiation.

1.4 The Force of Law

The unoriginal title of this book[20] is a play on words. It connotes the brute coercive force that law has at its disposal, to be sure. In everyday parlance, however, both for lawyers and for ordinary people, saying that a rule or prescription or command has "the force of law" is to contrast the prescriptions of law with mere suggestions or recommendations, with the commands of morality, and with the more conventional norms of our social existence. It is saying that *this* norm has been legally enacted and is legally valid. The very phrase "the force of law" entails that there is something distinguishing the norms that emanate from the legal system from those that do not.

But what distinguishes those norms that have the force of law from other norms? Is it a matter of governmental legitimacy? Is it because they come from the state rather than from God or from social agreement? Or is it, at least in part, because norms that have the force of law, in one sense, have law's force, in another sense, behind them? And thus the play on words is an attempt to suggest that law's force—its raw coercive power—has more to do with the very idea of law, and with what makes law distinctive, than has recently been assumed. That law's brute force—its violence, to some[21]—is the principal identifying feature of legality has in the past been the conventional wisdom.[22] It was Thomas Hobbes, after all, who famously observed that "[c]ovenants, without the sword, are but words, and of no strength to secure a man at all."[23] And James Fitzjames Stephen scarcely hesitated before proclaiming that "[i]ndeed law is nothing but regulated force."[24] But precisely the opposite—that force is not the characteristic or identifying feature of law—is now the conventional wisdom, a new conventional wisdom that has been in place, at least in some circles of academic legal philosophy, for more than half a century.[25] The initial goal of this book is to show the ways in which the previous conventional wisdom may have been more correct than is now understood and in which the current conventional academic wisdom may be less sound than is now widely accepted.[26] But to appreciate this aspect of law—to appreciate the force of law in two senses and not just one—is only the beginning. Once we grasp the importance of law's coercive, force-imposing, and force-threatening dimensions, new areas of inquiry open up before us. And thus this book seeks not only to resituate law's coercive dimension into the jurisprudential and philosophical understanding of law but also to begin to pursue some of the multiple paths of inquiry that this resituation reveals. There should be no expectation that the new paths revealed will be followed to their ends. But finding—or refinding—the beginnings may be accomplishment enough.

2

BENTHAM'S LAW

2.1 Law as Coercion—The Beginnings

The philosophical study of the nature of law—jurisprudence, to oversimplify—has a long and distinguished lineage. Plato in *The Laws, The Republic, The Gorgias, The Crito,* and *The Statesman* probed law's value and methods,[1] and he was followed in ensuing generations by Aristotle,[2] Cicero,[3] Aquinas,[4] Hobbes,[5] and countless others.[6] Yet in many important respects modern jurisprudence, at least in the analytic tradition, begins with Jeremy Bentham. As part of his unyielding campaign for comprehensive governmental and political reform, Bentham embarked on a systematic analysis of the phenomenon of law and the nature of a legal system. His effort to characterize the very idea of law was not, however, an abstract scholarly endeavor, nor even an entirely descriptive one.[7] Rather, Bentham viewed the accurate characterization of the nature of law as the essential first step in his fundamentally normative enterprise of attempting to destroy and then rebuild the legal system he knew best.[8] Bentham is one of history's great haters, and his hatred of the law, the field in which he himself was originally trained and in which his father had practiced, knew few bounds. Recoiling against William Blackstone's veneration of the common law[9] and Edward Coke's celebration of its "artificial reason,"[10] Bentham instead perceived the common law as scarcely more than a conspiracy between lawyers and judges to make the law unnecessarily complex and obscure. Both indeterminate[11] and highly complex law, Bentham insisted, required lawyers for its interpretation. Indeterminacy and complexity thus served the conspiracy by increasing the income of lawyers and the power of judges, all to the detriment of the public good. Bentham accordingly suggested, in all seriousness (which appears to be the only mode in which he operated), that it ought to be against the law to give legal advice for money.[12] Were such a prohibition in place, he believed, the incentives to make law more complex and less accessible to the ordinary citizen would disappear. And Bentham expressed a similar contempt for numerous other aspects of the then-existing English legal system. In describing legal fictions such as the law's presumption that a woman's husband was the father of any child born during the marriage, for example, he ranted that "the pestilential breath of Fiction poisons the sense of every instrument it comes near"[13] and that "[i]n English law, fiction is a syphilis, which runs in every vein, and carries into every part of the system the principle of rottenness."[14]

Bentham's opinions about legal fictions, legal complexity, and the indeterminacy of the common law are relevant to the present inquiry because the vehemence with which Bentham expressed his hatred of the characteristics and methods of English law highlights his contempt for almost all aspects of his own legal system at the time he was writing. And it was precisely this scorn which explains Bentham's deconstructive and consequent reconstructive goals—goals which led him to seek a descriptive and distancing, rather than sympathetic, characterization of law.[15] Only by seeing law as it actually is, warts and all, could he and those of like mind start the process of rebuilding it.[16] And only by recognizing that there could be (and often was) bad law could there be any hope of improving it. Modern legal positivism, which originated with Bentham, thus emerged out of his desire to describe law from the outside, free from sympathy or endorsement. Theorists have been debating the nature and commitments of legal positivism ever since,[17] but at the heart of the positivist outlook is the goal of distinguishing the description of law from its normative moral evaluation. Bentham and most of his fellow positivists, then and since, have thus aimed to challenge the natural law tradition which prevailed in Bentham's time. That tradition, and in particular the aspect of it against which Bentham rebelled, sometimes insisted that immoral law was simply not law at all. Moral acceptability, Blackstone and Cicero and a few others at times believed,[18] was a necessary property of law properly so called. A more plausible and now dominant version of the natural law tradition rejects the view that unjust law is no law at all—*lex iniusta non est lex*—but nevertheless subscribes to the position that morally defective law, while still law in one sense, is defective *as law* just because of its moral defects.[19] But whether in stronger or weaker versions, Bentham would have none of it. Introducing moral criteria into the identification of law and even into the evaluation of legality was for him a symptom of dangerous conceptual confusion. The existence of law was one thing, he insisted, and its moral value quite another.[20] By separating the descriptive identification of law from its moral assessment, Bentham believed, we would be better positioned to identify that which was, in Bentham's view, so sorely in need of radical reform. Far from seeing the legal positivist as an apologist for existing legal arrangements, as a common caricature has it,[21] the Benthamite positivist requires an entirely descriptive notion of law precisely for the purpose of evaluating it without empathy, and, in Bentham's case, of keeping one's moral distance from it. Bentham was, after all, a radical reformer, and his efforts to separate the identification of law from its moral evaluation was itself in the service of what were plainly moral and political ends.[22]

Bentham's contempt for the English legal system inspired him to understand the character of law largely in terms of its coercive power. If one believes, as Bentham did, that much of law's substance and process is rotten to the core, then an overwhelmingly salient feature of a legal system is its ability to compel compliance with its directives despite the system's glaring faults. For Bentham, law was uniquely capable of forcing obedience on its subjects, and law's force became most salient for Bentham because of his view of law's defects. And so, largely in a work now known as *Of the Limits of the Penal Branch of Jurisprudence*,[23] Bentham developed what is commonly labeled, two hundred years later, the "command theory" of law.[24] According to the command theory, law is a species of command, or, as Bentham sometimes put it, a mandate. But there are all sorts of commands all around us, and what for Bentham distinguished the commands of law from the commands of other enterprises or other normative systems is the legal system's ability to back its commands with the threat of unpleasant sanctions—fines, prison, or even death—in the event of noncompliance. Indeed, Bentham sometimes claimed that the possibility of such sanctions defined legal obligation itself. To have a legal obligation was simply to be under official state compulsion, and without the possibility of such force there was, he sometimes said, no legal obligation and no law.[25]

Bentham's emphasis on the role of sanctions in understanding law was based substantially on his own psychological theories of human motivation. Although he recognized that people could on occasion have purely social motives of benevolence and sympathy, and could even more often possess what he called the "semi-social" motivations to work for a common good from which they as individuals would proportionately benefit, Bentham believed that for most people most of the time—the "general rule,"[26] as he put it—these social or semi-social motivations would be decidedly secondary to people's self-regarding motivations—the desire to maximize their own well-being rather than that of others or that of the community as a whole. And thus if, as a contingent empirical matter, most people would most often prefer their own well-being to that of others or that of the community, then external force would be needed to prevent them from doing so, at least when their doing so would conflict with the common good. In *Constitutional Code,* Bentham states, "[W]hatsoever evil it is possible for man to do for the advancement of his own personal and private interest . . . at the expense of the public interest—that evil sooner or later, he will do, *unless by some means or other . . . he be prevented from doing it*" (emphasis added).[27]

Bentham's focus on coercion as lying at the heart of law was thus based on his empirical psychological assessment that other-regarding and social-regarding interests would rarely (but, it should be emphasized again, not never) be sufficient to motivate people to put aside their self-regarding motivations. To the extent that law seeks to promote the common good at the expense of individual preferences and interests, therefore, its ability to threaten or impose unpleasant sanctions emerges for Bentham as the principal way in which it can accomplish this end. More importantly, the threat of sanctions is for Bentham sometimes less a part of the *definition* of law than it is law's most prevalent modality and most pervasive characteristic. Coercion is something *added* to legal commands to make them effective by furnishing supplemental motives for compliance. Although Bentham describes the relationship of coercion to the very idea of law in various and sometimes conflicting ways, most often he did not take coercion to be part of the definition of a command, nor did he view coercion as a component of what, as a matter of definition, makes a command a legal command.[28] Bentham may on occasion have expressed the role of coercion and sanctions in such definitional terms,[29] but providing a formal definition of law was not his principal goal. Instead, he was mainly concerned with characterizing how law typically functioned, and the centrality of force in law's routine operation was for him a consequence of the likelihood—albeit not the certainty—that people would place the good of others or the good of society above their own well-being only if they were compelled to do so.[30]

Bentham's emphasis on sanctions as supplying motives for compliance with law[31] is important for three reasons. First, it enables us to distinguish the question of what a law is from the question of what might lead people to comply with it. Second, a sanction-dependent understanding of the nature of law incorporates a falsifiable, or at least investigatable, empirical hypothesis about the likelihood that people will, absent coercive sanctions, comply with law just because it is law. And third, such an understanding puts into proper perspective the less charitable interpretations of Bentham and his successors—interpretations that make it too easy to ignore the way in which Bentham understood legal coercion then and how we might best understand legal coercion now. But in order to pursue further these dimensions of coercion, we must turn our attention away from Bentham and instead to the most prominent of his successors, and indeed the successor whose influence on thinking about the nature of law itself has far outstripped that of Bentham himself.[32]

2.2 Enter Austin

For reasons that remain obscure, the work we now know as *Of the Limits of the Penal Branch of Jurisprudence* remained largely unpublished[33] in Bentham's lifetime, languishing unnoticed in the morass of Bentham's papers for more than a century. The manuscript was not discovered until 1939, and not published until 1945.[34] But although Bentham's writings about the nature of law were lost for many years, his ideas were not. Among his circle of friends in early-nineteenth-century London was a lawyer highly taken with Bentham's theories: John Austin. After failing at the bar, Austin, with the assistance of Bentham and James Mill, among others, was installed in a chair of law at the University of London. Taking up the chair, Austin delivered a course of lectures, hardly more successful than his law practice, in which he systematically expounded and expanded on the command theory of law and on Bentham's basic insights about the role of force and the threat of sanctions in understanding law.[35]

Austin's lectures were published in 1832 as *The Province of Jurisprudence Determined,* and subsequent editions, refined and actively promoted by Austin's wife, Sarah, after his death, added additional materials from the lectures.[36] And although Austin's intricate categorization of commands and elaborate typology of laws acknowledged some of the deficiencies in a pure command-based account of law and accordingly added many qualifications, he still followed Bentham in insisting on a rigid separation of moral evaluation from the criteria for identifying law:

> The existence of law is one thing; its merit or demerit is another. Whether it be or not is one enquiry; whether it be or be not conformable to an assumed standard, is a different enquiry. A law, which actually exists, is a law, though we happen to dislike it. . . . [37]

In distinguishing the existence of law from the assessment of its moral worth, Austin also followed Bentham in viewing the command backed by the threat of force in the event of disobedience as the central feature of law. In fact, Austin, whose normative commitments were less fervent than Bentham's but whose analytic proclivities (or perhaps obsessions) were stronger, incorporated the threat of force into his definitions of law and legal obligation. A law, for Austin, was simply the command of the sovereign backed by the threat of punishment for noncompliance. And it followed, for him, that to be under a legal obligation was equally simply to be the subject of a threat-backed command. Austin accordingly understood a command as the expression of a wish or desire, but, unlike other such expressions—requests or aspirations or hopes, for example—a command was the expression of a wish or desire backed by "the power and purpose of the party commanding to inflict an evil or pain in case the desire be disregarded."[38] Austin thus viewed commands and duties as correlative. The subject of a command was bound or obliged to follow it by virtue of the threat of evil in the event of noncompliance, and it was precisely by being obliged to obey in this sense that the subject of the command had a duty to follow it. "Being liable to an evil from you if I comply not with a wish which you signify, I am *bound* or *obliged* by your command, or I lie under a *duty* to obey it."[39] The binding nature of the command, and also the obligation or duty to follow it, was, for Austin, entirely a function of the ability of the commander to threaten to inflict evil or pain in the event of disobedience.

Plainly this understanding of a command is too broad to explain the idea of law, as Austin well understood. The gunman who says, "Your money or your life" or the parent who threatens to send a disobedient child to bed without dessert are both issuing commands in exactly Austin's sense. But unlike the parent or the gunman, law to Austin consisted of the commands of the *sovereign,* the entity by virtue of whose *position* (hence the term *positive law*) the commands of the state were to be distinguished from the commands of parents, gunmen, and everyone else. Consequently, law for Austin was the aggregate of only those commands of a political superior to a political inferior, where the threat of punishment was built into the very idea of a command. The notion of sovereignty then served the role of picking out the particular province of legal commands from the domain of commands generally.

There is much more in Austin's thinking than just this. His conception of "political superior," for example, required him to develop an elaborate theory of sovereignty, including a definition of the sovereign as the person or entity whose commands are habitually obeyed but who owes no such duty of habitual obedience to anyone else.[40] And Austin also distinguished occasional or particular commands—the police officer who tells me to get away from a crime scene or the judge who issues a ruling in a specific case, for example—from the general commands that constituted law. Laws, for Austin, were *general* commands and thus not limited to particular acts at particular moments of time. The generality of a legal command made it applicable to multiple people at multiple times in multiple contexts. The rule announced on the sign that proclaims "Speed Limit 60" would have been for Austin a law properly so called, but the police officer's warning to *me* to "slow down" would not.

These and other complexities in Austin's account of law are important, but it is the role of coercion that interests us here. And so we might ask why Austin thought coercion so crucial to understanding the nature of law. Despite the claims of some of his critics,[41] Austin appreciated that the institutions generally understood as legal could offer rewards as well as impose punishments,[42] and he was also well aware that many kinds of laws, as we will discuss shortly, did not really fit the model of a command backed by the threat of pain or other punishment.[43] Yet despite appreciating such qualifications and nuances, Austin still insisted on a definition of law "properly so called,"[44] and on accompanying definitions of legal obligation and legal duty, that were undeniably dependent on and restricted to law in its most baldly coercive aspect. Why, we might ask, did he do that?

As with most attempts to understand texts from earlier times, it is important to appreciate the position an author was arguing against. And in this case, Austin's foil, as it had been for Bentham, was to a significant extent William Blackstone narrowly and the overall natural law tradition more broadly. We know this from the historical record and from

Austin's and Bentham's other writings, but it becomes especially clear when we consider one of Austin's most memorable statements:

> Suppose an act innocuous, or positively beneficial, be prohibited by the sovereign under penalty of death; if I commit this act, I shall be tried and condemned, and if I object to the sentence, that it is contrary to the laws of God, who has commanded that human lawgivers shall not prohibit acts which have no evil consequences, the Court of Justice will demonstrate the inconclusiveness of my reasoning by hanging me up, in pursuance of the law of which I have impugned the validity.[45]

Read with modern eyes, the last phrase might be understood as suggesting that the crime was in impugning the law's validity, but that was not what Austin had in mind. Rather, he was insisting that a defendant's view of the morality or justice of a law was largely beside the point. The hangman has the last word. More specifically, Austin was arguing against Blackstone's spare version of natural law theory, according to which an unjust law is no law at all.[46] Many modern (John Finnis, most prominently) and not-so-modern (Aquinas, especially) natural law theorists reject this version of natural law theory, insisting both on a distinction between positive (or human) law and higher law and on a distinction between what might make law defective as law and what makes it simply not law at all.[47] But Blackstone, like Cicero before him[48] and Lon Fuller after,[49] maintained that morality was simply a criterion for law properly so called. For Blackstone, or at least the Blackstone that Bentham and Austin took as their target, any law that contradicted the laws of God was not a law at all.

With such a view widely accepted at the time, the point of Austin's little scenario is to emphasize the way in which an argument from law's immorality would be futile in a court—a court with its own view of morality and its own conception of the morality of the laws it is enforcing. Note that Austin is not taking sides on whether the defendant's act in this scenario is actually innocuous or beneficial, nor on whether a law prohibiting that which is innocuous or beneficial is truly contrary to the laws of God. Austin is simply maintaining that in an important domain of human life—the courts of law and their apparatus of enforcement—it is the law's own view that matters, and it is the law's power to punish that prevails. Austin is not so much insisting that Blackstone's argument about the nonlaw status of an unjust law is wrong as much as he is saying

that in an actual court and for an actual hangman, what is most important is the court's own view, regardless whether it is right or wrong in a
deeper sense.

Austin's pithy story is of a piece with his insistence that "the existence
of the law is one thing, its merit or demerit another." And so although
Austin, as with Bentham before him, fully recognized the possibility of
criticizing the law—evaluating its merit or demerit—he recognized as
well that a subject's ability to criticize the substance of the law was
largely irrelevant to the operation of the law as it actually existed. For
Austin the legal system was not a debating society. It was not the place
where a law's merit or demerit could be discussed, and that was precisely
and only because the law possessed the means of enforcing *its* view of a
law's merit and validity.

Law's coercive power was thus for Austin the key to understanding
the importance of the distinction between what the law is and what it
ought to be. Moreover, we must bear in mind that Blackstone was a
judge—and a judge in a common-law system in which judges retained
the power to make the law and to change it, even as they masked (or
simply denied) this power in the language of discovery rather than creation. Indeed, Austin, even more than Bentham, was among the first to
recognize the law-creating powers of the common-law judge.[50] And for
a judge—Blackstone, for example—to conflate what the law is and what
the law ought to be might not have been so surprising. After all, if you
have the power to make and remake law, then your view of what the
law ought to be can and, indeed, should dissolve into what the law is.

In describing the idea of the common law, A. W. B. Simpson observed
that "[i]n the common-law system no very clear distinction exists between saying that a particular solution to a problem is in accordance
with the law, and saying that it is the rational, fair, or just solution."[51]
But if, like Austin and Bentham, you have your own preferred metric of
what is rational, fair, and just, and if you believe that judges, in searching for the rational, the fair, and the just, are likely to get it wrong, then
you would certainly not want to see the law through the judge's eyes.

And that is why it is important that the defendant in Austin's story is
not the judge. He is a defendant, with the power neither to make law
nor to change it. For *him*, the distinction between what the law is and
what it ought to be is crucial, and for *him* the distinction is supported by
the law's power to punish. It is precisely the force of law that makes the
distinction between law's existence and its merit essential, for without

that force there would be no reason to recognize the importance of the law's own view of its merit. But by possessing that force, the law's view of the law's merit captures the high ground. If we are to understand law from the legal system's point of view, therefore, and if we are to understand the importance to everyone else of the legal system's point of view, we must understand, as Austin seems to be insisting, the force that makes the legal system's point of view not simply one point of view among many but one occupying a distinct position and a distinct conceptual space within the legal system.

2.3 The Conventional Wisdom, Circa 1960

Bentham and especially Austin erected an elaborate theoretical apparatus to explain how the threat of unpleasant sanctions was central to the idea of law and to the distinction between law and other normative domains, such as those of morality, manners, honor, and religion. Moreover, for Bentham and probably (at least until later in life[52]) for Austin, their view of the importance of coerciveness to law was an offshoot of their reformist program.[53] Because they were contemptuous rather than celebratory of the English law they knew, they found it easier to explain law's dominance by reference to its force than to its intrinsic soundness.

Yet although Bentham and Austin arrived at the importance of coercion to law by way of an intricate and normative theoretical route, their destination was hardly surprising. Not only does the ordinary citizen see law initially and predominantly in its coercive mode, but so too do those of a more theoretical bent. It is true that Bentham's most prominent positivist predecessor, Thomas Hobbes, drew a sharp distinction between law and imperatives backed by force, and he did so in the expectation that the populace would take the commands of the sovereign as dispositive as their part of the bargain that is the social compact. Hobbes obviously recognized that this expectation might not be satisfied in the conditions of actual social existence, but for theoretical purposes he was relatively unconcerned with the citizen who failed to understand the obligations of obedience that the social contract imposed.[54]

Moving ahead in time, however, Bentham's focus on the coercive side of law can be seen as increasingly less remarkable, and indeed even banal. T. E. Holland, the author of what was the standard English text on jurisprudence in the late nineteenth and early twentieth centuries, accepted with little question Austin's basic scheme, and what criticisms he had were plainly interstitial.[55] Others followed the same route.[56] Henry Maine, for example, thought little more of importance remained to be said about law's obviously "irresistible coercive power,"[57] believing the interesting issues involved when, where, and how that coercive power was or should be deployed. Somewhat later, W. W. Buckland, in a dyspeptic survey of the state of English jurisprudence, lamented the philosophical efforts to explain the fact of obedience to law and wished that theorists would perceive legal compliance in "a more pedestrian way," by which he meant following Bentham and Austin in their straightforward understanding of legal obligation in a less philosophical and more sanction-dependent manner.[58]

At the same time that English legal theorists were following the command-coercion model of law, much the same was happening in the United States, albeit from a different direction and for a different purpose. When Oliver Wendell Holmes famously observed that we should look at law from the perspective of the "bad man,"[59] he was following Austin, whom we know he read, in understanding "law as regulated coercion."[60] For Holmes, and then for Legal Realists such as Joseph Hutcheson, Jerome Frank, Leon Green, Herman Oliphant, Karl Llewellyn and many others from the 1920s through the 1940s (and, to some extent, thereafter),[61] there was a large difference between the law on the books—the "paper rules," as Llewellyn put it[62]—and the law actually applied. And what made this gap important was that the person affected by law, the "bad man," was somewhere between principally and solely interested in what would happen to him if he engaged in this or that conduct. The Realists were not nearly as concerned as Austin with defining "law" in some strict sense of definition, but for them the important part of law was its ability to impose sanctions. The Realists insisted, often correctly, that the legal system sometimes imposed its sanctions in ways that could not be explained by the paper rules of the written law, but there was little doubt that they accepted the basic Austinian point that the line between when the legal system imposed its sanctions and when it did not was central to understanding the very idea of law.

Nor was the widespread acceptance of coercion's importance limited to theorists in common-law and English-speaking environments. On the Continent, Hans Kelsen's highly influential theory focused on the systemic nature of norms and saw coercion and the state's monopoly of legitimate coercion as the keys to differentiating the legal system from all other norm systems.[63] Indeed, although Kelsen's theory of law diverged sharply from Austin's, he was equally clear about the role of coercion, insisting that "outward sanctions . . . are of the law's essence"[64] and that "[a]ll the norms of a legal order are coercive norms, i.e., norms providing for sanctions."[65] Likewise, the great sociologist of law Max Weber, who focused on the creation and function of various social institutions, maintained that law simply does not exist where there are no institutions for the coercive enforcement of society's norms, that being the entire point of setting up a legal system in the first place.[66] And various other figures in German and French legal philosophy took the coercive core of law to be so self-evident as barely deserving of extended commentary.[67]

Most importantly, however, the central place of coercion in understanding the phenomenon of law remained, as it remains today, an obvious proposition for that overwhelming proportion of the world not composed of legal theorists. Movie mobsters refer to the police as "the law," and although the poet Robert Frost thought he was being funny when he quipped that "a successful lawsuit is the one worn by a policeman," the humor in his remark turned on the ease with which ordinary people think of the law in terms of its capacity to compel compliance. Blaise Pascal observed centuries ago that "law, without force, is impotent,"[68] and much later Albert Einstein noted that "nothing is more restrictive of respect for the government and the law of the land than passing laws which cannot be enforced." Still more recently, Martin Luther King Jr. commended the law precisely because of its power of compulsion. "It may be true that the law cannot make a man love me, but it can keep him from lynching me, and I think that's pretty important."[69]

Among the highly visible facets of contemporary life is the tendency of the public, when the law is most visibly violated, to insist not merely that the perpetrators be criticized but that they be punished. For the public, it seems—as it did for Bentham and Austin and for James A. Garfield, among America's most learned presidents—that "[a] law is not a law without coercion behind."[70] But if it has seemed so obvious to the public and to presidents, to scholars and to activists, to scientists and to poets that law is all about force, then how could anyone deny it, and why would anyone want to? Chapter 3 is devoted to exactly that question.

3

THE POSSIBILITY AND PROBABILITY
OF NONCOERCIVE LAW

3.1 Missing Pieces in the Conventional Wisdom

It has long seemed self-evident—at least to ordinary people—that coercion, sanctions, threats, punishment, and brute force lie at the heart of the idea of law. And for most citizens, as well as for theorists in the tradition of Bentham and Austin, law's ability to compel compliance with its directives appears to be precisely what makes a legal directive different from a mere request or suggestion.[1] Moreover, the threat of force is what seems to distinguish law from the countless other prescriptions of which we are the targets. We exist, after all, in a normative world, constantly bombarded by people telling us what to do. They offer us advice, they give us instructions, and often they give orders and commands. Sometimes these people are parents or siblings or other relatives. Sometimes they are friends or teachers. Even perfect strangers and casual acquaintances tell us what to do. And public officials and advice columnists do it all the time. Moreover, we live our lives in a web of social norms, which, although less explicit, purport to dictate many aspects of our behavior.

Yet, against this background of what is often perceived as a pervasively prescriptive environment, law still stands out. And it does so in large part because when *it* tells us what to do, it has a way of backing up its prescriptions with the coercive power of the state. Or so it has long seemed. And it is just this distinction between enforced orders from the state and all other prescriptions, whether from the state or otherwise, that attracted the focus of Bentham and Austin and that has struck so many before and after them as the key to explaining the character and distinctiveness of law and the legal system.

Although law's seemingly singular ability to compel compliance with its directives appears at first glance to be especially important in understanding what makes law special, a host of legal theorists have nevertheless long observed that a force-centered account of the nature of law leaves too much unexplained. Writing in 1945, for example, Roscoe Pound, earlier the dean of Harvard Law School, wondered whether the Austinian picture omitted many aspects of law whose importance and status as law could hardly be questioned. "Might not one ask whether the legal canons of interpretation are law?" he suggested, and then asked, rhetorically, but "[i]f they impose duties on the judges (who else?), what punishment do they prescribe?"[2]

For Pound, the canons of statutory interpretation—the second-order rules[3] prescribing the methods for interpreting statutes—were obviously part of law. So too, by implication, were all the other rules (and principles, canons, maxims, standards, and other similar prescriptions[4]) that did not directly tell citizens how to behave but instead were directed to judges and specified the manner in which *they* were to perform their tasks. Yet these rules, while plainly *legal* rules, seem to have no sanctions behind them. According to the so-called Golden Rule of statutory interpretation, for example, judges should interpret statutes according to the ordinary meaning of their language unless the interpretation would produce an absurd result plainly unintended by the enacting legislature.[5] But no formal penalty awaits the judge who ignores that rule, or any other rule of that variety. For Pound it was important to acknowledge that such rules were clearly part of law even though they lacked sanctions to back them up. He knew that Austin and his followers had excluded them from the definition of law by stipulating that coercion was a necessary component of any legal rule properly so called, but Pound believed that omitting such obvious aspects of law from a definition of law was perverse. Indeed, although Pound's own scholarship and law reform efforts focused on the criminal law, he thought that Austin's implicit use of a criminal law paradigm appeared to miss much of importance about private law. In particular, Pound worried that legally constituted transactions—contracts, wills, the establishment of partnerships, and much else—could not be captured by the command model without some distortion. Some laws, he observed, "recognize[ed] or confer[ed] power," while others "recognized and conferred liberties and privileges," and still others "delimit[ed] recognized interests." "Reducing all this to commands," Pound complained, "is an over-simplification which does violence to more than one of them and does not conduce to better understanding of them."[6]

Pound was still not finished. Because he objected to conceiving all of law "in terms of the criminal law"[7] and remained unpersuaded by Austinian machinations to shoehorn "all that can be done by law or even by legislation" into a penal model, he wondered "[w]ho is 'made to suffer' when a court construes a will?" "We can't say that [those] whose expectations are disappointed are punished for something they did. They do not succeed in getting what they hoped to get, and this not because of anything pronounced or regarded as a wrong on their part, but because it was not given to them." And, further, "[i]f a court denies probate of a will because it was not executed in accordance with statutory requirements, does it allow pleasure to the virtuous collaterals next of kin, whom the testator considered unworthy of his bounty, and allot pains to the vicious friend of the testator whom he intended to provide for in token of gratitude for benefits conferred?" Moreover, "where a court construes a will or contract or a conveyance or instructs a trustee, is it taking a course of action against some one so as to make him a wrongdoer comparable to a felon or a tortfeasor?"[8]

Pound was harsher than most in maintaining that a sanction-dependent picture of law left too much of law unexplained, but he was hardly the first. As early as 1878, when Austin's influence was at its height, Frederic Harrison, foreshadowing Pound, catalogued a lengthy array of enabling laws of property, public franchises, governmental offices, and much else that were plainly law but that could not plausibly be understood as commands backed by the threat of force.[9] Other theorists in the late nineteenth and early twentieth centuries had also begun questioning whether Austin's coercion-based picture was as complete a portrait of law as he and Bentham imagined.[10] In 1931, for example, Carleton Kemp Allen observed, explicitly against Austin, that "a very great deal of law does not consist at all of . . . compulsion."[11] Allen then became even more specific:

> It has often been pointed out, in opposition to Austin, that many laws are not primarily imperative at all; they merely prescribe the means and the methods by which a person may, if he desires, effect an act-in-the-law— make a will, let us say, or a conveyance, or pursue a remedy in the courts.[12]

Such criticisms were not unanticipated by Austin,[13] and certainly not by Bentham.[14] At times Austin responded to these objections by acknowledging that such instances of law were simply not the principal object of his attention. More to the point, Austin, although like Bentham[15] offering an admittedly sanction-dependent account of the nature of law, relied on a conception of sanction broader than one limited to fines, imprisonment, and death. Austin observed, for example, that even the legally imposed nullity of a transaction could count as a sanction.[16] It is true that the sovereign is indifferent as to whether I enter into a contract, sell my house, or leave my money to a cousin upon my death. But if I try to accomplish such transactions without complying with the prescribed legal forms, the state will not enforce the transaction. The nullity of a transaction I desired to pursue will frustrate my intentions, make it impossible for me to do what I want to do, and perhaps even produce a result that is positively distasteful to me—for example, when the alternative and law-demanded beneficiary of my estate is another cousin whom I loathe. For Austin, this kind of legal nullity could operate as a genuine sanction, even if nullity's effect was only to make an optional act ineffective, as opposed to the sanctions attendant upon failure to comply with a mandate that I do something (such as pay taxes) or refrain from doing something (such as theft). The acts that legal nullity nullifies may have originally been optional, Austin believed, but when an expected outcome is nullified, the nullification, by virtue of frustrating the expectations of those who wished to consummate a transaction, seemed to him to fit within the idea of a sanction.[17]

We will return to the concept of the threat of nullity as a form of coercion. At the very least, the idea should be taken seriously. Requiring that I do something the state's way rather than my way is not totally unrelated to the idea of a command, and the penalty of not being able to do it at all if I do not do it the state's way is at least plausibly a form of sanction. But the sanction of nullity is also plausibly, as Pound and Allen first observed, coercive in only an attenuated way. And so they, with others, were led to conclude that much of what we normally understand as being part of law is not satisfactorily explained by coercion in even a broad sense. And if this is so, then coercion and sanctions may not do nearly as much work in accounting for the idea of law as Bentham and Austin supposed. What we should make of this, even if true, is the subject of much of Chapter 4, but in the meantime we must turn to the most influential version of the critique just sketched.

3.2 H. L. A. Hart and the Gaps in Austin's Picture

Allen, Pound, and others had long been exposing the gaps in Austin's picture, but what has become the canonical critique of Austin for overemphasizing coercion and slighting the noncoercive dimensions of law was the opening portion of H. L. A. Hart's *The Concept of Law*.[18] In laying the groundwork for what he described as a "fresh start" in thinking about the nature of law, Hart devoted much of the early chapters of his profoundly influential book to a critique of Austin. Indeed, so important has Hart's work become for legal philosophy in the Anglo-American tradition that the earlier challenges to Austin, not much different from what Hart later offered, have essentially been forgotten.[19]

Hart's critique of the Austinian model featured two major themes. The first tracked the earlier objections of Pound and others: that much of what is widely understood to be law is either ignored or unsatisfactorily explained by a sanction-based account. But Hart took these criticisms further. He not only reemphasized that coercion seems not to explain the legal status of contracts, wills, trusts, and other optional features of law, but he also explored a topic noted only briefly by Pound and Allen: the role of law in constituting such arrangements in the first place. Indeed, in Hart's 1953 inaugural lecture as Professor of Jurisprudence at Oxford,[20] he developed a theme later to become prominent in John Searle's distinction between constitutive and regulative rules.[21] Regulative rules, the most familiar sort of rule, govern conduct whose conceptual existence is logically prior to the rules. My ability to drive a car at 90 miles per hour may be a function of the car, the road, and my preferences, but it does not depend on the law.[22] This is also true of a person's ability to bring about the death of another. Humans killed other humans long before laws against murder or legal rules distinguishing murder from justified killing even existed. And thus rules or laws prohibiting driving at 90 miles per hour or killing other people govern conduct that could exist without law and whose conceptual existence is logically prior to the law. I do not need the law—any law—to drive at 90 miles per hour or to kill my neighbor.

But now consider those rules or rule systems that *create* possibilities that would otherwise not exist. To recall an earlier example, it is simply not possible to engage in castling without the rules that constitute the game of chess. Castling only exists *within* chess (although moving wooden pieces of a certain shape in a certain way on a board with squares is possible, even if pointless), just as home runs exist only within baseball.

So it is with law. Criminal law may regulate killing, and tort law may govern some forms of conceptually antecedent activity,[23] but a corporation or a trust or a will is like castling and not like killing. A group of people can run a business together without the law, but they can only create a corporation by virtue of legal rules that establish the very idea of a corporation. And the same is true of trusts, wills, pleadings, and countless other law-constituted and thus law-dependent institutions and practices.

How should we understand what the law is doing in constituting such institutions and practices? The law is hardly coercing anything or anyone, at least in the sense of requiring people to engage or not to engage in any of these law-constituted activities. Law constitutes corporations, but it does not mandate that anyone create one. That is what Pound and later Hart argued, and for both of them the neglect of law's constitutive dimension was a large part of their broader objection to excess dependence on coercion in explaining the phenomenon of law.

The argument from law's constitutive capacity should not be taken too far. If the point is to show the importance of law even when it is not being coercive by backing its prescriptions with sanctions, then we should consider the possibility that law, even in its constitutive mode, may be more coercive than is often appreciated. Sometimes, to be sure, coercion consists simply of telling people what to do, but sometime coercion exists when it tells people that what they want to do must be done in one way and not another. When law creates the very possibility of engaging in an activity, it often supplants a similar and law-independent one. And if the law-independent activity is part of people's normal behavior and background expectations, eliminating this possibility and compelling people to use law's alternative operates as a form of coercion.

Consider the legal idea of a contract. Contracts exist by virtue of law, and thus the concept of a contract is law-constituted in just the sense we are discussing. But even if there were no such thing as contracts, there could still be promises,[24] and the moral obligation to keep one's promises might well be enforced with the sanctions of shame, guilt, and reputational harm, among others. Yet once the law has created the institution of the contract, it turns out that promises, at least on the same topics encompassed by the law of contract, seem to have been pushed to the side psychologically, even if not conceptually. I can promise to sell you my house for a certain amount, but in a world with contracts, a background understanding emerges such that a contract to sell a house is the *only* way to promise to sell a house. To repeat, this is a psychological and not a logical claim, but that makes it no less sound. By moving into some domain of behavior, law often occupies the field, crowding out preexisting nonlegal alternatives. Consider the law of wills. A will is a creature of law, but leaving one's property upon death to designated individuals is not. A person could, after all, instruct her brothers and sisters and children that upon her death, her house and car should be given to one child and her bank accounts to another. In theory this could happen, and these wishes might well be carried out. But that is not the way it is done in our world. In our world, a world that uses wills, other ways of achieving the same end have been supplanted. Telling someone that he will get all my money when I die, and doing that outside of established legal processes, is less effective in a world that uses wills than in a world that does not.[25]

When legally constituted forms of conduct supplant similar law-independent forms of conduct, therefore, or when law regulates optional but law-independent conduct, the sanction of nullity becomes a real sanction. If I want to make a contract but do not do so in accordance with the forms prescribed by law, the contract is no contract at all. My expectations and desires will have been frustrated, and my disappointment will be palpable. If I wish to avoid that disappointment and achieve a particular goal by entering into a contract, the law's ability to frustrate these desires gives it a power of coercion not dissimilar to more direct coercion. The collapse of a complex transaction for reasons of noncompliance with law's mandates, for example, may be a far greater penalty for the parties engaged in that transaction than a $100 fine for exceeding the speed limit. As Leslie Green put it, "[N]ullity can be as inconvenient, distressing, and expensive as some penalties."[26]

Of course, sometimes nullity may not be disappointing at all, and then the threat of it loses its coercive force. As Hart points out, a contract that is invalid because one of the contracting parties is not of age may appear as no sanction at all to the minor who is no longer bound by the terms of the contract.[27] And although Hart overstates the case in saying that it is "absurd" to think of the nullity of a contract or legislation as a form of punishment,[28] the charge that speaking of punishment is out of place in the context of violating constitutive rules is apt when aimed at the idea that a chess player's attempt to move a rook diagonally is punished by a rule of chess—the rule that specifies that rooks cannot move diagonally. It is impermissible to move a rook diagonally, but it is odd to describe the player who attempts to do so as having been "punished."

Some violations of constitutive rules are thus so unlike sanctions that the Austinian picture again emerges as incomplete. But just because some conclusions of legal nullity are not plausibly perceived as sanctions or punishments, it does not mean that none of them are. To be sure, the invalidity of a contract is sometimes not experienced as unpleasant, but for most people making most contracts most of the time, the law's ability to say that it must be done in a particular way on pain of nonenforcement will be experienced as coercive. And though some judges will, as Hart notes, be indifferent to the validity of their orders,[29] judges commonly feel the sting of reversal and seek to avoid it, making the power of an appellate court over a trial judge a power that is experienced as coercive. In many ways, therefore, the power to impose invalidity will be the power to coerce those for whom invalidity is unpleasant or inconvenient, likely a larger number in many contexts than those for whom invalidity is a matter of indifference. Indeed, even the case that Hart sees as the *reductio ad absurdum* may not be so absurd at all. It is true that nullity is in some sense an essential component of any constitutive rule and thus that "if failure to get the ball between the posts did not mean the 'nullity' of not scoring, the scoring rules could not be said to exist."[30] And so nullity may best be understood as part of a constitutive rule rather than a conceptually distinct enforcement of an independent requirement. But once one is inside the game, whether that game be judging or contracts or football, the rules lose some of their constitutive power and appear regulative and coercive. The coercive aspect of constitutive rules thus becomes a phenomenological matter, and the power of those who make, change, and enforce the constitutive rules may well appear coercive to those who are inside the institutions that the constitutive rules constitute.

We must concede that law's ability to create the power to make wills and trusts and contracts, just like its ability to create the power to enact legislation and issue judicial decrees, is not completely captured by a coercion-based account of law. But even with this concession, we can also recognize that attempting to explain the operation of constitutive rules without recognizing the coercive dimensions of nullity is incomplete as well. Still, it seems an error to understand *all* legal rules as coercive. What to make of the widespread but nonessential presence of coercion-based reactions to law even in its constitutive mode remains a difficult question, and one to which we shall return. But for now, it may suffice to note that the claim that coercion is present for all law properly so called seems false, and in that sense the pure Austinian account is incomplete.[31] Just how incomplete it is, and why that incompleteness matters, is taken up presently.

3.3 The Internalization of Legal Rules

When Hart began writing about law, the view that large chunks of it could only with difficulty be explained by the command model had become, at least in jurisprudential circles, commonplace. Hart added his voice to these critics, but his more influential criticism of the command model cuts deeper. The problem is not merely that sanctions in the traditional sense are absent from much of what law does but also that even when law is in its most overtly regulatory and commanding mode, the existence of legal obligation is logically distinct from the sanctions and threats that law employs to enforce its commands and the obligations that law creates. As Arthur Goodhart, Hart's predecessor as Professor Jurisprudence at Oxford, put it in 1953, "It is because a rule is regarded as obligatory that a measure of coercion may be attached to it: it is not obligatory because there is coercion."[32]

Goodhart's idea, which was subsequently enriched by Hart, demands careful attention. For Bentham and especially Austin, sanctions were essential to the idea of legal obligation. Laws created obligations by backing their commands with threats. To be subject to a legal obligation—to be under a legal *duty*—was thus to be the subject of an official command supported by a threat of an "evil" for noncompliance. Force was not only an essential component of a legal command, but it was also an equally essential part of legal obligation and legal duty.

As Goodhart, Hart, and others have since pointed out, however, treating the threat of unpleasant sanctions for noncompliance as essential to obligation excludes the possibility of obligation without threat. For Hart, the distinction between being under an obligation and being threatened by force, as with the gunman who threatens my life if I do not hand over my money, is identified by and reflected in the linguistic distinction between being obliged, as in the gunman situation, and being under an obligation, as in being subject to a law. As a linguistic matter, Hart was mistaken. It is no error in English to say that one is morally obliged to care for a sick relative or to say that people have sanction-compelled obligations to pay their taxes or obey the speed limit. Indeed, it may be no linguistic error to say that the gunman imposed on me an obligation to hand over my money. It is far more common than Hart supposed simply to understand "obligation" as the noun form of the verb *oblige,* as when the Supreme Court of the United States said that "the heir in virtue of his liability as heir for the obligation of his ancestor would be obliged to respond for all the fruits and revenues as heir if not possessor,"[33] or when another American federal court announced that "[a]s the Order did not make the independent obligation delegable, CDSS was obliged to comply with it."[34]

That the linguistic distinction between being obliged and having an obligation does less work than Hart believed in marking the distinction does not make the distinction itself unimportant. Even aside from whether the distinction can be extracted from ordinary language, the difference that Hart meant to describe remains crucial, precisely because we can understand being under an obligation even without a threat for noncompliance.

The existence of obligations without sanctions is clearest with respect to moral obligations. Most people believe they have a moral obligation to care for their elderly parents, for example, but it is an obligation typically unsupported by the threat of sanctions. Yes, the sanction of criticism, especially public criticism, will be both effective and necessary to get some people to recognize or act on the obligation, but it is too impoverished an understanding of moral sensibility and moral motivation to believe that everyone who cares for an aged parent does so solely to avoid the sting of public criticism.[35] Consider, as another example, the ethical vegetarian who refrains from eating meat not for health reasons but because she believes it morally wrong to kill sentient creatures for food. There are many such people nowadays, but not so many that vegetarians risk condemnation, at least in most social environments. Nevertheless, the ethical vegetarian believes she has an obligation to refrain from meat-eating, and she believes that she would be in breach of that obligation—or duty—were she to eat a steak, a pork chop, or fried chicken. And so the very notion of a moral obligation, a notion familiar to most of us, shows that reducing the idea of an obligation to the threat of sanction is simply confused.

Such moral obligations can be described as having being *internalized.* The obligation to refrain from meat-eating is a reason for and guides our vegetarian's conduct. Under some circumstances she might even criticize others for eating meat, a criticism whose purchase derives from the vegetarian's internalization of the "don't eat meat" rule. Her criticism presupposes—Hart says "accepts"—the rule, and the criticism is made *from* the standpoint of the presupposed or accepted rule.

But if moral obligations can be internalized without sanctions, so too can legal ones. And this was the very point that Hart, a few of his predecessors, and almost all of his successors wished to emphasize. We need not confront complex metaethical questions about just where moral obligations come from to recognize that for all but the most irresolute subjectivists, they come from somewhere. In the minds of some people they come from God, for others from culturally and temporally contingent social norms, for others from their own intuitions, and for still others from an objective reality of right and wrong. But they come from somewhere, a notion that explains the difference between raw preferences and moral constraints. The committed moral vegetarian may well adore Beef Wellington and pork barbecue, and may even believe that a diet including meat and fish is healthier than one without them, but the moral obligation she has internalized requires her to set aside some of her preferences, some of her desires, and possibly even some of her needs in the service of her moral obligations. Her internalized moral obligations are second-order constraints on her first-order preferences.

Much the same applies to law, at least as a theoretical possibility. If people can understand and act on a sanction-free moral obligation coming from, say, God,[36] or from an objective notion of moral right and wrong, then there is no reason that the law could not have a similar status. As a logical and conceptual matter, people who do things because morality says they should (the locution is intentional, designed to suggest the common even if not necessary external phenomenology of moral obligation) could do things because the law says they must. People could perceive law as an independent source of obligation and could understand the law as imposing obligations even though the law threatened no sanctions. If it makes sense to say that I do something because morality tells me to do it, then it makes just as much sense, as a logical and phenomenological matter, to say that I do something because the law tells me to do it. In Hart's language, people can have an *internal point of view* vis-à-vis legal obligations. When they have such an internal point of view—when they have internalized the obligation—they recognize the fact of a legal "command" as creating an obligation and thus a reason for action in a way that is logically, phenomenologically, and empirically distinct from the possibility of sanctions for violating that obligation.

Legal philosophers since Hart have tended to accept this account of how law can create obligations, but they often make it more mysterious than necessary, typically by describing the issue in terms of a genuine puzzle about the source of law's "normativity."[37] But the issue is not nearly as puzzling as these theorists would have us believe. Whenever we are inside a rule system, we have obligations created by that system. If we understand morality as a system of rules (which not everyone does, to be sure), then moral obligation is constituted by the set of obligations created by a system of rules that one accepts. And when one is playing chess—when one has internalized and is thus inside the rule system that constitutes the game of chess—we might say, infelicitously but in a way that captures the idea, that one is under a chessal obligation to follow the rules of chess. Not an unconditional obligation, but an obligation conditional on being inside the game of chess and its rules. Similarly, when one is inside the rule system of, say, Victorian etiquette, then we could say that people are under an etiquettal obligation to follow the rules that the practice establishes. And if one internalizes the rules of fashion, then one is under a fashional obligation to follow the dictates of the ever-changing rules and norms of fashion. To be under an obligation is to be being within—and thus accept, or presuppose—the rules or commands of some system. The acceptance is conditional upon being inside the system. As a logical matter, moral obligation, religious obligation, chessal obligation, etiquettal obligation, and fashional obligation are all species of the same logical genus.

Legal obligation is another species of this same genus. Legal obligation can be like chessal obligation. If one accepts—internalizes, or takes as a guide to action—the system, then that system can create obligations for those who accept it. And the system can create such obligations for those inside it, as a conceptual or logical matter, without any reference to force, sanctions, or coercion.[38] This is what Joseph Raz called the "legal point of view,"[39] and as so expressed it is no more mysterious or puzzling than the chessal point of view or the moral point of view.[40] To be inside a system of norms is to have the ability to take actions, have reasons, make statements, offer criticism, and reach judgments *from* and not about the norms of that system. And thus the normativity of law presupposes (or is conditional upon) one being inside law's normative system. But once the contingent condition is satisfied, or the presupposition is accepted, then the normativity of law stands on the same footing as any other form of reason-giving from the standpoint of a presupposed system of rules or norms.[41] Recognizing what it is to make judgments (both about one's own behavior or in criticism or praise of others) from inside a system of rules was Hart's basic and profoundly influential point. *Contra* Bentham and *contra* Austin, there can be legal obligation independent of sanctions. To take sanctions, or the credible threat of them, as logically or definitionally part of the very idea of an obligation or a duty is, as Goodhart first put it, to confuse the very idea of an obligation with the instruments that are commonly used to enforce them.

To be sure, some of the theorists who continue to puzzle about normativity believe the foregoing account of legal obligation insufficient. Legal obligation is not merely relative to acceptance or being inside the system, they say, but, like morality, is unconditional. Just as I do not have to accept a system of morals in order to be morally wrong, so the argument goes, so too can I be legally wrong even if I do not accept the framework of the legal system. That is true enough, but there is no mystery about being *legally* wrong from the standpoint of the law. Perhaps, as it is said, the mystery resides in why being legally wrong is simply wrong, apart from the possibility (see Chapter 4) of there being a *moral* obligation to obey the law. But why would we even think there is something more to being legally wrong than just being legally wrong unless being legally wrong also meant being morally wrong just by virtue of being legally wrong? The puzzle of legal normativity is not the puzzle of trying to explain why there is a nonmoral and nonlegal wrongness to being legally wrong. It is the puzzle of why anyone would think there was in the first place.

3.4 Internalization and the Nature of Law

It is thus apparent that the sanction-independent internalization of legal obligation is logically and conceptually possible. Just as the moral vegetarian in an environment of nonvegetarians follows her moral calling in the absence of sanctions, people could follow the law just because it *is* the law (about which more remains to be said, and will be said in Chapter 4), and not for fear of sanctions. But is this more than just a logical possibility? And what does the existence of this logical possibility tell us about the phenomenon of law itself?

In large parts of the contemporary jurisprudential tradition, the mere possibility of sanction-independent legal obligation is sufficient to establish that sanctions—coercion—are not part of law's *nature*. And those who reach this conclusion do so by understanding the nature of something— of anything—as constituted by the essential or necessary conditions of its existence. To understand the nature of something, or, as some would put it, to understand the *concept* of something, is to be able to identify its essential or necessary properties. It may be that most birds fly, for example, but because some creatures are clearly birds and just as clearly cannot fly—penguins and ostriches, for example—it is a mistake to understand flying as an essential property of birdness. And because most people understand pineapple wine as wine, even if it is very poor wine,[42] it is similarly mistaken to include grapes as part of the concept of wine.

Just as an essentialist understanding of the concept of wine excludes being made from grapes as part of wine's nature, so too does a similar perspective exist, especially in recent decades, about the concept of law. Thus, to repeat a quotation from Chapter 1, Joseph Raz observed that what distinguishes legal philosophy from legal sociology is that "[t]he latter is concerned with the contingent and the particular, the former with the necessary and the universal. Sociology of law provides a wealth of detailed information and analysis of the functions of law in some particular societies. Legal philosophy has to be content with those few features which all legal systems necessarily possess."[43] Similarly, Scott Shapiro considers conceptual analysis generally, and conceptual analysis about law, to be a search for "truisms," which are not contingent empirical truths but are necessary truths about the entity that is being investigated.[44] Thus, he stresses that the truisms identified about law must be ones that are "in fact present in every legal system."[45] And Julie Dickson maintains that the nature of law is explained (and defined) by "those essential properties which a given set of phenomena must exhibit in order to be law."[46]

It is this essentialist understanding of the nature of law, or the concept of law,[47] or the nature of the concept of law that leads some theorists to view the possibility of sanction-free legal obligation and sanction-free law as profoundly important. If, as we have seen and as Hart and others have argued, there exists the logical possibility of law and legal obligation without force and coercion, then that very possibility, apart from the size of its empirical presence, causes coercion to drop out of the nature of law, at least for those who believe that the nature of something consists in and only in its necessary or essential properties. Even though all real legal systems employ a large battery of coercive devices to enforce the obligations they create, the fact that noncoercive law is possible and the fact that some parts of real legal systems appear to operate without coercion are sufficient reasons under an essentialist view to exclude coercion from law's nature. Coercion emerges as contingent and not necessary, useful but not essential, ubiquitous but not universal, and thus not part of the very nature of law itself.[48]

We have seen that it is possible for those inside the rule-based enterprise of law to internalize its commands without sanctions, just as it is possible for those inside the enterprise of chess to internalize *its* rules without sanctions. But what is the import of this possibility? Assume for the moment what no one denies: that sanctions are a large part of how all real legal systems enforce many of the obligations they create. But if this contingent and nonnecessary fact is not part of the nature of law precisely because of its nonnecessity, then we must consider what the nature of something consists of and whether necessity should be the touchstone of an inquiry into the nature of any phenomenon.

3.5 Generics, Concepts, and the Concept of Law

So what are we to make of the fact that coercion is not a necessary property of law, in the sense that there can be, and sometimes is, law without coercion? People can internalize legal norms independent of their methods of enforcement, and people, especially legal officials, as Pound first observed, sometimes do internalize, follow, and use legal norms even when sanctions are absent. But does this really mean that coercion should not be considered in an inquiry into the nature of law, as many legal theorists believe?[49] Perhaps it does, but maybe that view is based on a particular understanding of what a concept or a nature is, and maybe that understanding is erroneous.

Consider, again, birds. Most birds can fly, but some cannot. Yet if we ask someone to think of a bird, rarely will that person choose a penguin, an ostrich, or an eagle with a broken wing. And this observation is not just about birds. Cognitive scientists who study concept formation have almost universally concluded that people do not use concepts in the way that the "essential feature" view of concepts supposes. Rather, they understand that their concepts have central cases—birds that can fly, wine made from grapes, and clever mathematicians—as well as peripheral cases—birds that cannot fly, wine made from pineapples, and stupid mathematicians. They understand that permanently moored but floating houseboats are sort of like boats but are not central cases of boats and that houseboats are also sort of like houses but not central cases of houses.[50] In both their thinking and their speaking, people have prototype or paradigm or central cases of the concepts and the words they use, and other cases that are more debatable, less central, and more peripheral. Moreover, people think of concepts and categories in terms of properties—like flying for birds and grapes for wine—that may not hold even for all of the central cases of the category.[51] And although cognitive scientists debate about many things, this is not one of them, for it is widely recognized that a picture of concept formation that stresses necessary (and sufficient) conditions or properties is an inaccurate picture of how people actually think.

The same idea has been recognized from several different philosophical traditions. Most famously, but also most controversially, Ludwig Wittgenstein suggested the idea of a family resemblance as explaining at least some, probably most, and possibly all of language.[52] Using the example of games, he suggested that all the things we call games do not share common characteristics. Games have no necessary or essential properties, and there are no necessary or essential properties of all of the games we think of as central cases of games. It is not, or at least it was not for Wittgenstein and his followers, that there were central or prototypical or paradigmatic instances of games, such that we could identify the essential features of the paradigmatic cases—the things that made them paradigms—while recognizing that there were fringe or debatable cases that possessed some but not all of the properties of the paradigm. Rather, the things we call games, and even the multiple things that are central or paradigmatic cases of games, relate to one another as a family resemblance, like the strands of a rope rather than the links in a chain. Anything we understand as a game—as an instance of the concept of a game—shares some number of properties with some number of other games, but there are no properties that are shared by all games, not even by all of the games that are clear cases of games.

Not everyone agrees with the idea that family resemblance explains even games. Most notably, Bernard Suits argued that *all* games can be characterized as rule-based activities that are "voluntary attempts to overcome unnecessary obstacles."[53] And thus he purported to provide, explicitly *contra* Wittgenstein, a definition of games in terms of necessary and sufficient conditions. Suits's definition may not actually be correct. For example, would it apply to those who play sports for money? But even if Suits's definition is sound, it may not actually tell us very much of interest about games, and it may well be a definition offered at such a high level of abstraction as to be essentially uninformative.

But although Wittgenstein's views are hardly without dissenters, his and other forms of anti-essentialism have nevertheless been highly influential. The philosophers Max Black and John Searle discussed "cluster concepts"—concepts defined by a weighted set of criteria, with no single criterion being either necessary or sufficient for proper application of the concept, and no one of which is either necessary or part of a set of jointly sufficient criteria for proper application of even the central cases of the concept.[54] Still other philosophers have taken up a prototype theory of meaning that hews even more closely to what cognitive scientists have learned about concept formation.[55] And even more recently, there has been great interest in *generics*—characterizations that are usually or generally true but that tolerate exceptions.[56] It is not universally true that Volvos are reliable, that Swiss cheese has holes, or that birds fly, but it is not incorrect to say that Volvos are reliable, Swiss cheese has holes, or birds fly. It thus appears that an important feature of human cognition and human communication is the use of probabilistically but not universally true characterizations as a vital part of our cognitive and communicative existence.

This is not a book about cognitive science or the philosophy of language. That our language and our concepts, especially those that do *not* describe natural kinds such as gold and water, are best characterized in terms of prototypes, central cases, generic properties, clusters, and family resemblances is contested terrain.[57] But at the very least it is neither self-evident nor universally accepted that grasping and using a concept requires knowing the necessary and sufficient conditions for its proper use.[58] Assuming that understanding the nature or concept of law means understanding its essential properties or even the essential properties of its central cases is thus to rely on a premise whose empirical basis is shaky and whose philosophical provenance is highly contested.

It is worth repeating that the most important versions of anti-essentialism are not merely about peripheral cases. The issue is not whether there are core and fringe cases of law, just as there are core and fringe cases of pretty much everything else. Rather, the question is whether even the core or standard or central cases can be understood in terms of necessary features.[59] Many theorists claim they can, but many others argue they cannot, and the latter view—that even standard or central cases do not have essential properties—has its own substantial philosophical provenance and even more substantial empirical support. Neither this provenance nor the empirical support makes the anti-essentialist claim necessarily correct. And it is rarely a good idea to rely on the authority of anonymous or not-so-anonymous mass-academic opinion. "No one believes this anymore" is a bad argument, even though it sometimes represents an accurate empirical description. But the existence of live philosophical disputes and somewhat of an empirical consensus should caution against too quickly accepting the idea that looking for the nature of the phenomenon of law must be an exercise in searching, even in the central or standard cases, for law's essential properties.[60]

Even Hart, the inspiration for much of modern legal philosophy in the essentialist tradition, may himself have held nonessentialist views about the nature of law. Just as Hart memorably urged us to recognize core and penumbral instances of "vehicles" for purposes of applying a "no vehicles in the park" rule[61]—that trucks and other motor vehicles were core cases but that roller skates and bicycles and toy cars were on the fringe—he appeared to suggest, especially in the earliest pages of *The Concept of Law*, that not only might "law" be like "vehicle" in the sense of having central and peripheral cases, but also that "law" might itself be a family resemblance concept with neither necessary nor sufficient conditions for its proper application.[62] Whether this is what Hart actually meant or whether this view carried through to the remainder of his book is an interesting exigetical question, but it is not our primary concern here. At least we can recognize, however, that there is much support for the view that the concept of law, perhaps like all concepts and perhaps like only some concepts, is best characterized in terms of central cases not themselves identifiable in terms of necessary properties and whose properties may not be present in other arguably proper applications of the concept. Thus, law, like much—or perhaps everything—else, may well be a generic, a cluster concept, or a family resemblance.

If the concept of law, or the proper application of the word *law*, is best characterized in such an anti-essentialist way, or if the phenomenon of law simply has no essence, then the absence of coercion in things properly or at least plausibly understood as law is no longer fatal to coercion being an important feature of the central case of law. If, like generics in general, an unquantified statement about law is resistant to counterexamples, then the statement that "law is coercive" may be similar to statements such as "mosquitoes carry malaria" and "birds fly." Coercion may be to law what flying is to birds: not strictly necessary but so ubiquitous that a full understanding of the phenomenon requires that we consider it.[63] Conversely, noncoercive law may be like the flightless bird: useful in telling us something about all birds but hardly deserving of exclusive or even dominant attention. And thus if coercive law is the dominant instantiation of law as it is experienced, the fact that some law, even some important law, is noncoercive should be recognized but should not distort an inquiry into the nature of the social phenomenon that is law. That Bentham and Austin may have overstated the case for coercion is no excuse for facilitating an even great misunderstanding and inaccuracy by understating it.

3.6 In Search of the Puzzled Man

Proponents of an essentialist picture of the nature of law would deny at least some, and perhaps all, of the foregoing claims about the empirical and practical unimportance of coercion-free law. First, they would point out that legal systems have to "start" somewhere and that the officials who impose sanctions on others do not themselves internalize legal rules because of the threat of sanctions. Even this, however, may not be so. Judges may internalize the canons of statutory construction to avoid the penalties of reputational damage and to gain the rewards of professional prestige and advancement.[64] And many officials may internalize and apply legal rules simply because of fear of imprisonment or death. We know of societies that have elaborate systems of rules, including the rules about rules, which Hart called "secondary rules," in which the officials make and enforce the rules out of fear of the despot and his army and in which the despot and his army are motivated simply by the desire for wealth or power.[65] Perhaps some would deny that such systems are law at all, but an account of law that says there was no law in Zaire under Mobutu, or in the Philippines under Marcos,[66] or in some number of other nation-states may depart too much from an ordinary understanding of law to be very helpful.[67]

I do not wish to fall into the trap I have just accused others of failing to avoid. Legal systems in which no one at all, not even the officials, internalizes law except out of fear of sanction are possible, and sometimes they exist, but they are rare. Far more common are legal systems in which at least some officials are committed to the system for sanction-independent reasons.[68] Therefore, it is a mistake to ignore coercion-free internalization entirely. The sanction-independent acceptance of a legal regime by officials at the pinnacle of that system is an important part of most legal systems and thus deserves the kind of analysis that much of the modern jurisprudential tradition has provided.

But although it is wrong to neglect sanction-independent internalization entirely, there is a more profound claim made by those who have succeeded in relegating coercion to the jurisprudential sidelines. Hart made reference to Holmes's image of the "bad man," whose behavior vis-à-vis the law was entirely a function of what the law would do to him or not do to him if he engaged in this or that conduct.[69] But this ignores the "puzzled man," Hart said, the person who wants to know what the law requires not so he knows what he can get away with but so he can do what is required by the law—sanctions, punishment, and coercion aside.[70] The puzzled man is disposed to comply with the law *just because it is the law,* and an account of law that fails to take account of the puzzled man simply does not, Hart said, "fit the facts."[71]

More recently, Scott Shapiro builds on the same idea. In developing what he calls the "planning theory" of law, a theory whose details are not germane here,[72] Shapiro demonstrates how an entire legal system could be erected and would be needed without any coercion whatsoever. And he explains the importance of this admittedly hypothetical system in terms of telling us something about the "many people" who are in fact like Hart's puzzled man—that is, who are inclined to follow law's mandates because they are law and not because of what people with uniforms and guns and robes might do to them if they do not.[73]

Hart, Shapiro, and many others thus justify their attention to coercion-free law and their departure from Bentham and Austin not only on the conceptual grounds we have been discussing but also because of their belief that by stressing coercion, Bentham and Austin were empirically misguided, underestimating the importance of the puzzled people in most societies whose inclination to follow the law is robust and who would follow law's mandates without the need for threats of force. It turns out, therefore, that the case against Bentham and Austin is not only conceptual and philosophical but also empirical. It is thus time to turn to the empirical issue, to examine what lurks behind the image of the puzzled man, and to see just how many of them there really are.

4

IN SEARCH OF THE PUZZLED MAN

4.1 Taking Stock—and Moving Ahead

So where are we? It is time to recapitulate the argument so far.

A portion of Chapter 3 focused on questions of methodology, but these questions are important not because the answers reveal new ways of searching for the necessary features of law but because the importance of the methodological inquiry lies in the way that rejecting an essentialist understanding of the nature of law removes a barrier to careful theoretical consideration of the role of coercion in law. Having shed the belief that properties that are not conceptually necessary are of little philosophical or jurisprudential interest, we are better situated to think about those aspects of law that are ubiquitous and typical but not conceptually essential. Coercion is surely one of those aspects, and freed from the necessity of limiting our examination to conceptual essences, we can recover the theoretical and philosophical examination of coercion in law from the exile to which a dubious essentialism has cast it. Or, to recast the same point less tendentiously but more directly, methodological questions about the philosophical significance of noncoercive law should not distract us from recognizing the truth and importance of the contingent empirical fact that law as we experience it is overwhelmingly coercive.

The significance of law's coerciveness is highlighted by the omnipresence of law in the modern regulatory state. Hart, some of his predecessors, and most of his followers criticized Bentham and Austin for attempting to shoehorn too much of law into a criminal and tort law paradigm,[1] but if anything, the modern regulatory state makes that paradigm more rather than less important now than it was in Bentham's and Austin's time. Today, individuals, businesses, and associations operate within the constraints of the administrative state to a much greater extent than Bentham and Austin could ever have imagined in the nineteenth century. And, importantly, the modern administrative state is an environment of pervasive regulation, with a mass of detailed regulations being enforced by the threat of criminal fines, civil liability, loss of privileges, and a panoply of other sanctions. Moreover, much of the contemporary regulatory environment, although often effective in implementing worthwhile environmental, health, safety, consumer protection, financial stability, and other policy goals, rarely inspires voluntary compliance. The owner or manager of a typical business may not need to be coerced into refraining from murder or outright fraud, but only rarely will she view the intricate regulation of securities transactions, anticompetitive agreements, and even worker safety with the same spirit of voluntary compliance. And the French cheese maker whose traditional use of raw milk has been declared unsafe by those he sees as meddling Brussels bureaucrats is little more inclined to comply with these regulations absent coercion than is his American counterpart whose workplace is regularly examined by inspectors from the Occupational Safety and Health Administration. For a vastly larger range of human and commercial activities than was the case even as recently as half a century ago, the state's power to regulate and punish is the overwhelmingly salient feature of law, even as that power has made life for millions, and even billions, of people far better than it was in the past.[2]

Not only does modern public law make the legal system's regulatory side vastly more important in the full scheme of social life than it was in earlier generations, but we now see as well a far greater regulatory intrusion into the seemingly voluntary transactions lying within the purview of private law. The legal implications of contracts, wills, and trusts, for example, are far more wide-ranging than in the past, and the tax consequences of effectuating such transactions in one way rather than another add a new element of coercion into the legal systems of modern states. And thus it is not just the man on the Clapham omnibus but almost all of us, in expanding aspects of our lives, who encounter law substantially in terms of the force it can bring to bear in the event of noncompliance. We should appreciate more today than in Austin's day that an examination of the nature of law cannot ignore the obvious fact of law's pervasive coerciveness. Denying the importance of law's force seems ever more perverse, even if we accept that coercion is not a necessary feature of all possible legal systems or of all aspects of the actual legal systems with which we are most familiar.

Although it is obvious that the coerciveness of law is important, it is not as obvious that it is jurisprudentially important. And thus we are led to consider the very question of importance, for one way of understanding the methodological debate is in terms of how we should treat the important features of law as we know it. Indeed, even those who believe that examining the nature of law must involve a search for its essential properties widely accept that we are only searching for those properties that are, in addition to being essential, also important.[3] After all, the essential properties of law include that it does not play the clarinet or explode before our eyes, but we have learned nothing of interest by including such properties within an account of law. And thus, even for those who hold an essentialist view of concepts and of the jurisprudential enterprise, the features we identify as being part of the nature of law must be those that appear to be important to the phenomenon under inspection and to our deeper understanding of it. But if it is pointless to examine those properties that are essential but not important, then perhaps one way of understanding the argument up to now is by stressing that it is far from pointless to examine, even philosophically, those properties that are important but not essential.[4]

Appreciating the role of importance in focusing the inquiry allows us to situate the concern for what Hart called the "puzzled man."[5] Even as we accept that noncoercive law is important in appreciating multiple dimensions of what law does, much of the argument for treating coercion as decidedly secondary in understanding the phenomenon of law is the view that in the typical advanced society law's unenforced obligatoriness—its normativity, as it is sometimes put[6]—is a substantial determinant of human behavior. After all, law has value as a distinct phenomenon, a distinct institution, and a distinct category largely insofar as it affects human behavior. Perhaps law might be of interest even were it causally inert, because examining a society's laws might reveal some feature of interest of which law was the consequence. From that perspective we might (and perhaps should) be interested in law as indicator and not as cause. Realistically, however, and certainly in this book, our principal interest in law and legal systems lies in their capacity to shape and influence what people do. Hart's puzzled man, who seeks to know what the law is in order to inform his behavior,[7] is the embodiment of this view.

It is possible to think of the puzzled man and thus of law's normativity from an entirely nonempirical perspective. We might wish to explore in a purely conceptual manner the way in which law—as law, and not as a reminder of what we should do even without it[8]—can provide its subjects with reasons for acting in accordance with the law just because it is the law, and can do so without regard for any possible sanctions. Sanctions would then be understood as a way of enforcing law's normativity, but not, *contra* Bentham and Austin, as a necessary component of law's normativity itself.

Yet, in the face of a purely conceptual inquiry in which the puzzled man is a potentially hypothetical construct and not an empirical description, some people might respond with a simple "So what?" If unsanctioned law does not actually influence human behavior, then why should we care about it? And at just this point in the dialectic, Hart's puzzled man (this is no longer 1961, so we will talk about the puzzled person) emerges in a different light. The image of the puzzled person is Hart's rejoinder to the "So what?" argument. The puzzled person is the one who actually does take sanction-independent legal obligation as a reason for action, and as a reason that can and often does influence her behavior and her decisions.

But even if *legal* obligations can in theory exist and be conduct-guiding without the state's army to back them, the extent to which people actually do internalize those obligations remains a serious empirical question. More specifically, our (not so) imaginary objector might respond, the actual number of people who take law's norms as reasons for action absent some form of coercion or incentives is so small as to be hardly worth worrying about.[9] Coercion is pervasive, the objector continues, precisely because the person who follows the law just because it is the law may be a theoretically instructive construct, but is not representative of many people we encounter in our everyday lives.

But now Hart has a further response. The puzzled person is not just a theoretical possibility, he argues, but the representation of people who exist in sufficient numbers that ignoring them gives a false picture of what law is and how it actually operates.[10] Hart, after all, used the puzzled man in conjunction with his charge that Austin's coercion-dependent picture did not "fit the facts" or recognize the "complexity of facts" of our actual existence under law.[11] Moreover, and more famously, the puzzled man is the central feature of Hart's response to what he understands as the import of Oliver Wendell Holmes's image of the "bad man."[12] Now we should not make too much of Holmes's language. There really are, of course, genuinely bad people, and for them the law is a looming threat to their exclusively self-interested and amoral or immoral proclivities. But there are also many people who are not "bad" in any conventional sense of that word, but who plan much of their lives and many of their activities in what has been called "the shadow of the law."[13] The editor of a newspaper whose editorial decisions are influenced by the probability of a libel judgment is not ordinarily a bad person, nor are the individuals whose decisions about whether to use marijuana, to drive above the speed limit in favorable conditions, or to engage in technically illegal but harmless sexual practices are influenced by the likelihood of actual enforcement of the laws.

If we thus put aside the unfavorable connotations of the "bad man" image, we see a contrast between the individual whose inclinations to obey the law are determined substantially by the likelihood of punishment and the individual who is inclined to obey the law just because it is the law and without regard to the possibility of punishment. The former class is what Bentham, Austin, and Holmes, among many others, all had in mind, and the latter is Hart's puzzled person. And if Hart and his followers are correct in their belief that puzzled people exist in significant numbers, then law's commands as laws are important even if and when they are backed by no sanctions at all. But if instead Bentham, Austin, and Holmes are correct in supposing that such puzzled people might exist in theory but only rarely in actual practice, then an account of the phenomenon of law that stresses coercion is not nearly as incomplete as many have believed. Bentham, in particular, recognized that people might behave for other than self-interested reasons, but he also believed that the demands of self-interested prudence would so often dominate the demands of altruism and community that law needed to use force to provide the motivation to do what the law required.[14]

The question is thus revealed as an empirical one. Hart offered the puzzled man as an empirical claim, but he provided no empirical support for that claim beyond bald assertion.[15] We can understand and agree that too insistent a focus on coercion may leave parts of law unexplained, and we can understand as well that following Austin in *defining* legal obligation in terms of coercion seems confused. But even conceding these objections, we may still wonder how important law without coercion really is. And when we do, the answer to that question turns out to depend largely on the extent to which people actually do take the law's commands as reasons for action, sanctions aside. If many people do so, as Hart and others have supposed, then it is indeed a mistake to put too much stock in coercion as an important element of the phenomenon of legality. But if sanction-oblivious law-followers are rare, and if puzzled people are few and far between, then it is not the account stressing coercion but the one setting it aside that presents a distorted picture of law as it is experienced.[16] And so, although Hart accused the Austinian account of failing to "do justice to the complexity of the facts,"[17] the soundness of that charge rests on an empirical claim that must now be examined with care.

4.2 What Is It to Obey the Law?

The image of the puzzled person is that of someone who wants to know what the law is so she can obey it and who is consequently inclined to obey the law just because it is the law but without having to be coerced. But although we can more or less easily understand what it is to be free of the threat of sanctions, at least in the standard case, the question of what it is to obey the law is a bit trickier.

Consider the laws against theft. Suppose I covet a much nicer car than the one I now own, and one much nicer than I can afford. And then suppose that one day I am strolling down the street and I see just the car I would like to have, parked at the side of the road, with the windows open and the keys lying invitingly on the driver's seat. The owner is presumably in a nearby shop, but there is no one on the street or elsewhere in sight. With little effort I could open the door, put the key in the ignition, and drive off in the car of my dreams.

Like many others, I like to think I would not steal the car. And I would not steal the car even if, counterfactually in a world of vehicle identification numbers and registrations and license plates, there were no possibility of apprehension, and even if, more counterfactually still, there were no laws against stealing at all. For me, and I believe (and hope) for many other people, the wrongness of the act would keep me from doing it, even though at a shallower level stealing the car would satisfy my immediate desires.

There are, of course, laws against theft, and those laws make it illegal to drive off in someone else's car without permission, even if the owner's carelessness has made it easy. And thus when I refrain from stealing a car, my behavior is consistent with the law. I have not violated the law, but, still, I have not behaved as I did *because of* the law. Even if stealing a car were not illegal, I still would not do it, and thus my actions in not stealing the car are not actions I took because of the law. We might say I acted *consistently* with the law, but I did not *comply* with the law. I do not, however, want anything to turn on a linguistic distinction, if one exists, between consistency and compliance. It is the underlying distinction that is important, and not whether the English language happens to recognize it. Similarly, we might say, and I would say, that it is only acting consistently with the law because of the law and not acting consistently with the law for reasons other than the law that counts as obeying the law, but, again, nothing in this argument turns on what the word "obey" means.[18] The point is only that there is a crucial difference between doing something because of the law and doing something for law-independent reasons that happens to be consistent with the law.

So now consider my dog. When I put food in front of her and command her to "Eat!," she eats. Every time. But of course she is not obeying my command. She would eat the food placed before her even if I said nothing at all.[19] And it is the same with the commands of the law. When the law tells me to do what I would have done anyway, the law's commands are no more causally consequential than commanding my highly food-motivated dog to eat. Our interest in law is largely an interest in law insofar as it is causally consequential, and for that purpose the distinction between law that makes a difference to behavior and law that makes no difference is of central importance. If we are interested in obedience to law, we must focus on law's effect on people who, but for the law, would have done something other than what the law commands. Or, to put it differently, we are interested in the cases in which what the law commands differs from what a subject of the law would have done for law-independent reasons.

There are many kinds of law-independent reasons, but two are particularly important here. First is the domain of law-independent personal preferences, desires, values, or tastes. It is illegal in most legal regimes to engage in cannibalism—eating the flesh of a deceased person, even if the eater has not caused the death. And it is illegal in many regimes—although perhaps not quite so many—to have sex with animals. But most people refrain from eating the flesh of human beings or having sex with animals for reasons having nothing to do with the law, even though their refraining from these activities puts them in compliance with the law. If the laws against such activities were repealed, most people's culinary and sexual practices would not change at all. These actions may be illegal, but most people do not avoid them because of the law. They avoid them because they simply have no desire to engage in them in the first place.

Second, sometimes people do desire to engage in what happens to be prohibited behavior but refrain from indulging these first-order or solely self-interested preferences because morality in the broadest sense constrains their behavior. I do not steal even the objects I covet, for example, because I believe that stealing is, usually, wrong. I do not throw heavy objects at those of my colleagues who speak interminably at faculty meetings not because I do not want to but because, even apart from the prudence of worrying about retaliation, I believe that such a reaction would be morally wrong, however much it might satisfy an immediate desire. And I refrain from likely profitable insider trading not because it is illegal but because I believe it is often wrong to take advantage of undisclosed informational disparities in commercial and business transactions. Of course, theft, assault, and insider trading are all illegal, but their illegality is no determinant of my behavior. Even when I have self-interested desires I would like to satisfy, I often refrain from satisfying them for reasons (or desires) of morality. The fact that the morally wrong thing to do is also illegal is interesting, and it might be important to others, but for me, at least on these and many other topics, illegality is no part of the equation.[20]

I make no claim that I am more moral than most. I might even be less. The point is only that most people make decisions about what to do and what not to do based on some complex mix of reasons of preference, prudence, and morality, but it is a mix that need not include the law. For most people most of the time, much that they do is consistent with the law, but is not done because of the law. Indeed, once we recognize that people can have altruistic, sympathetic, cooperative, and public-spirited motives,[21] that such motives often produce behavior consistent with those motives, and that these motives are neither self-interested nor caused by law, we can recognize the false dichotomy between Hart's law-motivated puzzled person and Holmes's self-motivated bad man. For in addition to law-motivated people and self-motivated people, there are other-motivated and morally motivated people. These other-motivated and morally motivated people are not only interested in furthering their own interests, but also can and often do take account of the interests of others even without the guidance of the law.

The point that concluded the previous paragraph is worth underscoring, for the false dichotomy between law-governed and self-interest-governed actions is ubiquitous. Consider the following, from a sociologist of law:

> Why do some people comply with the letter of the law, even when there is no threat of sanctions against their noncompliance and even though they know that following the law is not in their self-interest and will cost them in material and other terms? The answer to this question takes us to the heart of law's normativity.[22]

No, it doesn't. The leap from some people making decisions for reasons other than self-interest to *law*'s normativity assumes both law's causality and the lack of non-self-interested causality, most obviously from morally produced altruism, sympathy, cooperation, and public-spiritedness. But once we recognize that these latter motivations are real and frequently causal of human behavior, that people might behave for reasons of morality rather than self-interest, and that such behavior will often be consistent with the law even if not caused by the law, we are left with the question of what causal contribution, if any, the law makes to people's non-self-interested behavior when there are no legal sanctions or other forms of coercion in the offing. The contribution might be substantial, or it might be negligible, but posing an exclusive dichotomy between self-interest on the one hand and *law*'s normativity on the other ignores even the possibility of morality's normativity and thus makes it virtually impossible even to glimpse an answer to the question of how much law, *qua* law, contributes to people's decision-making processes.

Now that we have added moral, altruistic, cooperative, and sympathetic motivations to self-interested motivation, the question of law's effect becomes more complex. Consider, therefore, the person who has decided on a course of action on the basis of the full array of law-independent reasons, an array including both the self-interested and the moral. But then she discovers that the law prohibits what she has otherwise decided to do, or requires what she has otherwise decided to avoid. Under these circumstances, the question is whether she will do what the law requires even when the full array of law-independent reasons—what Joseph Raz calls the "balance of reasons"[23]—says otherwise. And bear in mind that we have stipulated that this is a person—the puzzled person—for whom law's coercive force is not relevant. That is, we are putting ourselves in the place of someone who thinks that she ought to φ on the basis of the full array of law-independent reasons, who then discovers that the law requires not-φ, and who then, *because of the law,* proceeds to do not-φ, and proceeds to do it without regard to the possibility of punishment or any other form of legal coercion. This is the puzzled person according to Hart's formulation. The question, however, is whether she exists.

4.3 Refining the Question

The question now before us is whether there are people, and if so in what quantity, who take the law *qua* law, and without the prudential reasons that threats of sanctions for violation may provide, as a reason for action. If such people exist in significant numbers, then, as Hart argued, explaining law largely in terms of its coercive force is a poor representation of the role that law serves in most people's decision-making processes. But if those who take the very fact of law as a reason for action or reason for decision are few and far between, then coercion resurfaces as the likely most significant source of law's widespread effectiveness and its longstanding appeal in achieving various social goals.

It is worth emphasizing that we are considering what is often referred to as law's *content-independent* authority.[24] The question is not whether we should follow the law because of the substantive content of the law. Yes, we should follow the laws against murder, rape, and price-fixing, but that is because murder, rape, and price-fixing are wrong. Laws against these activities should be followed because of the soundness of their content. Consequently, we should avoid such behaviors even if they were not illegal and thus without regard for the law. By contrast, accepting the law as obligatory in a content-independent way is accepting that the very fact of a law—its very existence independent of its content, or its very status as law rather than as something else—is a reason to obey it. Our question is whether law is in reality understood in this way by its subjects—whether people follow the law not because of its content but because of its existence.

Two important refinements need to be added to the stark way in which the issue has just been presented. First, law's putative effectiveness in providing reasons for action must be distinguished from its possible conclusiveness. As a long-standing literature about duties, obligations, reasons, and rules has stressed, there is a difference between a reason and a dispositive reason.[25] If I promise to meet you for lunch, I have a reason—an obligation—to meet you for lunch, but if a close relative falls ill in the interim, the reason I have to meet you for lunch will be overridden by the even stronger reason stemming from my obligation to assist ill relatives. At times, this idea of a not-necessarily-conclusive reason is described in terms of a *prima facie* reason, and at times as a *pro tanto* reason, but the idea is the same. What we have a reason to do is different from what we *should* do, all things considered. And thus, if the simple fact of law is a reason to behave in compliance with its directives, it will not necessarily always (or even usually) be the case that people actually follow the law. One can believe in the obligation to obey the law while believing that the obligations of morality and prudence are often stronger.

This qualification should not be taken too far. As an empirical and not a conceptual matter, we would expect that a real reason would actually make a difference in some cases. If we were to discover that over a run of a very large number of instances the law, as law, never determined the outcome, we would have reason to suspect that the law did not operate as even a weak reason. Only if in at least some cases did the presence of law produce an outcome or a decision different from that which would otherwise have prevailed could we plausibly conclude that law was actually operating as a reason.

Second, and relatedly, the distinction between the law and the array of law-independent reasons should not be taken as suggesting that decision makers necessarily bifurcate or sequence their decision-making processes in this way. Sometimes they do, and a nice example is President Franklin Roosevelt's suggestion to the U.S. Congress in 1937 that they consider the merits of a proposed regulation of the coal industry entirely as a matter of politics and policy, putting aside even "reasonable" potential legal and constitutional objections.[26] But sometimes the law exists as one of a number of nonsequentially ordered reasons affecting decisions in a less serial and less bifurcated matter. When this is so, the law is among multiple more-or-less simultaneously considered factors, as opposed to being consulted only after a law-independent decision has been reached. But even when this is so, it would again be highly unlikely, even if not logically impossible, for law to have the status of an actually internalized reason for action unless it made a difference in at least some instances. If law never made a difference—if it never produced an outcome different from the outcome produced by an array of reasons not including the law—then we might conclude, as an empirical matter, that it did not actually function as a reason at all.

The distinction between legal and all other reasons is thus a construct designed to isolate the question whether law figures in the decisions and actions of law's subjects. Without this construct, we would be unable to ask the question whether law actually matters. We could, of course, just choose to assume that law matters, but at this point the bare assumption that law matters begins to resemble an assumption that there are unicorns. We know what unicorns are (or would be), but the mere fact that we can describe a unicorn tells us little about whether there are actual unicorns in the world. Similarly, we can describe and understand legal normativity—the ability of law to make a practical difference[27]— but we should also want to know whether the law, without regard for the sanctions that might contingently back it up, actually plays a role in determining the actions and decisions of its subjects. And for purposes of this inquiry, distinguishing law-free decisions from those in which law is part of the array of reasons internalized by a decision maker remains important.

Yet, we should not be too quick to assume that the distinction between law-free and law-influenced decision making is merely an analytical fiction, however useful that fiction may be. In fact, just this kind of law versus everything else bifurcation appears to occur as often in reality as in fiction. Businesspeople often strike their bargains in a business-informed, not law-informed, way, and then only after agreeing on the fundamentals of the transaction will they call in the lawyers to make it legal or tell them how it might not be. And, in much the same way, policy makers often make policy decisions without regard to legality, only thereafter securing the advice of government counsel to determine whether they can pursue those policies in accordance with the law.

The question is thus refined: If we distinguish the reasons provided by law from the reasons provided by morality, policy, prudence, and everything else, and if we distinguish the reasons provided by law from the various forms of enforcement that law typically employs to assure actual decision according to those reasons, then to what extent do these sanction-independent legal reasons actually influence decisions? Hart's puzzled person is the implicit answer to this question. But we do not know whether Hart's answer is correct.

4.4 The Ought and the Is

Obedience to law *qua* law—taking the very existence of law as at least a *prima facie* reason to follow it—is a topic with a distinguished history. But almost all this history is normative and not descriptive. As far back as Socrates and his insistence on acknowledging his obligation to the law even as he believed it to have condemned him unjustly,[28] philosophers and ordinary people have argued that there is a content-independent moral obligation to obey the law. Thomas Hobbes and John Locke, among others, found the basis of such an obligation in the social contract.[29] John Rawls and others even more recently have located the source of the obligation in principles of fairness and reciprocity.[30] Still others have seen the obligation to obey the law as arising from a notion of consent,[31] from law's ability to coordinate collective action in the face of diverse and suboptimizing incentives to individual preference satisfaction,[32] or from our obligations to respect our fellow citizens in the process of making the law.[33] But all these theories share the goal of justifying an obligation on the part of people to obey the law just because it is the law, and thus to obey—or at least have a reason to obey—even those laws with which they disagree.

Along with this tradition of seeking to justify a moral obligation to obey the law is a conflicting and more recent tradition denying that there is a moral obligation to obey the law at all.[34] Often called "philosophical anarchism" these days, this more recent tradition rejects all of the existing reasons to recognize a content-independent obligation to obey the law. Philosophical anarchism thus concludes that although the moral citizen has a moral duty to do the right thing, she has no moral duty to follow the law just because it is the law, and thus has no moral duty, and no reason, to follow those laws (or other manifestations of the state's assertion of normative authority) that conflict with her own best all-things-considered moral calculation about what to do.[35]

The debates about the existence (or not) of a moral obligation to obey the law are interesting and profoundly important. But our concern here is different. For present purposes, the question is not whether citizens *should* follow the law because it is the law but whether, and to what extent, they actually do so. For if citizens (or officials, as we shall explore in Chapter 6) rarely obey the law just because it is the law, and if puzzled people, in Hart's sense, are few and far between, then coercion reemerges as a phenomenon empirically even if not logically necessary for law to do what is expected of it. The importance of looking at obedience to law *qua* law descriptively and empirically rather than normatively is that the importance—albeit not the possibility—of sanction-free law presupposes a critical mass of obedient subjects. If a significant proportion of the population does not need to be coerced into following the law even when the demands of the law are at variance with subjects' otherwise best law-independent judgment, then coercion may be a useful support for law, but is hardly central to it. But if the significant proportion does not exist—if there is no critical mass of people willing to subjugate their own judgment to that of the law unless they are forced to do so—then sanction-free law is more theoretical possibility than empirical reality. And if sanction-free law is empirically rare, then coercion, which even Hart acknowledges is a "natural necessity,"[36] is revealed, as it was for Austin and Bentham, as a central feature of the legal systems that actually exist.

The stage is now set for examining this empirical question, informed and clarified by the understanding of obedience to law that generations of legal theory have helped us to see. We know that mere consistency with law is not enough. We want to see whether people make decisions or take actions *because* of the law. And we want to know whether people who make decisions or take actions because of the law do so without regard to the law's threats of force or other sanctions. And that, precisely, is the focus of Chapter 5.

5

DO PEOPLE OBEY THE LAW?

5.1 Complying with the Laws We Like

In an influential book, the social psychologist Tom Tyler asked *Why People Obey the Law.*[1] The title is revealing. A book entitled *Why Humans Are Omnivores* would be expected to focus on the causal explanation of what we know to be plainly the case, but a book entitled *Why Humans Have Antlers* would probably intrigue us because the title presupposes a fact that is in reality false. Human beings do not have antlers, so explaining why they do makes no sense.

Tyler's title is not confused in so obvious a way, but it does assume that people *do* obey the law. But is the assumption sound? *Do* people obey the law? The answer is not obvious, and it hinges not only on clarifying what it is to obey the law but also on the empirical answer to the question as so clarified. We thus need to look closely at the question whose answer Tyler takes to be self-evident. Do people actually *obey* the law?

In concluding that people do obey the law, and in using that conclusion to inquire into why they do so, Tyler's main point is that people obey the law for reasons other than fear of punishment or other sanctions. He is interested, as we are in this book, in the causal role of law in influencing behavior. And Tyler is especially interested, as was H. L. A. Hart in referring to the "puzzled man,"[2] in the extent to which law influences behavior even when the law's directives are unsupported by the threat of coercive sanctions in the event of noncompliance. Yet, although Hart and others[3] have simply asserted or assumed that puzzled people exist in large enough quantities to support a sanction-independent account of the nature of law, Tyler believes that much the same conclusion is supported by systematic empirical investigation. More particularly, he and his colleagues take themselves to have established, largely by survey research, that sanctions are of decidedly secondary importance in ex-plaining legal compliance. Rather, they conclude that "morality [is] the primary factor in shaping law-related behavior."[4]

Put aside for the moment the ambiguity of the phrase "law-related behavior." We will return to it and to the distinction between behavior correlated with law and behavior caused by law. But first we must at-tend to an essential preliminary issue. And that is that Tyler derives his conclusion that morality is the principal determinant of law-related be-havior by setting up a contrast with his principal foil: the belief that people ordinarily behave for entirely or principally self-interested rea-sons. That this is Tyler's target is made clear by his arguments explicitly aimed at the "self-interest model"[5] and his claim that "the study of law-related behavior [has] been dominated by [economic] analysis."[6]

Whether economists actually believe that self-interest and the fear of unpleasant sanctions (or the hope for personal rewards) are the sole or dominant human motivations is a question best left to economists. But Tyler nevertheless posits a dichotomy between self-interested behavior and law-related behavior, as if self-interest and law exhausted the uni-verse of human motivation. But if there are motivations that are neither self-interested nor law-related, then the move from the absence of moti-vation by self-interest to the presence of motivation by law is an error. More particularly, if the motives of law-independent morality (or altru-ism, cooperation, and working for the public interest) also impel human action, then Tyler's conclusion about the effect of law from the premise of non-self-interest is fallacious. If people frequently engage in morally or socially motivated rather than purely selfish behavior, and if they do so without reference to the law, then the conclusion that morality is the primary factor in shaping law-related behavior tells us little about law and even less about law's effect on behavior.[7]

That people can be altruistic, cooperative, moral, social, sympathetic, and other-regarding not only in their attitudes but in their behavior has long been established by extensive empirical research.[8] It is true that self-interest is an important and often dominant motivation for many people in many contexts, and indeed it may even be a natural human impulse.[9] Yet we know that when people perceive a form of behavior to have substantial moral (or religious) or "prosocial" implications, they will often relegate their own personal interest to secondary importance behind what they believe is the right thing to do.[10] But if moral motivations and internalized moral norms lead people to refrain from activities that are both self-interested and illegal—if they keep people from stealing even when it would be profitable and from committing assault even when it would be pleasurable—we do not know whether the cause of people's non-self-interested actions is the illegality or the immorality. And without distinguishing the two, we do not know how much of a causal contribution, if any, the illegality is making to people's decisions.

The existing research on human motivation thus supports what should be hardly surprising (except to those who believe that self-interest is the only human motivation): that people often do what they believe is right, questions of law aside. But insofar as that is so, then law's contribution can be understood largely in terms of constraining moral outliers rather than in affecting the behavior of the majority. The majority may well often engage in morally motivated behavior that happens to be consistent with the law, but it is not clear why we would want to call such behavior "law-related." Maybe we should just call it "moral." And if we did, it would be easier to focus on the distinction, as an empirical matter, between consistency with the law and actual obedience to the law. If moral people do not shoplift, then the fact that their nonshoplifting happens to be consistent with the law is compatible with law being causally inert for them. It is worthwhile knowing that people will behave consistently with those laws that track their own moral preferences,[11] but this conclusion tells us nothing if we are interested in examining the effect of sanction-independent law on human behavior and decision making.

If we thus seek to distinguish morally motivated consistency with law from law-motivated behavior, another aspect of Tyler's research seems initially more fruitful. And that is his conclusion that the perception of legitimacy, while not as important as morality in determining conformity with law-related behavior, is an important factor. More specifically, Tyler concludes that when the probability of sanctions is low,[12] subjects' beliefs in the law's legitimacy are more important than the threat of sanctions in bringing about law-consistent behavior.[13] Thus, one of Tyler's secondary conclusions is that people tend to obey the law for reasons other than fear of punishment when they believe that the laws are the product of a system they believe legitimate. And legitimacy, Tyler maintains, is largely a matter of procedural regularity, opportunity for citizen input, and the respectful treatment of citizens by those in authority. When people have a say in the laws that bind them, when those laws are made through fair and open methods, and when people feel respected by their officials, Tyler concludes, they will be inclined to obey the law just because it is the law.

But now consider the laws that are Tyler's predominant focus: primarily the minor prohibitions of the criminal law, such as shoplifting, littering, making excessive noise, and the laws regulating driving and parking.[14] But in almost all the cases in which Tyler finds that people claim they would follow the law for reasons other than fear of sanctions, the laws are ones the followers likely think are good laws, even if application of those laws disadvantages them personally. Few people who shoplift think that prohibiting shoplifting is a poor idea, and so too with laws against excessive noise, littering, speeding, and even overtime parking. The people who break these often do not believe that societies should not have those laws, but only that it is advantageous to them at some particular time to break what in the abstract they believe to be a good or necessary law. And so it turns out that people who claim to be following laws they believe to have been enacted legitimately are also following laws they believe to be good laws. And again it is not clear that law *qua* law is playing any causal role. If a perception of legitimacy increases the likelihood that people will obey laws they think are good but that "cost" them personally, we have learned something about compliance but little about the extent to which the fact of legality leads people to obey laws they think wrong and not merely costly, frustrating, or inconvenient. Or, to put it differently, we have learned nothing about people's willingness to defer to the law's judgments about correct and incorrect courses of action when our field of vision is limited to people who agree with the law's judgment but would still prefer to do what they acknowledge is wrong but which will benefit them personally.[15]

More promising is the question in Tyler's survey[16] asking respondents whether they agree or disagree with the statement "People should obey the law even if it goes against what they think is right."[17] On this, 33 percent of the respondents strongly agreed, 52 percent agreed, and the remaining 15 percent disagreed or disagreed strongly.[18] If these responses are to be believed, it does appear that many people are willing to obey the law just because it is the law even when they think the laws are unwise.[19]

Yet although this question is aimed at whether people will obey laws with which they disagree, a problem remains because the question does not exclude the possibility of reaction to sanctions. Tyler's research does indicate that, at least at low levels of enforcement, fear of sanctions is not as strong a motivation for compliance as belief in the wrongness of the act or belief in a law's legitimacy. But without excluding sanctions from abstract statements of willingness to comply with laws that one believes are wrong, we cannot reach strong conclusions about the extent to which sanction-free law *qua* law is providing people with a reason to avoid engaging in behavior they would, the law aside, have considered desirable.[20]

This is not to say that the research in this vein is without value. Many laws do track people's law-independent decisions about what to do, and enforcing those laws against outliers is important. And so is enforcing those laws in the face of personal interests in noncompliance. If a sense of legitimacy will increase compliance rates under those circumstances, it is a valuable tool for policy-making purposes. But our interest here is in whether, absent sanctions, the very fact of law makes a difference to the reasoning and decision-making processes of ordinary people. For this purpose, Tyler's research provides some support for the conclusion that legitimacy makes a difference, but it also supports the conclusion that the level of sanction-free compliance with laws with which people disagree remains very low. At the very least, the research provides at best weak evidence for the empirical claim that Hart and others have found so important: that significant numbers of puzzled people take the bare fact of a norm being a legal one as a reason for action or a reason for decision— that is, who follow the law just because it is the law.

5.2 Isolating the Effect of the Law

As referenced above,[21] a long-standing body of research finds that people commonly act for reasons other than self-interest.[22] Often they tell the truth even when it would be beneficial to lie. They help strangers in need even at personal cost. They do not take others' belongings even when there is no possibility of detection. And in many other ways, to borrow the words of the filmmaker Spike Lee, they "Do the Right Thing."[23] Moreover, even when self-interest in the broad sense predominates, we know from the research on collective action and cooperative and coordinating behaviors that individuals will frequently engage in short-term self-denying acts in order to reap the benefits of longer-term coordinated action.[24]

There are numerous competing or overlapping explanations of why people seem frequently, although hardly always, to set aside their self-interest in the service of moral or other values. Under some accounts, certain moral intuitions explain much of moral behavior.[25] Other accounts emphasize moral behavior as a function of the internalization of social norms and social expectations.[26] Others attribute non-self-serving moral behavior to the way in which morality and altruism make us feel better about ourselves, and thus be self-serving in a deeper sense.[27] And still others are attracted to Freudian,[28] evolutionary,[29] or neuroscientific explanations of moral, altruistic, and genuinely cooperative behavior.[30] But whatever the deeper cause, it seems clear that behavior other than the self-serving is often a significant motivation of human action.

The import of this conclusion is that it is a mistake to view human motivation as based either on self-interest or on law. Setting up this false dichotomy between law and self-interest was Tyler's mistake. And, earlier, it was Hart's mistake as well. In framing the issue of obedience as an opposition between the bad man—who cares only for self-interest—and the puzzled man—who wants to know what the law is so he can follow it—Hart ignored the moral person: the person who acts for reasons other than self-interest but who does not need the motivations or prescriptions or instructions of the law to get her to do so.

If people often act for non-self-interested reasons, inquiring into the effect of law thus requires distinguishing law-produced reasons for action not only from self-interested reasons but also from law-independent moral reasons. Because people sometimes act morally for reasons other than self-interest and other than law, we need to know what, if anything, law adds to the equation. More precisely, we need to know not only what people do when law conflicts with their self-interest but also, and often more importantly, what people do when the law conflicts with their all-things-except-the-law-considered best judgment. The question now is whether people, when they have reached this all-things-except-the-law-considered judgment, will, sanctions aside, subjugate *that* judgment to the prescriptions of the law. Will people do what they believe is wrong (or silly, pointless, unsound, immoral, improvident, unwise, etc.) just because of the law and without regard to the threat of sanctions?[31]

Hart's puzzled person is thus someone who follows the law just because it is the law even when what the law requires seems not only not in her best interest but also contrary to her best judgment. There is a reason that philosophers grappling with the issue are fond of imagining "Stop" signs in the middle of the desert,[32] and that is because the example creates a situation in which the likelihood of apprehension and punishment is close to zero and in which acting in accordance with the law appears otherwise pointless. The example is artificial, but it does present the issue clearly, and it captures, as we shall see, a rather wide range of real-world circumstances in which what the law commands diverges from what its subjects would otherwise do and in which the likelihood of sanction is negligible. It is in such circumstances that Hart supposed that his puzzled person would likely follow the law, or at least take the law as a sometimes dispositive reason for action. And it is with respect to such circumstances that the question of sanction-independent obedience to law *qua* law arises.

To formulate a question is not to answer it. But proper formulation steers us in the right direction and keeps us from wrong ones. More specifically, the correctly formulated question about obedience to law points us to research focused precisely on how people behave and decide when their own best all-things-considered analysis indicates one course of action or decision and the law indicates another. At times this divergence will reflect someone's belief that the law is morally or otherwise mistaken, as with the now-common beliefs about laws restricting the use of marijuana and other so-called soft drugs, or laws prohibiting various sexual practices that conflict with the contemporary majority's moral notions. And at other times people believe that the law's mandates are mistaken not because the entire law is, by their lights, misguided, but because a good law appears by virtue of its generality to have produced a poor result on a particular occasion.[33] Most people who violate traffic laws, for example, do not object to traffic laws as such, or even to the particular traffic laws they violate. Rather, they believe that the traffic laws have indicated a bad or silly result on some particular occasion, as with a speed limit that seems far too low on a clear, dry, and traffic-free Sunday morning or a "Don't Walk" sign that tells pedestrians to wait at the curb even when there is no approaching car as far as the eye can see.

Whether because of a belief that an entire law is wrong or only that a good law would produce a bad result under particular circumstances, people often face situations in which their all-things-except-the-law-considered best judgment indicates one course of action and the law indicates another. It is in such cases that Hart and Tyler, among others, believe that many people will follow the law's indications even absent sanctions. But both the existing research and ordinary observation appear to provide virtually no support for their conclusions.

To be specific, little actual empirical research focuses directly on the question whether people obey the law, sanctions and their own best judgments apart, just because it is the law. And what research there is appears more consistent with the conclusion that the law makes little difference under such conditions than with the opposite conclusion: that adding law to the decision-making process makes a substantial difference apart from the sanctions the law may have at its disposal. Of course, there is a difference between lack of support for a conclusion and support for the opposite conclusion. Here, however, there appears to be little support for the conclusion of law's sanction-independent influence and some, albeit weak, support for the conclusion of law's sanction-independent noninfluence.

Thus, in one study, researchers asked subjects whether they would, as a teacher, violate a rule (which in this context can be considered equivalent to the law) mandating so-called blind grading of papers when following the rule would produce injustice. And although the subjects professed to have general attitudes favoring rule adherence over rule-independent good outcomes, these general attitudes withered in the face of a concrete example. When given a specific example as opposed to being asked for their abstract opinion, subjects preferred the good outcome to the rule-directed one. And this was so not only for lay subjects but also for law students and lawyers.[34] The law students and lawyers were somewhat more inclined to follow the rule even when it produced what they deemed to be an unjust result, but subjects in all categories took their own sense of a just result to be more important than following what they perceived to be the governing law. Thus, this particular study—only one study, to be sure—not only suggested that there may be less law-following for the sake of law than others have supposed but also that abstract attitudes about the importance of law-following may be less reliable as predictors of law-following behavior than some of the earlier research—Tyler's, in particular—has assumed.

Other research has produced similar results. In one pair of studies, law students were found more willing to make decisions in accordance with their own policy preferences than in accordance with the law, even when the law was clear, even when they were given incentives to follow the law, and even though they tended to believe that their policy preferences should not have and did not have any effect on their legal decisions.[35] Again, these studies indicate not only that being guided by law *qua* law is less prevalent than often assumed but also that the importance of legal guidance is systematically overestimated even by the decision makers themselves. We *think* that law ought to matter, and thus we think that law *does* matter, but in fact it may matter less than we think, at least when our law-independent judgments are inconsistent with the law's judgments and when force, coercion, and sanctions are removed from the equation.

These conclusions should not be surprising. We know that preferences influence judgments, the phenomenon being what psychologists sometimes call "motivated reasoning"[36] and sometimes "myside bias."[37] And the more specific application of this phenomenon is the tendency of legal decision makers, including ordinary people deciding whether the law constrains their actions, to understand and interpret the law in light of their outcome preferences.[38] Indeed, this was the core claim of the American Legal Realists, who argued that judges often or even usually understood and interpreted the law in light of their nonlegally determined outcome preferences.[39] And although the empirical conclusions of the Realists were often underresearched and overclaimed, subsequent research has confirmed at least some of the basic Realist insight that judges frequently perceive and locate the law in light of their preferred outcomes.[40] And thus, insofar as even lawyers and judges often find or interpret the law in ways that produce their desired outcomes, it should come as little surprise that ordinary people do the same thing.[41] We know, for example, that lay jurors generally prefer what they perceive as the right decision over the legally mandated one when the two conflict.[42] And thus, to the extent that both lay and legally trained people treat the law as less important than their law-independent judgments, the empirical foundations of the notion of law operating, absent coercion, as an external constraint on people's preferred courses of action are undercut even further.

Indeed, when we turn from experimental research to data on actual legal compliance, we find substantial support for the hypothesis that unenforced law that does not track people's law-independent preferences and judgments (including moral judgments) is often ineffective. Before computers facilitated the process of tracking down people who did not appear in court in response to citations for traffic violations, for example, the nonappearance rate was 60 percent, even though in such cases the legal "command" was directed to a particular person to engage in the particular act of showing up in court.[43] Much the same can be said about people who are individually summoned to appear for jury duty, where compliance rates absent stringent sanctions have been found to be as low as 20 percent, and are often in the 30 to 50 percent range.[44] Similarly, the scofflaw rate for parking meters in San Francisco was 40 percent in 2007,[45] and official reports indicate that compliance rates for mandatory pet licenses in New York, New Jersey, and Pennsylvania are below 20 percent for dog licenses and, at least in New York, around 3 percent for cat licenses.[46] In Australia, noncompliance with High-Occupancy Vehicle lane laws was 90 percent without enforcement and was estimated at over 50 percent in the United States.[47] Similarly, fare evasion in cities and countries with so-called honor systems of fare collection on public transportation has been reported at equivalently high rates.[48] Compliance with motorcycle helmet laws in Jamaica has been estimated at 6 percent,[49] and one study found that under circumstances of low enforcement, the degree of compliance with a Hong Kong law prohibiting tobacco sales to minors was below 19 percent.[50] Most recently, the California law restricting the sale of marijuana and its use only for medical reasons is widely disregarded, and the *New York Times,* tellingly, describes the widespread disregard for the law as creating "few problems," presumably on the assumption that disregard for the law itself is not problematic.[51]

A great deal of interesting data come from studies of compliance with tax laws. An unfortunate tendency in the tax-compliance literature is referring to taxpayer-provided information and payments as "voluntary" to distinguish taxpayer reporting and payment from point-of-income payments, as with the common (and required) practice of withholding taxes from salary payments.[52] But failing to report income is a crime, as is intentionally failing to pay the taxes that are due. And even when the level of culpability does not rise to the criminal, underpayment of taxes often brings substantial civil penalties. As a result, so-called voluntary tax compliance is voluntary only in the same way that someone who drives under the speed limit rather than be stopped by the police and required to pay a fine is voluntary, and only in the same way that the would-be thief who refrains from theft to avoid imprisonment can be said to have acted voluntarily. In may be true that someone who chooses compliance rather than punishment has made a voluntary choice in some sense, but describing an act of legal compliance under threat of punishment for noncompliance as voluntary is inconsistent with our ordinary understanding of voluntariness and incompatible with our effort here to focus on coercive dimensions of law.

When we put aside the confusing connotations of the word "voluntary," we discover that genuinely uncoerced compliance with the tax laws is hardly common.[53] In the United States, many forms of income are reported directly by the payor (such as an employer) to federal tax authorities, making the opportunities for undetected evasion small. But for income neither withheld nor directly reported in this manner—income not subject to information reporting, as it is put—and thus for income whose existence is known primarily by the taxpayer, estimates of the rates of noncompliance range from 50 percent upward (the Internal Revenue Service estimated 54 percent in 2007)—and this under circumstances in which taxpayers know that failing to report is a crime involving serious penalties. Although rates of tax compliance vary greatly across countries, these figures are hardly atypical internationally.[54] Indeed, the data from the United States, where compliance is thought to be higher than in many other countries, suggest that truly uncoerced and unthreatened obedience to the tax laws is far rarer than the image of the puzzled person would suggest.

This collection of studies and reports provides considerable support for the conclusion that when sanctions are removed from the equation, and when the laws at issue are not ones that track people's salient and law-independent sense of what they ought to do, compliance with the law just because it is the law is far less widespread than Hart, with his reference to puzzled person, and Tyler, in presupposing that people *do* obey the law, assume. Indeed, looking carefully at Tyler's reference to "law-related behavior" is particularly instructive. Behavior can be law-related if it correlates with law even if it is not caused by law, and it can be law-related if it is caused by the sanctions that accompany the law (or a perception of those sanctions) and not the sanction-independent internalization of a legal norm as a norm of behavior. But when we remove the instances in which we see correlation but probably not causation, and when we remove sanctions, what we are left with is an empirical claim about the prevalence of obedience to law *qua* law that appears largely unsupported by the available evidence.

5.3 On Obedience to Authority

But what about Milgram? From 1963 to 1974, the Yale psychologist Stanley Milgram conducted a series of now-notorious experiments in which subjects were instructed to inflict increasing amounts of pain (through electric shocks) on various victims, allegedly as part of an experiment on the effect of punishment on learning.[55] In fact, the victims did not receive any electric shocks, and the experiment was not about the effect of punishment on learning but about obedience to authority. The subjects, however, most of whom followed the instruction to inflict pain, did not know that at the time. The Milgram experiments have thus been widely cited as supporting the conclusion that people will obey authority even to the point of doing things they would not otherwise do, and which they would otherwise find unacceptable for moral or other reasons. And, not surprisingly, many people believe the Milgram experiments explain why so many people blindly followed orders from authority to engage in the appalling acts we now refer to as the Holocaust.[56]

For our present purposes, it appears that the lesson we can take from the Milgram experiments is that people will do things an authority figure tells them to do even if their own authority-independent judgment tells them not to. And because law is a practice of authority in which the law claims the right to tell its subjects to put aside their own judgment in favor of the law's judgment,[57] then do not the Milgram experiments suggest that people might blindly or at least presumptively defer to the law in the same way that they deferred to the authority figure in the laboratory? Because our inquiry at this point is empirical, the Milgram experiments seem to support the conclusion that people can and will obey, in the strict sense of "obey," an authority. Just as the subjects appeared to set aside their own judgments and moral compass in favor of following the researcher's instructions, then it would seem that much the same might apply to the willingness of people to set aside their own judgments in favor of the commands of the law.

As several decades of commentary on the Milgram experiments have suggested,[58] however, it is hardly clear that the subjects understood themselves to be following an authority, as opposed to trying to please someone with whom they were in close contact or as opposed to participating in a collective small-group enterprise. Indeed, when subsequent experiments attempted to isolate obedience as such, and thus exclude various forms of interpersonal cooperation, it became less apparent that following an authority figure just because he or she exhibited the trappings of authority or possessed formal authority was very much of an identifiable phenomenon.[59] At the very least, the subsequent research cautions against reading too much into the Milgram experiments and against taking them as plainly establishing the willingness of people to obey authority simply because it is authority.

Just as we should not take the lesson of the Milgram experiments too far, neither should we put too much emphasis on the subsequent skepticism about the experiments. People frequently do follow authorities and often consider their instructions and commands as valid reasons for action. Sometimes, of course, this obedience grows out of a fear of sanctions, and it is hardly unusual for people to set aside their own judgment in favor of the those of sergeants, parents, teachers, deans, police officers, and others just because of what such authority figures can do to them if they do not obey. And sometimes the obedience is indeed sanction-independent. It is implausible to claim that the directives of parents, teachers, and religious and political leaders, even when not backed by sanctions, never or even rarely have an effect on behavior. [60]

The premise that people often obey authorities, however, does not entail the conclusion that people obey *legal* authorities with the same frequency. I might trust the sergeant's judgment but doubt that the law systematically has the same degree of experience or expertise. I might obey my parents out of respect but not have the same respect for the law. And I might understand that numerous social tasks require someone to be in charge without believing that law is very often the best candidate for that role. Indeed, law's very distance from its subjects might make legal obedience less likely than in some of these other examples, and law's distance from its subjects might make it more necessary for law than it is for sergeants, parents, teachers, and lifeboat commanders to have sanctions at their disposal. To offer that hypothesis is to get ahead of things a bit, but at least at this point in the argument it is wise not to draw too many inferences about sanction-free legal obedience from instances of obedience in far different contexts.

5.4 Does Law Cause Morality?

One potential objection to the empirical analysis in the previous sections is that it assumes a false dichotomy between law and morality, or between law and someone's all-things-other-than-the-law considered best judgment. If the very idea of "law" included a wide range of political, moral, empirical, and policy considerations, then making any attempt to isolate the effects of a narrower conception of positive law would be a fundamentally misguided enterprise. If the very category of law encompassed the factors I have been supposing are the components of a law-independent decision, then the distinction between the legal and the nonlegal would be rendered incoherent.

This objection has overtones of Ronald Dworkin's perspective on law and his capacious understanding of the category of law.[61] For Dworkin, law itself is the best interpretive understanding of a wide range of legal, moral, and political inputs, and he thus rejects what he describes as the "positivist" inclination to separate out a distinct realm of the legal from this larger array of normative considerations. Consequently Dworkin would find it hard even to understand an inquiry premised on isolating the effect of a narrower conception of law.

Such an understanding of law, however, defines away what would otherwise be a range of important questions. Most significantly, too capacious a conception of law makes it virtually impossible to determine the effect on the decisions of judges, policy makers, and the public of what the ordinary person and the ordinary official take to be law: the category of materials largely dominated by statutes, regulations, reported judicial decisions, written constitutions, and the conventional devices of legal analysis. Following Ruth Gavison, we might label this skeletal category of materials "first-stage law."[62] Whether first-stage law is all or just some of law is an interesting and important question, but it is not the only interesting and important question. After all, when such famous practitioners of civil disobedience as Henry David Thoreau, Mahatma Gandhi, Bertrand Russell, the Suffragettes, and Martin Luther King engaged in what they took to be acts in contravention of existing law, *they* understood their acts as violations of law understood in a narrower and more concrete way. *Their* question was whether and when first-stage law should be violated in the service of what they perceived as a higher moral calling. But only with a grasp of a category such as first-stage law does their (and our) understanding of their acts even make sense, because the very conflict they perceived and articulated dissolves if law includes the moral issues they believed conflicted with the law.[63] And thus, only with something like the category of first-stage law in hand can we understand the perspective on law not only of most ordinary people but of the legal system itself. When we are interested in whether people obey the law, we require such a relatively narrow understanding of law to make sense of the question. If "law" is simply the label we attach to a judgment with a far more capacious set of inputs—if obeying the law collapses into doing the right thing—then inquiring into the effect of law on decisions becomes pointless, defining away a question that has endured at least since the death of Socrates.[64] So whether we call the category first-stage law, positive law, human law, or something else, a persistent issue is whether people should and do act in accordance with the mandates of the components of that category. At least here we are asking whether this category as a category has an effect on people's behavior and, if so, when, how, and why.

The more serious false dichotomy objection, however, accepts that there are important differences between law and the nonlaw set of moral and social norms but claims that law, even in the narrow "first-stage" sense, has a causal effect on what people believe that morality requires. Even steering well clear of the metaethical question of what morality actually is, there is still the question of where people's moral beliefs come from. And if the law has a causal effect on what people believe morality requires, then law is potentially doing more work than a skeptical conclusion about law's persuasive effect would acknowledge.

The research on the effects of law on perceptions of morality is, again—and not surprisingly—mixed. In the 1930s and 1940s, a group of legal theorists called Scandinavian Realists started with the assumption, derived from the Logical Positivism that was fashionable at the time, that morality itself was an inherently subjective and entirely psychological phenomenon.[65] The Logical Positivists believed that the very concept of morality was meaningless except as the outgrowth of the contingent beliefs that people happened to have, and the Scandinavian Realists believed that law was a significant contributor to these beliefs. In short, the Scandinavian Realists believed that public official pronouncements in the form of law had a causal effect on what people believed to be right and what they believed to be wrong.

The Scandinavian Realists were not sophisticated social scientists, and their conclusions about the causal effect of law on beliefs about morality were largely speculations, hypotheses, assumptions, and perhaps just hopeful guesses. In the ensuing years, however, social scientists have become interested in the question, but the research on the effect of law on opinion formation remains inconclusive.[66] Although some studies have found that making an activity (attempting suicide and littering, for example) illegal appeared to have no effect on the percentage of people finding the activity immoral,[67] others have found some effect of law on moral beliefs in the context of acts such as public drunkenness and failure to prevent suicide, although the latter studies did not distinguish between the effect of law and that of peer opinion.[68]

A contemporary example illustrates the issue. There is little doubt that many countries have seen a rapid change in opinion about homosexuality in general and same-sex marriage in particular. And much of that change has taken place in parallel with or subsequent to legal change, including the proliferation of laws and judicial decisions prohibiting discrimination on the basis of sexual orientation, and including the increasing number of jurisdictions legally recognizing same-sex marriage. But these changes have also taken place in parallel with and subsequent to a dramatic increase in the favorable portrayal of gays and lesbians in the mass media, particularly in movies and on television. And there has also been an equally dramatic increase in the number of gays and lesbians who are willing to be open and explicit about their sexual orientation, and thus an increase in the number of heterosexuals who have regular contact in school, at work, and in social interactions with people they know to be gay or lesbian. As a result, it is not surprising that the research task of sorting out direction of causation among these multiple factors is daunting and that the results have been largely inconclusive on the precise question that interests us here. Believing that the law is the predominant factor in attitudinal change seems to attribute to law more importance in attitude formation than the research conclusions justify, but attributing to law no or only a small effect seems equally unjustified.[69] At the moment we just do not know the answer, but that does not make the question any less important.

Much the same can be said about some number of other topics that combine high public and legal salience. American constitutionalists, in particular, are fond of attributing to the Supreme Court's decision in *Brown v. Board of Education*[70] in 1954 a substantial causal effect on changing racial attitudes, but the lawyer/political scientist Gerald Rosenberg has offered evidence that the *Brown* decision's effect on people's beliefs may be less than that of changes in popular culture, mass-media reports of important public events, and various official acts and pronouncements less obviously associated with the legal system as such.[71] Yet, there is some evidence that Supreme Court decisions may have produced attitudinal change with respect to prayer in the public schools.[72] And we might hypothesize the same about laws relating to the environment. Many more people now believe that environmental preservation is of fundamental moral importance than believed the same thing fifty years ago, and there are far more laws protecting the environment than there were fifty years ago, but sorting out the causal pathways is extraordinarily difficult, and perhaps intractable.

For our purposes, the issue is even more complex. Even if law is itself a contributor at one remove to what seem to be law-independent moral and policy judgments, we do not know how much of law's effect on moral and policy attitudes is a function of law's sanction-independent content and how much is a function of the emphasis supplied by the sanction. Could law have the opinion-forming or opinion-influencing it has, however much that may be, without the way in which the sanction arguably underlines the importance of the legal norm itself? We simply do not know, and it is not clear how we could find out given that the causal terrain is so complex. But although it would be a mistake, as much of this chapter has argued, to equate behavioral consistency with compliance, it is also a mistake to assume that the factors that produce seemingly law-independent behavioral motivation are entirely divorced from the symbolic and persuasive power of the law. Lawyers and legal academics are, not surprisingly, prone to exaggeration of this power, but it seems difficult to claim that it is entirely inconsequential.

5.5 The Cultural Contingency of Obedience to Law

Europeans—especially Germans, Austrians, Swiss, Finns, and Scandinavians—who travel to the United States are often surprised at the extent to which American drivers and pedestrians ignore various signs telling them how to drive and where and how to cross the street. And Americans who travel in Germany, Austria, Switzerland, Finland, Norway, Sweden, and Denmark are often equally surprised to see a Finn, for example, standing obediently on the sidewalk when facing a "Don't Walk" sign when there is nary a car or police officer to be seen.

There is no reason to believe that the Finns are right and the Americans are wrong, or vice versa. But the cultural variability on such a trivial matter illustrates the way in which the empirical question of obedience to law is itself culturally variable in a larger way. We know, for example, that subsequent replications of the Milgram experiments show people from Russia and Japan to be more deferential to authority figures in a hierarchical structure than are Americans.[73] We know that dog license compliance is far higher in Calgary, Alberta, than in New York.[74] And we know that rates of tax and traffic law compliance vary widely across countries, although, again, the many cross-cultural legal and nonlegal variables make it difficult to draw strong conclusions from this fact. Still, the fact that United Nations diplomats from some countries are vastly more likely than those from others to park illegally in New York confirms the folly of attempting to assume that obedience to law is similar across different times and different cultures.[75]

If the puzzled person is merely a useful analytic construct, then none of this makes a difference. If we are interested in how law *could* make a difference, then the fact that it makes more of a difference *qua* law in some countries than in others is almost entirely beside the point. But if the puzzled person is not just an analytic construct but the empirical underpinnings of the claim that we have good practical reasons to take noncoercive law seriously, then the actual presence of such persons, and to what degree, becomes important. And what we can conclude from the existence of cultural variation is that there are plainly more puzzled people in some countries than others, and the prevalence of Tyler's sanction-independent compliers, although likely much less than he supposes, will nevertheless vary with time and place, as well as with a host of more fine-grained cultural variables.

This variation may doom the very process of trying to find very much about law itself that is not culture-specific. If we cut off all avenues of inquiry that vary in interesting ways across legal systems, we may find that the legal systems of the United States, Germany, Zimbabwe, North Korea, Fiji, and Saudi Arabia do not share very much in common. And reaching this conclusion might not be a bad thing. There is no reason that law must have a cross-cultural essence, and "law" may merely be the label attached to a diverse collection of sociogovernmental phenomena neither joined by shared properties nor interestingly connected across different systems. But law's coercive force, even if not necessary for law's existence, may be more persistent across cultures than law's coercion-independent normative power. And if this is so, then we may learn as much, if not more, about law wherever and whenever it actually exists by focusing on coercion than by looking exclusively at a phenomenon that not only varies widely across cultures but may well be relatively empirically unimportant even when and where it is most prevalent.

6

ARE OFFICIALS ABOVE THE LAW?

6.1 Turtles All the Way Down

In a widely known but apocryphal story, an eminent scientist or philosopher (William James in some versions, Bertrand Russell in others, and various unnamed Westerners traveling to the allegedly inscrutable Orient in still others) embarks on a foreign journey to give a series of lectures on the origins of planet Earth and its place in the universe. At one of the lectures a member of the audience (the ubiquitous little old lady in some versions, and a mysterious Far Easterner in others) stands up to point out that the lecturer is mistaken. Everyone knows, the questioner announces, that Earth rests on the back of a giant turtle. "But what holds up the turtle?" the scientist asks. The audience member replies that of course the turtle is sitting on top of another turtle. And when the scientist, thinking himself clever, asks what is holding up *that* turtle, the interlocutor, amazed at the scientist's ignorance, triumphantly says, "Why it's turtles, turtles, turtles, all the way down."[1]

The turtle legend is surprisingly relevant to questions about law. We saw in Chapter 5 the importance of distinguishing obedience to law from consistency with law. And having drawn this distinction, we can see that sanction-independent genuine obedience to law is far less common than is often assumed. Yet because it is often necessary to secure such genuine obedience in order to protect social or moral norms against outliers and to enforce socially valuable law against mistaken individual judgment or excess self-interest, sanctions enter the picture. And thus in an environment in which genuine and sanction-independent obedience is rare, coercion through the threat of sanctions emerges as the principal mechanism for securing the obedience that turns out to be so often necessary.[2] Even if, *contra* Austin, sanctions are not an essential component of the very idea of legal obligation, they seem nonetheless crucial in promoting a motivation to obey and thus in promoting compliance with law. Having sorted out the very idea of obeying the law *qua* law, we can now see the importance of sanctions in motivating people to do something other than what they would have done absent the law.

Still, the sanctions that motivate obedience to law do not just emerge from the ether. They must be imposed by someone. But we are then led to inquire into why those who impose the sanctions actually impose them and what is it that leads the officials who impose or threaten sanctions to impose or threaten those sanctions and not others. Why do the police and the courts impose the sanctions they do, especially when they might prefer to impose greater or lesser or different sanctions, or simply to impose whatever sanctions are most consistent with their own best judgment, without regard for the law?

The quick answer to this question would be that the enforcers of law are in turn required by still other laws to enforce the law—and to enforce it in a particular way. But that would be too quick. After all, we could ask the same question one level up and inquire into why those who make and enforce the rules that constrain the police and the courts make *those* rules and not other ones. And so on up the ladder. At any level of the official hierarchy, we might say, and Austin would certainly have said, that even those who make and enforce the rules are subject to the coercive force of those above them in the law-making and law-enforcement hierarchy. And consequently, an important motivation for officials as well as for citizens might be the rewards (a subject to which we shall return in Chapter 8) and punishments, or the incentives in the broadest sense, that apply to those officials in the performance of their official roles.

Once we understand that the enforcers of the law are at the same time the subjects of still other laws, we can draw on the resources that Bentham and Austin and others have provided in understanding much of official compliance in terms of sanctions and incentives. Yet, as H. L. A. Hart and others have pointed out,[3] at some point that explanation runs out, and we find ourselves at a loss to explain in sanction-dependent terms the existence of law-constrained behavior at the pinnacle of the legal hierarchy. The picture that Hobbes, Bentham, and Austin drew was an essentially vertical one. For them an unconstrained sovereign loomed at the top of the hierarchy,[4] but their account appears incapable of accounting for the fact that certainly now, and even to some extent when they were writing, those officials even at the pinnacle of the hierarchy are themselves constrained by the law. Hobbes denied this,[5] but actual modern official behavior seems to belie Hobbes's conclusion. These days even the highest officials both talk and act is if they were constrained by law. But if legal constraint is solely a matter of obeying orders from those above, then the fact of obedience to law when there is no one above to impose sanctions appears to be a puzzle that Hobbes, Bentham, and Austin could not solve.

Indeed, much the same puzzle applies to judges, especially in their law-finding, law-applying, and dispute-resolving modes, rather than when they are simply part of the law-enforcement apparatus in passing judgment and imposing a sentence. Why do judges follow the law? Why do judges make decisions according to the law, assuming they do, when such decisions might diverge from a judge's preferred law-independent outcome? Again, an incentive-based account might in some systems explain why judges do what they do, for even judges might rule in one way rather than another because of fear of sanctions from those with power over them.[6] But at this point, in what is again beginning to resemble an infinite regress, we are pressed to ask why those who apply the incentives apply them based on the law rather than on other factors or on *their* own best all-things-except-the-law-considered judgment—and so on. The spatial metaphor of the top of the hierarchy may clash with that of the bottom turtle, but the idea is the same: if we try to explain constraint by law in terms of incentives imposed from above, then at some point it is no longer possible to explain the fact that even those with no one above them seem themselves to be constrained by law.

6.2 The Nonlegal Foundations of Law

The point of the turtle story is to demonstrate that the "turtles all the way down" explanation is an ultimately unsatisfactory account of the nature of the universe.[7] But it is also an unsatisfactory account of the nature of law.[8] Those who sanction may do so under threat of sanctions from those above them, who may in turn respond largely to the threat of sanctions from those above *them,* and so on, but who can threaten the supreme sanctioner? We need to worry not only about *Quis custodiet ipsos custodes?*—Who guards the guardians?—but also *Quis coercebit ipsos coercentes?*—Who coerces the coercer? Even if, as seems plausible, a focus on sanctions and coercion may explain much of why people and even officials at most levels of the official hierarchy comply with the law *qua* law, still at some point the inherently hierarchical sanction-based account runs out, and we find ourselves at a loss to explain in sanction-dependent terms why the sovereign, to use Austin's term, internalizes the law. And as a result we also find ourselves at a loss to locate the ultimate foundations of a legal system.

Indeed, the problem of law's ultimate foundations need not be understood solely in terms of a hierarchy of coercion. Even if we (temporarily) set aside force, coercion, sanctions, and the various external motivations to legal compliance, the very same regress appears if we consider the question of legal *validity*. We know that laws are made valid by other laws, and those other laws by still other laws, and so on, until we run out of laws. But what determines the validity of the highest law? What keeps the entire structure from collapsing? On what does the validity of an entire legal system rest?

When our inquiry into the foundations of a legal system is framed in this way as a series of questions about legal validity, we find ourselves with still another aspect of Hart's arguments against Austin and against a sanction-dependent account of the nature of law. Once Hart had cast aside (perhaps mistakenly, as we have seen) the importance of sanctions and coercion in explaining the everyday phenomenon of law, he introduced the idea of a rule of recognition, the secondary rule, in his terminology, that enabled citizens and officials to determine whether some primary rule regulating conduct was or was not a valid legal rule.[9] The prohibition on littering is a *legal* rule, but the prohibition on being rude to your mother is not, and that is because another legal rule, a secondary rule of recognition, makes it so.[10] The rule of recognition *recognizes* the primary rule against littering as a legal rule and does not recognize the rule against being rude to your mother as a legal rule, even though it may well be a social rule. Moreover, the rule of recognition distinguishing the legal from the nonlegal is itself a legal rule. And what makes the secondary rule of recognition a *legal* rule of recognition is that still another legal rule of recognition, typically a constitution, makes it so. To offer a concrete example, American factories are required to provide their workers with hearing protection if the factory noise level is above a specified decibel level.[11] The requirement is imposed by a federal administrative agency called the Occupational Safety and Health Administration, and that requirement is valid because the rule containing it was issued in conformity with the Administrative Procedure Act,[12] an Act of Congress, and because the Occupational Safety and Health Administration was created by another Act of Congress.[13] And these acts are themselves valid because they were all enacted in accordance with the provisions of Article I of the Constitution of the United States, which empowers Congress to make laws and establishes the procedure for doing so.

But the turtles are still with us. The Constitution of the United States empowers Congress to make laws that purport to bind citizens and officials, but what makes the Constitution valid? In a word—nothing. Or, to be more precise, the Constitution is the ultimate source of *legal* validity, but *its* validity is simply a matter of, as Hart explained, social fact.[14] The Constitution derives *its* validity from what Hart called the ultimate rule of recognition, but the validity of the ultimate rule of recognition is not a legal matter. *It* is valid, if that is even the right word, simply by virtue of its acceptance, and it is that fact of acceptance that makes the Constitution the final source of legal validity.[15] It is the bottom turtle, and it rests on the brute fact that it is simply accepted as such. I could write a constitution today, designate it as the Constitution of the United States, and write it in such a way that its validity was dependent only on my signature. When I then signed it, it would then become valid according to its own terms, just as the Constitution that sits behind three inches of glass at the National Archives is valid according to *its* own terms. Both it and my constitution purport to be the Constitution of the United States, and both are valid according to their own terms. Most importantly, no further legal rule specifies that the one in the National Archives is the real one, while mine is a sham. Both, after all, are equally internally valid.[16]

Yet although the real Constitution and my self-drafted and self-ratified one are equally valid according to their own terms, the one in the National Archives is plainly the real Constitution and mine just as plainly is not. This much is obvious, but Hart's basic and profoundly important point is that this conclusion is not itself a legal one. Law ultimately rests on nonlegal foundations, and it is the nonlegal fact of acceptance of the National Archives constitution and the equally nonlegal fact of nonacceptance of my constitution that support the bottom turtle of the legal system.[17] The thrust of Hart's argument is that the ultimate rule of recognition is neither legally valid nor legally invalid. It just is, as a matter of social fact.[18]

Questions about the ultimate and nonlegal foundations of a legal system are of more than pure theoretical interest. Consider, for example, the situation in what was called Southern Rhodesia until 1964 and Rhodesia from 1965 and for some years thereafter. In 1965, Rhodesia was a self-governing British colony in which voting rights and political power were held exclusively by the white minority. When the British refused to allow Rhodesia full independence until it enfranchised black Rhodesians and made moves toward majority rule, the Rhodesian government, led by Prime Minister Ian Smith, issued what was called the Unilateral Declaration of Independence (UDI), declaring Rhodesia's independence from Great Britain and seeking to preserve white rule. Great Britain and most other nations refused to recognize the new government, creating an impasse that was as much jurisprudential as it was political.[19] From November 11, 1965, the date of the UDI, on, both the Smith government and the British claimed legal sovereignty over the same geographic area, and thus there existed two alleged legal systems on the same portion of the planet. The question, then, was just which of the two systems was actually the legal system of Rhodesia.

The UDI was, of course, illegal under British law, but that is neither here nor there. After all, the American Declaration of Independence of 1776, on which the UDI was modeled, was also illegal under British law. The ultimate legality of the UDI could not be conclusively a matter of British law, because whether the relevant law was British law or post-UDI Rhodesian law was exactly the matter at issue. As a result, the situation in Rhodesia was analogous to the conflict between the Constitution of the United States and my self-ratified constitution purporting to govern the same territory. And it is at precisely this point that we confront the nonlegal foundations of a legal system. When competing legal systems both claim to represent the law of a particular piece of physical territory, questions about which is the real legal system have real and pressing importance, but the answers to those questions cannot lie in law alone.

Many of the questions about the identity of the Rhodesian legal system after the UDI had arisen a few years earlier in the context of what is now Pakistan. From 1956 to 1958, a series of coups d'états had produced on multiple occasions the situation in which competing political forces each claimed to be the government of Pakistan, and each of the competing governments claimed to have in place its own legal system. And thus, in both Rhodesia and Pakistan, the issue was about just what constituted a legal system. Which was the *real* legal system?

What we have learned from both Hart and Hans Kelsen,[20] each in their own quite different ways, is that determining the conditions for the existence of a legal system cannot itself be considered a legal determination.

Something outside the legal system determines a legal system's identity, and thus something outside both the British colonial legal system and the post-UDI Rhodesian legal system determined which constituted the legal system of Rhodesia. But what is it? What holds up the legal order? And why is it that the Constitution in the National Archives is the Constitution of the United States and my silly self-drafted constitution is not?

An important answer to such questions, it turns out, lies not in the domain of law or legal theory but in economics, political economy, sociology, and all of the other realms of inquiry that explore the nature and origins of cooperative behavior. We know that people do engage in cooperative behavior and that they do so in ways that appear outside of or antecedent to law. When groups develop the norms of cooperative behavior, those norms may, once developed, be enforced by sanctions such as ostracism or reputational attack, but the development of the norms themselves is logically and temporally prior to the effect those norms have. And thus if we ask what leads people to develop those norms in the first place, and often to continue to adhere to them, we cannot rely on sanctions but on the more complex dynamics of human interaction that lead to cooperative and coordinated behavior. The economist Thomas Schelling[21] and the political scientist Elinor Ostrom[22] have won Nobel Prizes for theorizing this dynamic, and others in law (Robert Ellickson, most notably[23]), political science (Robert Axelrod, especially[24]), and philosophy (David Lewis, for example, in the context of language,[25] and Edna Ullman-Margalit, with reference to prescriptive norms of behavior[26]) have contributed influentially. And, indeed, one can find many of the origins of this perspective with respect to law in the writings of Thomas Hobbes, who understood why people in a state of nature would seek cooperative arrangements for the common good, but who also recognized that punishment of defectors would be necessary for the arrangement to work. "[C]ovenants without the sword are but words," Hobbes wrote, but he also recognized that the original act of making the covenant, including the part of the covenant that sanctioned defectors, was an act that emerged from people in the state of nature, rather than being imposed by some higher authority.[27] But the basic idea is that people often do engage in cooperative behavior for the common good, and do so even under circumstances in which it may seem irrational for any individual cooperator to participate. And when they do so, they can create a legal system, resting not on force but on a shared commitment to advance the common legal enterprise and the collective goods it can produce.[28]

The identity of a legal system can accordingly be traced to just such a cooperative agreement, an implicit compact to treat a certain system as law. And thus, at least part of the answer to the problem of dueling constitutions and dueling legal systems lies in this notion of acceptance and in the fact that a polity may choose to accept one system rather than another for reasons that are more about cooperation and coordination than they are about force. That polity may use force to keep the system in place, but the initial choice of the system need not be, and often is not, determined by coercion in any straightforward way.

6.3 Force and the Foundations of Law

Yet although legal systems can come into being by virtue of coordination and cooperation rather than compulsion, it is not strictly necessary that the foundations of law rest on some such initially cooperative arrangement. A sufficiently powerful individual despot might well create a legal system by his own coercive power alone. Ronald Dworkin observed, for example, that "[m]any officials of Nazi Germany obeyed Hitler's commands as law, but only out of fear."[29] And thus, as with captains of ships in the age of sail—leaders who possessed the only firearms on board—the despot might possess resources of compulsion[30] sufficient to ensure the cooperation of subordinates and the obedience of subjects solely by the threat of unpleasant sanctions. And the despot might also, in the service of efficiency, enforce public order and common goals not by individual orders but by a system of primary rules of behavior and secondary rules about the primary rules. There would thus be a system of general rules, both primary rules of conduct and secondary rules about the primary rules, looking in important respects, and maybe even in all respects, like a legal system. But in the end the entire structure would rest on the raw power of a single individual or, more plausibly, of a small group that came to power, and continue to hold onto that power, by force alone. In such cases, assuming again the conjunction of primary and secondary rules that Hart took to be central to "the idea" of law[31] and to the "heart of a legal system,"[32] we would have what appears to be a legal system in which raw force explained the behavior of everyone except the despot and in which, perhaps, the joy of power, the accumulation of wealth, or other selfish motives provided the sole explanation for the despot's own decisions. Seen in this way, it appears to be a mistake to assume that a legal system that relies solely on force is a conceptual impossibility.

If we look at force in a more capacious way not limited to the brute power of guns and armies, the role of force in undergirding a legal system seems even more pervasive. Consider again the question of competing claims to be the authentic legal system, as in the Rhodesian and Pakistani examples. Sometimes in such cases the ultimate determinants are the realities and dynamics of popular acceptance. When a population accepts a legal system as authentic, or legitimate in the very thin sense of acknowledging its right or simply its power to make and enforce the laws, then the legal system so accepted will simply *be* the legal system. But acceptance is a slippery notion. Austin described a "habit of obedience," but the habit is to be contrasted with an environment of widespread disobedience or, at the extreme, rebellion. Perhaps at certain times a population accepts a legal system because of a normative belief in its legitimacy, at other times simply because of the force of habit, and at still other times because of the advantages of implicit coordination with others who have the same habit. But the habit nonetheless rests on the unwillingness of the population to engage in concerted disobedience. When such concerted disobedience takes place, a legal system will commonly collapse, and in this possibly attenuated sense we can see even widespread acceptance of a legal system as the exercise of the raw power of a population by virtue of its numbers to reject by force a legal system of which it disapproves.

Although internal acceptance by a population is often necessary and often sufficient for the existence of a legal system, at times the existence of a legal system, especially in cases of competing legal systems as in Rhodesia and Pakistan, will be determined by the dynamics of international recognition. Insofar as regimes, especially in the modern world, need to engage in various transactions and arrangements with other nations, the determination of the international community of which regime is the real regime will often, as was in fact the case with Rhodesia, be decisive in establishing which regime will prevail and, thus, which legal system will be the actual legal system.

It is often the case, however, that a legal system will rest simply on the exercise, threat, or concentration of raw force. Consider, for example, the situations in Egypt in 2011 and 2013. As in Pakistan in 1958 and Southern Rhodesia in 1965, during the early months of the revolution in Egypt, both the revolutionary movement and the existing government of President Mubarak claimed to be the legitimate government of Egypt, and both claimed ultimate legal and political authority. And the issue was temporarily resolved, if that is the right word, not by judges, or even by the people, but by the army, because once the army cast its lot with the revolution, it was clear which of the competing governments and legal systems was primary. But the fact that it was the army and not the post office or schoolteachers or tax collectors is what was most important. In the final analysis, it was the decision of the ultimate repository of raw force that determined which was the legal system of Egypt and which was not. And thus, when in 2013 there was another transformation, one that some called a revolution and others called a coup, the ultimate determination, still in flux as of this writing, rested in the hands of the army.

Egypt is hardly unique. It has sometimes been claimed, for example, that the Thirteenth, Fourteenth, and Fifteenth Amendments to the Constitution of the United States are unconstitutional, insofar as their ratification was secured—achieved by the ratification of three-fourths of the states—not by a sufficient number of freely elected legislatures but by a total number of state legislatures that included, in the states of what had been the Confederacy, legislatures installed by the Union.[33] But if we think of the Constitution as having been remade at the conclusion of the Civil War,[34] then we can recognize as well that the ultimate determination of what was the real legal system of the United States, and of the states that comprised it in 1865 and thereafter, was not determined by a document written in 1787 but rather on the field of battle. There were two competing legal systems in the Confederate states from 1861 to 1865, and it was Lee's surrender to Grant at Appomattox Courthouse in 1865 that resolved the question,[35] just as the surrender of Cornwallis to George Washington at Yorktown in 1781 resolved the question of which legal system would govern what had been the thirteen British colonies in North America, and just as the decision by the Egyptian army resolved the question of which government, and thus which legal system, was the legitimate legal system of Egypt in 2011, and perhaps again in 2013. It is a mistake to assume that the legal status of a legal system necessarily ultimately rests on the use or threat of force, but it is just as much of a mistake to assume that it never or rarely does.

But of course we do not want to fall into the same trap against which we cautioned in Chapter 3. We do not want to equate the possible with the likely, or the conceivable with the actual. When we do so, we may ignore what is important in the typical but not universal, and thus what may be most important in the phenomenon under inspection. Therefore, we need to recognize that, in reality, complex cooperative enterprises, whether they be lifeboats at sea, organized crime families, or municipal legal systems, typically rest on the decisions of multiple individuals to create a common enterprise for what they perceive as their own collective good, or maybe even the larger common good. Those who are at the apex of such cooperative enterprises may then rely heavily or even exclusively on force to make the enterprise work and to ensure its continuation and its effectiveness, but at the foundation we are most likely to find a group engaging in a cooperative enterprise for reasons other than force or fear. It is conceivable that the bottom turtle rests only on a gun, but in reality it typically rests on something that cannot be explained by coercion alone.

But although it is thus true that many legal systems rest on an original noncoerced cooperative compact among a group of founders or elites, it is just as much of a mistake to underestimate the role of coercion as it is to overestimate it. Even if the ultimate foundation is one better explained by agreement than by coercion, such agreements, once they reach a certain not-very-big size, almost always employ sanctions of some sort to keep potential defectors from defecting.[36] This was most famously theorized, again, by Hobbes, who noted that "[t]here must be some coercive power to compel men equally to the performance of their covenants by the terror of some punishment greater than the benefit they expect by the breach of their covenant."[37] Three or perhaps even thirty people can sustain their mutually beneficial agreement without coercion, but to expect that three hundred or three thousand can do the same thing, at least when there is a benefit to the individual defector from defecting, is fantasy. And thus, as Hobbes predicted, force is necessary to keep the social contract together once it reaches a certain size. Some might describe the organized coercive force necessary to keep the contract in place as "governance,"[38] but others might simply call it "law." Moreover, not only is coercion typically necessary to keep the essentially horizontal agreement at the foundation (or pinnacle, depending on how one conceives the appropriate spatial metaphor of law and governance) of any legal system in place, but coercion is a pervasive feature of the vertical and hierarchical arrangements that characterize more complex legal and governmental structures. Once we descend below the pinnacle of the governmental hierarchy, we see officials whose legal responsibilities are enforced not by their general agreement to obey the law *qua* law but by coercive powers designed to ensure, as it is often put, that no person is above the law.

6.4 The Question of Official Obedience

Although one of the persistent critiques of the sanction-focused account of law offered by Bentham and Austin was its failure to recognize that people could, in theory, internalize, apply, and follow legal rules even were no sanctions attached to disobedience, another has been that the top-down model of law implicit in Bentham's and Austin's accounts could not explain the fact that in modern legal systems the officials themselves are expected to obey the law and, even more importantly, that they typically do so.[39]

We have seen that it is possible, albeit hardly universal, for legal systems to rest, ultimately, on force-independent cooperative agreements. But when we are looking at officials, and especially at the lower levels of officialdom, it seems a mistake to assume that rewards and punishments play no or little role in ensuring official obedience to law. Police officers in most constitutional democracies are subject to countless rules and regulations, some but by no means all of constitutional origin. And most of these rules and regulations are backed by sanctions.[40] Police officers who break the legal rules constraining their actions can be and are punished, and so too with tax collectors, customs agents, workplace safety inspectors, and most other administrative officials. Once we see the extent to which even officials operate in a law-constrained and sanction-enforced environment, we can appreciate that there may be little to distinguish questions about citizen compliance from questions about official compliance, at least at comparatively low levels of officialdom. Citizens are expected to obey the law, and although in theory they could do so for reasons other than fear of sanctions or hope for rewards, we have seen that citizen compliance is typically dependent on, and at the very least reinforced with, coercive sanctions. And so it is for police officers and countless other bureaucrats. Thus, the complaint against the Austinian picture is not that it cannot accommodate the laws that constrain the police and other officials but that it cannot accommodate the legal constraints on the people who make laws that constrain the officials or that, ultimately, it cannot constrain the people who make the laws that constrain the people who make the laws that constrain the police.

The acceptance of and obedience to law even in the absence of sanctions at the top of the legal hierarchy is indeed a puzzle to which the Austinian account has no answer, but there also remain important questions about official obedience even at lower levels of the hierarchy of officials. Judges who disobey the laws that allegedly constrain their behavior, for example, are often subject to no sanctions at all. The judge who ignores a governing statute might be reversed by a higher court,[41] but when the highest court ignores a governing statute, the judges in the majority are typically subject to no sanctions at all.[42] And although legislatures are expected to obey the constitution, it is frequently the case that formal enforcement of that obligation is largely absent. Often, and certainly in the United States, for example, a police officer who conducts an unconstitutional or otherwise illegal search or arrest is subject to administrative punishment and possibly even civil liability,[43] but a member of a legislature who votes for a law authorizing police officers to conduct an unconstitutional search is subject to no formal sanctions whatsoever. Consequently, the hard questions about the role of coercion in supporting a legal order arise largely in the context of the courts and legislatures whose accountability is only to the constitution, and whose constitutional obligations seem typically to be unsupported by sanctions in the ordinary sense.

We can therefore ask the question directly: Do officials obey the law? We have examined citizen compliance in Chapter 5, concluding that citizen compliance with law, if understood as genuine obedience to law just because it is law, may well, for all of its obvious temporal and geographic variation, be less than the conventional wisdom supposes. But what about officials? Do they follow the law because of acceptance and not because of force? Are sanctions less important to officials than to citizens? And might the percentage of puzzled officials, precisely in the sense we have been exploring, be greater than the percentage of puzzled citizens?

These questions are interesting and important not only in their own right but also as an important indicator about compliance generally. As just noted, in many developed legal systems, low-level and midlevel officials who violate the statutory and constitutional laws designed to constrain their official actions are subject to relatively ordinary sanctions. They might be internally punished by their superiors, they might be subject to lawsuits and required to pay monetary damages if they are found to have violated the law, and they might be vulnerable to criminal penalties including prison and criminal fines. But often none of these sanctions is available against relatively high-level executive, legislative, and judicial officials. In the United States, for example, members of Congress are subject to no sanctions (except at the ballot box, which we will examine more closely presently) for voting for blatantly unconstitutional laws, and judges, prosecutors, and many upper-level executive officials have immunity from the type of civil liability that is typically available against police officers, municipal officials, and others of similar rank who might violate the Constitution or various state and federal laws limiting their actions.[44] As a result, these officials operate in a world in which formal sanctions for illegal actions are absent, giving us an interesting setting for evaluating the extent to which the subjects of law, regardless of status or official position, will obey the law just because it is the law when sanctions are not on the table. And to the extent that the sanctions available for such official illegality are imposed by the political process—in the court of public opinion, as it were[45]—the imposition or nonimposition of such political sanctions can also tell us something about the extent to which the public itself values compliance with the law when what the law requires varies from what the public's law-independent moral and policy preferences would otherwise be.

That the question of official obedience in the common sanction-free environment is a useful window into legal obedience generally should not blind us to the importance of the question of official obedience itself. Consider the "rule of law," for example. Of course there are almost as many views about the rule of law as there are viewers,[46] but there exists wide agreement that at least one of its multiple components is the requirement that officials obey the law.[47] If officials are not themselves subject to legal constraints, and if they are not, by and large, bound by the same rules they apply to ordinary citizens, then the ultimate rule is not by law but by the people who control the resources of raw power.

But although the idea of the rule of law appears to require official obedience as a normative matter, the descriptive question is whether they in fact do so. In important ways, the answer to that question is clearly "yes," at least in most democratic societies. Officials occupy their offices—they become officials rather than just people—by virtue of the law, and law in its constitutive role plays a major role in establishing a government itself. There are, to be sure, countries in which the implicit constraints of constitutive law are too easily cast aside in the service of political advantage and raw power. But most of the time in most democracies—or all of the time in all democracies, depending on one's definition of "democracy"— elected officials who leave office after losing elections do so because of the constitutive power of law, and so too with the willingness of officials not to implement legislation that has not been enacted by the requisite procedure. In these and many other ways, law is important just in establishing the very structure of government. As we saw in Chapter 3 when we explored the distinction between constitutive and regulative rules, and thus between constitutive and regulative law, law does, in theory and in practice, play an important role in regulating and constraining behavior, including the behavior of public officials, by establishing the very nature of their powers.

But law has its regulative as well as constitutive side, and the answer to the question whether the regulative side of law actually constrains legally constituted official behavior is rather more difficult. Often, as noted above, officials will follow the laws that constrain them, but they will do so precisely because of the coercive force of the sanctions that attach to disobedience. But when the constraints on public officials are not, as we have just noted, backed by sanctions, do officials actually put aside their own best moral, political, and policy judgments in favor of the law? That is the question whose answer we will now address.

6.5 When and How (If at All) Does Law Constrain Official Policy Making?

Consider the widely discussed legal question about the American manned and drone air strikes on Libya in 2012. When Libyan revolutionary forces attempted to oust the government of President Mohamar Qaddafi, the American government, for a complex array of humanitarian, strategic, and political reasons, came to the support of the revolutionary forces, and did so by way of using airstrikes and unmanned drone bombers to attack the government forces. What made these attacks a contested legal issue in the United States was the existence of a 1973 law called the War Powers Resolution,[48] which required the president, as commander in chief of the armed forces, to secure the approval of Congress for any involvement in foreign "hostilities" lasting more than sixty days. There was no question that the airstrikes and use of drones lasted more than sixty days, and there was no question that Congress had not given its approval. Faced with what seemed to be clear case of illegality, the Obama administration initially attempted to claim that the use of drones, which involved little risk to Americans, did not even constitute "hostilities" for purposes of the law.[49] This argument was widely mocked, even by the president's political allies,[50] and thus it was broadly accepted that the president's actions were unlawful. But no American lives were lost, and the outcome of the intervention undeniably included the removal from power of a man widely regarded as a sadistic despot. And in the face of what appeared to be a favorable policy and political result, the fact of illegality, which attracted a day or two of media and political attention and criticism, was soon forgotten. In the absence of any plausible legal enforcement mechanism, and with the presence of a positive policy result, the fact of illegality turned out to make virtually no difference at all.

At least in the United States, this outcome was hardly unusual. Quite often, officials who are immune for one reason or another from formal legal sanctions violate the law with some frequency and suffer few if any political or personal repercussions for doing so. To be more precise, when officials take actions that turn out to be successful on political and policy grounds, the fact that they are illegal appears to make little to no difference. When, correctly anticipating the changing tide of public opinion, the mayors of San Francisco, California, and New Paltz, New York, performed same-sex marriages in plain contradiction of existing state law at the time, they suffered no formal or political penalties.[51] Similarly, some members of Congress have in recent years proposed congressional salary suspensions as a way to create a real and symbolic motivation to deal responsibly with budget deficits. Yet although such seemingly self-sacrificing salary suspensions without an intervening election would clearly violate the plain words of the Twenty-Seventh Amendment to the Constitution, constitutional objections to the proposals have been dismissed as largely irrelevant. And when a federal law called the Posse Comitatus Act[52] prohibited the use of federal troops for Hurricane Katrina disaster relief without a formal request from the governor, a request that had not been forthcoming, New Orleans mayor Ray Nagin, with scant objection, announced explicitly that he did not care about the law and demanded that the troops be sent immediately.[53] And thus, on these and many other occasions, the illegality of official policies and decisions that turned out well as policy was largely ignored.[54] When the actions turn out to be unsuccessful as policy, the illegality does appear to increase the political penalty, and thus it is a mistake to think that the regulating law makes little difference.[55] But when there is a clear conflict between what the law requires and what a political official believes to be the best all-things-except-the-law-considered policy decision, numerous examples suggest that the power of the unenforceable legal constraint is minimal. Indeed, David Hume identified the phenomenon centuries ago:

> In 1662, [King] Charles, pleading both the rights of his supremacy and his suspending power, had granted a general indulgence or toleration; and, in 1672, he renewed the same edict: thought the remonstrances of his parliament obliged him, on both occasions, to retract; and, in the last instance, the triumph of law over prerogative was deemed very great and memorable. In general, we may remark that, where the exercise of the suspending power was agreeable and useful, the power itself was little questioned:

where the exercise was thought liable to exceptions, men not only opposed it, but proceeded to deny altogether the legality of the prerogative on which it was founded.[56]

Thus, the claim here, tracking Hume's insight in 1778, is not that there cannot be political or public opinion sanctions for illegality. There can, but the question is whether political sanctions tend to be imposed for illegality by itself or whether the political sanctions tend to track the first-order substance of the decisions, with legality and illegality themselves making little difference. And a plausible conclusion is that the latter picture is often the correct one, with the processes of politics and public opinion formation rarely taking the law itself as an important determinant of political rewards and political punishment.[57]

Although Hume was talking about England, most of the foregoing observations are restricted to the United States, and thus may be less sound elsewhere. It may be, that is, that voters, the press, and the other constituent elements of public opinion and political power place a greater weight on legality per se in other countries than they do in the United States.[58] And because of this possibility, the American example here is not intended to make a global claim or even a definitive claim about the United States. Rather, it is presented to suggest that, just as with citizens, official obedience to the law, absent the threat of formal legal sanctions, may well be less than is commonly assumed.

Indeed, the issue may be even more important for officials than it is for citizens. Countless personal and political dynamics will lead officials, even well-meaning ones, to have great confidence in the wisdom and even morality of their policy conclusions. But law exists, in part, because neither good faith nor confidence is a particularly reliable indicator of official wisdom. Policies enacted with the best of motives and with few doubts on the part of the enactors may be and frequently are mistaken. And if even those officials who act in good faith and with much confidence in the wisdom of their actions are nevertheless often mistaken, then an important role for law is to constrain not only those who motives are suspect but even the well-intentioned inclinations of officials.

This role for law is especially apparent in the context of constitutions. It is commonly believed that the principal purpose of a constitution is to prevent self-interested or evil officials from operating to the detriment of the public good. And although that is certainly one purpose of a constitution, arguably a more important one is to keep even well-intentioned officials from making erroneous decisions. To put it differently, a constitution exists in part to keep bad officials from doing bad things, but it also, and more importantly, exists to keep good officials from doing what they think are good things, or may even be good things in the short run, to the detriment of the long-run public interest. And if these kinds of second-order constraints on even seemingly sound first-order policy decisions are often important, then we can begin to glimpse why sanctions may be even more important in the context of public law than in private.

7

COERCING OBEDIENCE

7.1 The Argument So Far

Were we searching for the essential properties of law, examining the empirical descriptive side of the obligation to obey the law would be a fool's errand. After all, something that looked very much like a legal system *could* exist without coercion or any other form of externally imposed incentives to obedience.[1] And as long as there could possibly be a coercion-free legal system, coercion would no longer be a conceptually necessary property of law. So if our inquiry were into the necessary or essential properties of law, the mere possibility of a coercion-free or sanction-free legal system would make it pointless to investigate the extent to which people actually obey the law just because it is the law.

Yet although we know that a legal system could in theory exist without sanctions and without coercion, we know as well that, with somewhere between few and no exceptions, no such legal systems actually exist.[2] Even H. L. A. Hart, whose argument against Austin is commonly understood to have definitively established that coercion is not an essential property of the concept of law, acknowledged that coercion is a "natural necessity" in all actual legal systems and that every existing legal system appears to recognize the need for some way of coercing compliance with the law.[3]

Everything thus turns on the nature of the inquiry. If our task were the pursuit of law's essential properties in all possible legal systems in all possible worlds, there would be little point in being much concerned with force, sanctions, coercion, and the various incentives of self-interest. In a community of angels,[4] a society of individuals universally committed to cooperation for collective benefit, law would be necessary to manage coordination and cooperation, but obedience to law *qua* law would be sufficiently widely accepted that coercion would be unnecessary. And as long as we can imagine such a community of angels universally committed to using coercion-free law to promote a common goal or plan, then coercion emerges as no longer noncontingently *necessary* for there to be law. The very fact that the community of angels, hypothetical but conceivable, would not need coercion would cause coercion to lose its place in an account of law's conceptually necessary properties.[5]

But what if our inquiry is into what is typical of law rather than what is necessary for it? Or what if it is into what is universal but only empirically and contingently so? In that case, as we concluded in Chapter 3, what Hart called a natural necessity comes back into the picture. Yet, even for Hart, and even recognizing the ambiguity of his own commitment to methodological essentialism,[6] the natural necessity of coercion was still not much in the picture. And that is largely because Hart viewed the puzzled person—the person inclined to obey the law just because it is the law and who is thus curious about what the law requires—as an important feature of the legal landscape in most modern advanced societies.[7] If such societies are widely populated by people who are inclined to obey the law without the need for coercion, then an emphasis on coercion, even if it is necessary to constrain the outliers, is empirically distorting. The reluctance of Hart and some others to focus on coercion in explaining the phenomenon of law thus appears to be based not only on a preoccupation with law's conceptually necessary properties but also on a presupposed existence of puzzled people in substantial quantities.[8] Resistance to seeing coercion as central to legality as it is experienced may thus signal, as it did for Hart, a belief in the proposition that the very existence of law is often a significant reason for action for most citizens and most officials.

As we saw in Chapters 5 and 6, however, a belief in the widespread sanction-independent internalization of law *qua* law is likely mistaken. The matter is empirical, to be sure, and varies with time and place, but there appears to be much assertion and little empirical support for the general proposition that so-called puzzled people exist in significant numbers in modern legal systems.

Even apart from its likely empirical inaccuracy, accepting the proposition that many citizens have internalized the value of following law just because it is law is also problematic because it may lead us to ignore important, albeit contingent, empirical features of the phenomenon of legality. One relates to the scope of the phenomena we are setting out to explain. In many societies—call them nondemocratic, totalitarian, or despotic—law appears to exist even in a pervasive climate of fear. Despots set out rules, their underlings enforce them, and people comply with the rules for reasons that are almost entirely about fear. In most tyrannies the ratio of the fearful to the fear-imposing is typically very large. Indeed, this dominance of fear may be definitional of what constitutes a tyranny in the first place. But although tyrannies are plainly not good societies, they do appear to have what looks like law. Their laws may be substantively flawed and procedurally defective, but their subjects nevertheless understand them as law. And it is far from clear that these subjects are mistaken in doing so. Tyrannical legal systems are, after all, connected with internationally recognized political states. Moreover, their leaders and perhaps a small group of allies have typically internalized an ultimate rule of recognition. And in such systems there are ordinarily not only primary rules of general application but also secondary rules that enable citizens and officials to identify the primary rules and adjudicate disputes under them.[9] Although in typical tyrannies almost all of the primary rules and most of the secondary rules are made effective by the threat of force, we still see the union of primary and secondary rules that for Hart, at least, was the key to understanding the nature of a legal system and the transformation from a prelegal to a legal society.[10] And thus if we seek to understand law in tyrannical and nondemocratic societies as well as in nice countries like New Zealand and Norway, it seems a mistake to ignore the role of force in supporting and pervading the large number of legal systems whose regime of primary and secondary general laws is made effective largely at the barrel of a gun.

There are, to be sure, some legal theorists who would take issue with the conclusion that a regime claiming (or demanding) nothing more than force-based obedience would even count as a legal system. Joseph Raz, most prominently, argues that it is an essential feature of law that it claims (but does not necessarily have) legitimate authority.[11] Relatedly, Scott Shapiro maintains that having moral aims is necessary for an alleged system of legal rules to count as genuinely legal.[12] But to adopt either of these constraints on the definition of the legal seems to exclude too much. After all, many alleged legal systems of many alleged countries claim nothing or little more than the power to do bad things to their subjects in the event of disobedience. Consider, for example, those nation-states focused only on accumulating wealth and power for the leaders, such as the Philippines under Marcos, Zaire under Mobutu, Indonesia under Suharto, Serbia under Milošević, and Haiti under "Papa Doc" Duvalier. These nations, sometimes semijokingly referred to as "kleptocracies," rarely claim to have moral goals,[13] so they are not the same as countries that have goals they claim to be moral but are decidedly not, such as Nazi Germany and Russia under Stalin. And rarely do the kleptocracies even claim legitimacy, other than the legitimacy that comes from raw power, more guns, and the imposition of fear. But such regimes do claim to have law, and the law they claim to have is typically not just a collection of the unsystematic particular commands of the despot.[14] They have written primary rules of conduct that their subjects are punished for violating, and they have internalized secondary rules, even though the ensuing legal systematicity is solely in the service of efficiency, and even though the efficiency is solely for the benefit of the despots or a ruling elite. Indeed, in many such states there is not even the claim of or pretense to legitimacy. But if our goal is to explain and understand the phenomenon of law, it is hardly clear that we would want to conclude that large numbers of state-based and organized rule–based systems of social control are not law at all[15] and hardly clear that many current and past members of the United Nations, for example, have no law at all. If we wish, therefore, for purposes of explanation and understanding, to include the legal systems of tyrannies and kleptocracies within the realm of what we are seeking to explain, we become hard-pressed to deny the central role of coercion in sustaining such systems. Expanding the realm of the phenomenon we seek to explain thus gives us a new window through which to view the legal importance of coercion, for it is coercion in the most basic sense that enables us to understand law as it exists in bad societies as well as good.

Even apart from the issues about which legal systems we wish to understand, erroneously assuming the widespread existence of puzzled people will lead to mistaken conclusions about the nature and experience of legality even in nontyrannical modern legal systems. Once we clarify carefully exactly what it is to obey the law just because it is the law, and once we understand the error in assuming that all morally motivated and non-self-interested actions that happen to be consistent with the law are in fact based on law, we can see that the existence—or not—of puzzled people even in advanced liberal democracies emerges as an important issue. It may be valuable for some purposes to develop a theory that attempts to understand legal obligations from the perspective of the puzzled person, but if most real legal systems are populated by many who are "bad"[16] and few who are puzzled, a theory of the puzzled person will fail to provide a satisfactory account of the phenomenon of law as it is actually experienced by judges and citizens alike. If, as we have seen, it is far from clear that puzzled people exist in the quantities that Hart, Tyler,[17] and others suppose, whether for the citizenry or for officials, then we have come a long way toward understanding the natural necessity of coercion in all or virtually all of the legal systems we know. If people are generally disinclined to obey the law *qua* law, then coercion reemerges as the obvious way in which even advanced legal systems in mature democracies can secure compliance. As James Madison famously observed, "If men were angels, no government would be necessary,"[18] but he could as easily have been speaking about the law.

The scarcity of puzzled people, whether among citizens or among officials, should come as no surprise. Once we understand that people really do often behave morally and altruistically,[19] law emerges as not one but two steps removed from self-interest. There is self-interest itself and then there is the documented willingness of people and officials to do the right thing as they see it (including engaging in cooperative behavior and abiding by salient social norms), and even at some personal sacrifice. But then there is the law, which achieves its bite and much of its importance precisely when it tells people that even what they think is the right thing to do, and even when the right thing to do is not necessarily in their personal interest, is not what they should do. And when seen this way—when we understand that law's value often rests on its ability to get people to put aside not only their self-interest but also their not-necessarily-self-interested best judgment—the challenge of securing obedience to law just because it is law becomes much more understandable. As Christopher Morris put it, "Coercion and force are needed when the state's claimed [legal] authority is unappreciated, defective, or absent,"[20] and it could well be that theorists, in particular, are often the ones who do not appreciate just how often the state's authority is unappreciated.

Having thus liberated ourselves from the intellectual shackles of believing that jurisprudence or legal theory is necessarily and exclusively a search for the essential criteria of law or, even worse, a search for individually necessary and jointly sufficient properties, we are free to look for law's ordinary or typical or contingently universal characteristics.[21] Coercion is hardly the only such characteristic, but it seems to be among the most important. And coercion's nonnecessary importance is a function of the relative scarcity of so-called puzzled people and puzzled officials, for reasons that we are now well situated to understand. Because the commands of law, when they make a difference, are typically two steps removed from individual self-interest, and even one step removed from even individual best judgment, coercion appears necessary to motivate both citizens and officials to take actions so removed from their own interests and their own considered judgments. This is why coercion in law is so ubiquitous, and it is why coercion may be the feature that, probabilistically even if not logically, distinguishes law from other norm systems and from numerous other mechanisms of social organization.

7.2 The Incentives to Compliance

The basic empirical idea being offered here is that although people might be willing to sacrifice self-interest in the service of morality or in the pursuit of wise policy for the common good, there is scant empirical support for the view that people are willing voluntarily to subjugate their own best judgment of what morality and policy require to what they consider law's mistaken moral or policy judgment. Accordingly, if law is to do what it needs to do—which is often to impose a collective sense of good policy or wise actions on people's individual and often mistaken sense of good policy and wise actions—it must find a way to motivate people to make judgments or engage in behaviors that are not only not in their own self-interest but which they also often believe involve moral or policy error.

Obviously one way to make people do things they consider self-sacrificing or unwise is to force them to do so. Bentham thought that the threat of force was the most effective way to motivate people to follow the law, and Austin may have believed that it was the only way, but such a view is too crude. People wish to avoid the hangman and to avoid less final forms of punishment or unpleasantness, but human motivation is more complex than this. Bentham and Austin may have excluded rewards and other nonpunitive incentives from their definition of law, but even they understood that the incentives to compliance and to action in general were complex and not simply about avoiding unpleasantness, a subject to which we shall return in Chapter 8. They and we understand that people respond to rewards as well as to punishments, and just as people are often willing to subjugate their self-interest or best judgment in order to avoid negative sanctions, so too are they often willing to do much the same thing in the hope of a reward or some other gain. Indeed, the complexity of the external factors that might motivate compliance is so much richer than the crude model offered by Bentham and Austin that we devote all of Chapter 8 and much of Chapter 9 to exploring them.

By way of preview, therefore, we might note now that even equating negative sanctions with the particular unpleasantness of most forms of punishment is too narrow. Criminal punishment, civil and criminal monetary fines, various forms of disablement (losing a driver's license or a business license, for example), and reputational harm, among others, are conditions that most people seek to avoid, and each of these has its positive analogue. People wish to avoid having bad reputations, for example, but they also seek good ones, maybe even better ones than they deserve.

All of the foregoing can perhaps be encapsulated by the economist's focus on *incentives,* a concept that seeks to capture a much larger range of positive and negative stimuli than mere monetary reward and physical (and painful) punishment. Some economists make the mistake of thinking that the incentives of self-interest exhaust the range of incentives and exhaust the domain of human motivation, but incentives may, for the reasons explored in the previous section, have a particularly large role to play in inducing compliance with the law. We explore this issue further in succeeding chapters, but it is worthwhile noting even here that it is best to understand the related ideas of coercion, force, and sanctions more metaphorically than literally and that all of these terms encompass a wider range of external incentives than Bentham and Austin had in mind. We have reached the point in the argument where we should accept that some form of motivational assistance will commonly be necessary to produce a socially desirable degree of legal compliance, but we should be careful not to understand the array of possible forms of that motivational assistance too narrowly.

7.3 The Occasions of Law

In the not-so-distant past, signs on the Massachusetts Turnpike, a high-speed limited access highway, warned drivers that they were not to back up on the roadway if they missed their assigned exit. At the University of Oxford, announcements posted by the proctors at examination time remind students taking examinations that they are prohibited from throwing flour, eggs, and whipped cream in the examination room.[22] And prominently displayed at the BMI Terminal at London's Heathrow Airport are placards reminding passengers that it is against the law to assault airline employees.

These signs share the characteristic of producing an element of surprise. Most of us, or so I hope, would never consider backing up on a highway, throwing food during an examination, or assaulting a ticket agent. But obviously some people would, for otherwise the signs would not be there. Indeed, the signs tell us a great deal about the kinds of behaviors that might exist absent warnings or legal prohibitions.[23] The very fact that the signs exist provides useful information about the law-independent behavioral proclivities of Massachusetts drivers, Oxford undergraduates, and British airline passengers, information that, as in these examples, is often as surprising as it is illuminating.

All of these examples involve signs telling people what the law is, rather than being the law themselves, but it is the same with underlying law. The Third Amendment to the Constitution of the United States, for example, prohibits government from forcing citizens to quarter troops in private homes, a constitutional prohibition existing nowhere else in the world.[24] The prohibition exists, however, because it attempts to guard against what was, in 1791, perceived as a genuine possibility, a possibility informed by the actual pre-Revolutionary British practice of just a few years earlier. And the fact that there are in some jurisdictions specific prohibitions on cannibalism[25] suggests that some people might be inclined to engage in a practice that I and most others find unthinkable.

In commenting about language and not about law, the philosopher John Searle some years ago argued that there is no remark without remarkability.[26] The point is profound. The very fact of saying something presupposes the genuine empirical possibility of its negation. Were that possibility nonexistent, there would be no cause for the assertion in the first place. The conversational implicature, to use the correct technical term,[27] of an assertion is a context in which the opposite of what is asserted is sufficiently plausible for some people that there follows a good reason for the assertion. And thus if I observe, entirely correctly, that a colleague is sober today, that very remark implies that he is not sober on some other days, or at least that some people believe he is not sober on other days, a possibility that might not have occurred to my listeners had I not commented accurately on his sobriety.

So it is with the law. As the examples at the beginning of this section illustrated, legal prohibitions typically presuppose an inclination on the part of at least some people to engage in the prohibited activities. Were there no such inclination, or at least were there no suspicions of such inclinations, there would be no need for laws. That is why the French Constitution does not prohibit the quartering of troops in private homes, why the examination regulations for Swedish universities do not prohibit the throwing of food, and why passengers on privately hired executive jets are not warned against assaulting the pilot. Just as there is no remark without remarkability, there is rarely law without the real and antecedent possibility of the behavior that the law finds a need to prohibit.

Yet although legal prohibitions presuppose the genuine and nontrivial possibility of the conduct that the law seeks to control, there are important conceptual and empirical differences among the kinds of behavioral inclinations that inspire legal restrictions. According to the laws of the United States and the Commonwealth of Virginia, I am required to pay taxes, abstain from using marijuana, and avoid engaging in cannibalism. But these laws are different from one another in how they intersect with my own best judgment and my own self-interest, and it is a mistake to assume that all laws operate in the same way with respect to individual or population-wide motivation. Until we can understand the different ways in which law intersects with its subjects' law-independent preferences, we cannot begin to understand the role of incentives and coercion in motivating legal compliance.

Consider first the laws against cannibalism. As just (perhaps unnecessarily) noted, most people do not engage in cannibalism. Moreover, most people would never consider the possibility, even were there no legal prohibitions at all. And we might say the same, perhaps a bit more optimistically, about the legal prohibitions on murder, rape, and child molestation. In a society with no law at all, these behaviors would still, we think and hope, be quite rare.

But they would not be nonexistent. And thus, we can identify one of the occasions of law—one of the reasons for having legal prohibitions—as the effort to enforce widespread and typically self-enforcing social and moral norms against outliers. On a wide range of topics, most people do not need the law to tell them what to do, and most people will do the right thing most of the time. But there is a difference between "most" and "all." And it is precisely because of this difference that we see one of law's primary modalities as guarding prevailing social and moral norms against a relatively small number of outliers. In such circumstances, we can easily grasp the necessity of coercion, because there is little reason to believe that someone who rejected the underlying social norm or moral requirement would accept a coercion-independent obligation to obey the law. Doing so is not logically impossible, of course. In theory people could reject the obligation to avoid murder, rape, and theft while accepting the obligation to obey the law. But because such people are in reality either rare or nonexistent, coercion becomes necessary when the law seeks to guard law-independent social and moral norms and practices against the occasional outlier.

In other instances, however, the face of law seems very different. Many of the people who have no inclination to commit rape or engage in cannibalism do have law-independent desires to drive at high speeds or avoid paying taxes, and thus have little aversion to leaving others to shoulder the costs of collective governance and the risks of collective existence. Similarly, many businesses that even without legal prohibitions would not engage in fraud or blatant misrepresentation seem often willing to cut the costs of worker safety or offer inflated, if not false, claims about the quality of their products. In such cases the simple observation that people and businesses often do the right thing for law-independent reasons seems insufficient, and here law is concerned not merely with the occasional outlier, as in the case of cannibalism, but with a host of issues in which self-interest appears to dominate the morality of cooperating for the public good. In such cases coercion again seems necessary, but in a more pervasive way. Moral beliefs vary in strength, and people who would not seriously consider engaging in personally satisfying theft or assault, even absent the possibility of apprehension and punishment, often feel differently about tax avoidance or dangerous (to others as well as to themselves) driving while intoxicated. It is not that such people do not recognize or even internalize the moral negatives of the practice. It is just that both altruistic morality and self-interest vary in strength. And thus, when it is expected that the demands of morality are perceived (even if incorrectly) as weak, and the pull of self-interest is perceived (even if, again, incorrectly) as strong, coercion, as Bentham reminded us, is often necessary to put a heavy thumb on the right side of the balance.

Coercion may be most necessary, however, when significant numbers of law's subjects simply disagree with law's goals. And this is hardly an unusual phenomenon. Not only do we have instances in which large segments of a population simply have the wrong views, as with the enforcement of school desegregation in the American South in the 1950s and 1960s, but law also plays a substantial role in imposing what start out as minority norms and only later become widely accepted. The laws protecting the environment and endangered species, for example, were initially supported only by a small but committed minority of the population, and it would be foolish (and without evidential support) to suppose that simply changing the law will induce a substantial degree of compliance without the assistance of coercion and sanctions of various types. But the psychological and sociological dynamics are complex. One possibility is that the mere enactment of a legal prohibition, just because it is a statement of the law, will induce both attitudinal and behavioral change. This is certainly possible, although it seems more likely on a subject as to which people had no views prior to the legal change than when they had views contrary to what the law came to be. That the simple fact of legal change, without coercion, caused significant numbers of people who were previously hostile to racial integration to become more sympathetic seems highly unlikely. But when the law prohibited certain actions detrimental to endangered species, a subject about which most people might previously have had no views whatsoever, the power of the sanction-unsupported legal change might well have been considerably greater.

But the matter is even more complex than this. As long as coercion is ubiquitously even if not necessarily conjoined with law, coercion may be perceived as a necessary indicator of law's seriousness. When a legal prohibition is simply hortatory, against a background of law being (and being perceived as) generally sanction-backed, the targets of the hortatory prohibition may believe that the law is not serious about its prescriptions and thus that those prescriptions need not be taken seriously by its subjects. The Constitution of the Republic of Ireland, for example, contains a number of explicitly unenforceable rights to various aspects of social welfare, but it is far from obvious that the existence of such unenforceable provisions has produced governmental action different from what have occurred had the unenforceable constitutional provisions not existed at all. Coercion may accordingly operate indirectly to encourage legal compliance by reinforcing the seriousness of the prescription itself. And coercion may also encourage compliance by some people, which will change the sociological terrain in a way that noncoerced compliance by others becomes more likely. Insofar as legal change produced a change in attitudes about racial segregation, for example, it may be that coerced legal change put people more in contact with those of races other than their own, which in turn changed attitudes in a more widespread way. Similarly, prohibitions on smoking in public establishments may have forced at least some people to recognize the possibility of enjoying a restaurant or a pub without a cigarette. As a result, their preferences and attitudes may have changed as a result of the law, but only in a less direct way.

Some of these causal pathways between legal coercion and attitudinal change are explored further in Chapter 10, when we take up the relationship between law and social norms. But it is at least worth mentioning them here, if only to signal that the relationship between legal coercion and behavioral change is a complex one. Coercion may well be more necessary for legal effectiveness than the misleading image of the puzzled person suggests, but the connection between coercion and legal effectiveness may be rather more complex than Bentham, Austin, and their followers found it necessary to consider.

7.4 The Settlement Function of Law

Apart from law's role in controlling potential outliers to widely accepted social and moral norms, and apart from the way in which legal coercion adjusts people's motivations when self-interest is strong and moral sensibility is weak, there are also, as just noted, instances in which law is the instrument of genuine attitudinal and behavioral change. Law may have served this role, for example, with respect to questions of racial discrimination, gender discrimination, and environmental protection. In such cases, law may have helped change the views of the majority rather than simply protecting preexisting majority views from outliers. And insofar as law serves this role of shifting what we might call the weight of public moral or policy opinion, coercion has an important role to play, precisely because law is attempting to shift views away from what people who hold those views believe (mistakenly, in the law's view) is right. Yet, although law does occasionally operate in this way, it is far more common for law to function less in changing people's moral or policy views than in resolving a practical question in the face of moral and policy disagreement.[28] We can call this law's "settlement function."

At its most obvious, law's settlement function operates when widespread agreement on the need for settlement is combined with little of consequence turning on the substance of the settlement. The stock example is the requirement that people drive on only the left or the right side of the road. Almost everyone agrees that a rule requiring one or the other is necessary, and almost no one much cares whether the chosen rule requires driving on the left or on the right. Under such circumstances law can serve a valuable settlement function in choosing one or the other, and it is highly unlikely that coercion would be necessary to support the law's choice. As long as people agree that one or the other must be chosen, and as long as few people would feel aggrieved even by a choice different from the one they would have made themselves, people are unlikely to need the threat of punishment in order to comply with the law's choice. Law would be necessary to help locate the focal point—the locus of coordination or agreement[29]—but as long as there is widespread agreement that there needs to be some focal point, then sanctions may not be needed for law to serve its purpose. After all, most people who drive on the wrong side of the road are drunk or reckless, and thus are usually guilty of something else. There are very few—perhaps no—cases in which people sanctioned for driving on the wrong side of the road are people who believe that it is right or even in their self-interest to drive on the side other than the one the law has chosen. And thus, in such cases law can serve its coordination function without any need for coercion.

In other cases, however, law can settle, even if only temporarily, and even if only for the purposes of necessary action, serious disagreements about the substance of morality and policy. Many people in France, for example, believe that public religious displays, including many forms of religious garb, ought to be prohibited. But others, including many French people, believe such practices ought to be permitted. And some of the people who believe that such practices ought to be permitted believe as well that they, personally, should wear appropriate religious garb at all times, even in public. French law has, albeit temporarily and with difficulty, settled the dispute in favor of the first position, but there is little reason to believe that those in the second and especially in the last-mentioned group would comply with the law except for law's threat of punishment. Thus here, and on a large number of similarly morally contentious issues, law provides an important settlement function. In a world of moral and political disagreement, law can often provide a settlement of these disagreements, a settlement neither final nor conclusive, but nevertheless authoritative and thus providing for those in first-order disagreement a second-order resolution that will make it possible for decisions to be made, actions to be coordinated, and life to go on. It is precisely because of deep underlying disagreement that settlement is often necessary, but at the same time, underlying disagreement is what makes effectuating the settlement without coercion virtually impossible. Even if there were people in drive-on-the-right countries who believed that driving on the left was preferable, it is unlikely that they would insist on driving on the left without coercion. That is not so in many other cases, however, and there is little reason to believe that those who believe

that wearing religious garb in public is desirable or (religiously) mandatory would suppress their beliefs solely because French law has resolved
or settled the issue against them. In these and countless other cases, law
serves a settlement function, but the settlement will be effective only if
those whose views are at odds with the agreed settlement are compelled
to comply with the settlement. Law enables societies to function by set-
tling deep moral and political disagreements for purposes of action, but
it does so by mandating with the threat of force that those who disagree
will nevertheless act in accordance with the imposed settlement.

7.5 Mistaken Angels

James Madison famously observed that if men were angels, no governments would be necessary. But Madison's observation, however perceptive it was and however memorable it has become, may regrettably have
failed to draw an important distinction between those who are evil and
those who are simply mistaken. Yes, there are nonangels—calling them
"devils" seems a bit harsh, but "amoral" is closer to the mark—who constantly seek their own advantage, even at the expense of others. Such
people are rarely if ever altruistic, they are almost never morally motivated, and they consistently avoid working for the common good as
opposed to their own personal benefit. But even those who are altruistic,
who do indeed recognize the interests of others, and who are willing to
contribute to the common good are not necessarily as wise as they are
well-meaning. Indeed, the history of the world often appears to be as
much if not more a history of well-meaning errors as of genuine evil or
even of more benign moral failure. We know, for example, that the vast
majority of drivers think their driving skill is above average,[30] and this
often-replicated finding is but one example of the widespread tendency
of ordinary people not only to overestimate their own decision making
abilities but also to assume that the degree of confidence they have in
their decisions is a reliable indicator of the soundness of those decisions.[31] It is the same for officials. Societies rarely—perhaps never—
select officials for their modesty and self-doubt, and so it should come as
little surprise that the people who happen to find themselves in public
elected or appointed office are as likely as ordinary people to overestimate their decision making skills and thus their ability to make sound
decisions for the benefit of others or for the benefit of society.

Consider, for example, the case of the lay Good Samaritan. We know
that people often fall ill or are injured when there is no physician pres-

ent. And we know that bystanders or companions will, to their moral credit, often come to the aid of the afflicted in such situations, sometimes even at personal risk or cost. But we also know that although many of these well-intended interventions are effective and life-saving, many others are life-threatening and produce worse outcomes than would be produced by nonintervention. The effects of snakebite are often worsened, for example, by well-meaning interveners who make cuts across the fang marks and attempt to suck out the venom. Similarly, the well-intentioned but medically ignorant bystander at an accident will sometimes exacerbate a fracture or spinal cord injury by altruistically attempting to move the victim out of danger or removing a victim's motorcycle helmet. And most of us know that the neighbor who generously and genuinely offers to repair your car or your lawn mower is at least as likely to make it worse as to fix it.

Obviously the causes of such well-meaning but mistaken interventions are psychologically and sociologically complex. Some are caused by simple ignorance or by a lack of sufficient training and expertise to make certain kinds of decisions. Many are the product of the numerous deficiencies in reasoning that contemporary psychological research has shown to plague even the smartest and most careful among us.[32] Much of this research has been focused on factual error and seemingly irrational mistakes in basic reasoning, but many of the same sources of cognitive error are often sources of moral error as well.[33] And simple hubris also plainly plays a large role in some instances, as does the more general inclination of many people to desire to be heroes, to want to take charge, and to drastically overestimate their own abilities in various other ways. But whatever the causes, the mistaken intervention is a sufficiently widespread phenomenon that it should lead us to be wary of assuming that even those with seemingly well-meaning motives will have a degree of skill or judgment that is even close to commensurate with their good intentions.

The phenomenon of the well-intentioned and admirably motivated blunderer is even more apparent with respect to officials.[34] On a daily basis we observe a large number of bad policies or unfortunate applications of good policies that are less the product of ill will as much as they are the consequence of bad judgment, predictable cognitive irrationalities, moral mistake, or insufficient knowledge or experience. And to the extent that this is so, then one of the functions of law is to create the motivation for people in general and officials in particular to relinquish their own best judgment in favor of a judgment they (mistakenly) think mistaken. The official who blindly follows the law or who follows the rules to an unfortunate outcome is regular fodder for popular and journalistic contempt,[35] but those who mock the law in such circumstances would likely recoil at the prospect of empowering police officers, customs agents, or tax collectors simply to use their best judgment in deciding whom to arrest, whom to search, and whom to tax. Not only do we often and appropriately worry about the mistakes that such officials may make in the well-meaning pursuit of their duties, but we may also be concerned that the incentives of various official roles may lead those who hold them to ignore other socially valuable ends. Tax collectors may often, and not surprisingly, understand their roles in terms of revenue maximization, and police officers and prosecutors in terms of arrest numbers and conviction rates. But the law, from a larger perspective, will often recognize other and frequently conflicting goals.

Once we understand, however, that in such cases society is asking officials to suppress their own best judgment about policy or to reject their own considered decisions about what actions to take on some particular occasion, we can appreciate that sanctions have an especially important role to play. Yes, officials might, in theory, recognize that the judgment of the law is often better than their own personal judgment. Yet little that we know about people's assessment of their own abilities would give much cause for optimism about the likelihood that officials would relinquish their own judgment in such cases. After all, overconfidence is a widespread and widely documented phenomenon.[36] Moreover, it is hardly a revelation that those whose official office puts them in a position of being treated obsequiously by subordinates and supplicants—high elected officials, judges, deans, and military officers seem often to fit this characterization—are especially likely with some frequency to fall prey to the vice of overestimation of their own decision-making abilities. And to the extent that such decision-making pathologies are systematic and predictable, then some form of coercion—some system of positive rewards and negative sanctions—will often be necessary as a way of motivating officials to follow the law rather than what they, individually on this occasion, think is best.

Indeed, the importance of suppression of individual judgment increases insofar as an official's best judgment may actually be the best judgment for some particular constituency but not for the larger community. Consider the prohibitions on economic protectionism, whether in individual countries such as the United States[37] or in groups of countries, as with the European Union. When an Italian official promotes protectionism for the Italian pasta industry, he is not only behaving responsibly from a moral or policy perspective, but he is also serving the genuine needs of his primary constituency. So too when the officials of the state of Hawaii decide to assist the indigenous pineapple wine industry by granting it tax preferences over the non-Hawaiian producers of other types of wine.[38] But we know that when multiple officials in multiple countries or states or provinces behave in such a fashion, the overall economy suffers. And thus the law often prohibits just this kind of protectionism precisely because protectionism may be good for some parts of a larger economy but bad for the economy as a whole. But the likelihood of an official following the law for the larger good even at the cost to his own primary constituents is small, and we should not be surprised that courts and the associated coercive enforcement mechanisms emerge as necessary mechanisms precisely to allow law to serve the larger good. To be sure, law does exist, in part, to prevent bad leaders from making bad decisions. But law also exists to keep good leaders from making good first-order decisions that turn out to be detrimental to various second-order interests or to the long-term general welfare.[39]

It is thus an error to think that officials who will not voluntarily obey the law are necessarily venal, selfish, or power-mad. They may simply be serving their constituents or relying in good faith on their best and not self-interested judgments. But as long as those judgments might be mistaken or inattentive to certain larger interests, law has a role to serve, and a role that it is difficult to imagine law serving without the assistance of various institutions and techniques of compulsion. What those institutions and techniques are and might be, in the context of both citizens and officials, is the subject of Chapters 8 and 9.

8

OF CARROTS AND STICKS

8.1 Austin's Apparent Mistake

It is simply mistaken to assume that people behave entirely according to their self-interest. To repeat what was discussed in Chapter 5, there is more than ample evidence that altruistic conduct and moral motivation do exist, as do a host of cooperative (or what the psychologists call pro-social) behaviors that might not even rise to the level of pure altruism. To be sure, efforts have been made to explain the entirety of altruistic, pro-social, and other-regarding moral behavior in terms of even deeper happiness or other forms of self-interest, but most of those efforts appear strained and reductionist.[1] Even Jeremy Bentham, frequently and mistakenly caricatured as having an entirely egoistic or other self-interested view of human nature, understood that people often recognize their duties to others[2] and at least sometimes act for reasons of sympathy, benevolence, and friendship.[3] Yet, although many anecdotes and even more serious research reveals that it is mistaken to assume that all human behavior is driven by self-interest,[4] it is equally mistaken to assume that none of it is. To a significant extent, people do attempt to maximize their own well-being or, as Bentham put it, to maximize their own pleasure and minimize their own pain.[5] For most of us, our decisions are driven, as Bentham recognized, by some mixture of moral and other-regarding motivation on the one hand and prudential self-interest on the other.

Even to the extent that behavior is determined largely or entirely by self-interest, however, individuals appear often to be motivated not only by a fear of unpleasant sanctions but also by a hope for rewards. Although many people would prefer to avoid military service, for example, the shift in many countries from military conscription to an army of volunteers has been facilitated by the promise of education, specialized and civilian-relevant training, early and generous retirement, and in many cases a higher salary and better food and shelter than might otherwise have been available for those who volunteer.[6] Obviously there are distributional and equity concerns of such a shift, for the marginal value of the financial rewards accompanying military service is far greater for those who start with far less than for those who start with more. But although these issues of equity are important dimensions of public policy, they are not directly relevant to the present inquiry. For our purposes, the volunteer army as it exists in much of the developed world is a good example of the use of rewards and not more direct and more negative forms of coercion as a way of getting people to do what they would otherwise prefer to avoid. And as many parents and teachers, supported by legions of pop psychologists as well as by some serious research, know, children often respond better to promised rewards than to threatened punishment.[7] Indeed, in an important way it all started with the rats. Behavioral psychologists, following the original path set out by B. F. Skinner and his theory of operant conditioning,[8] have studied the behavior of rats (and pigeons, and sometimes even people) and have concluded, to oversimplify, that rats and other experimental subjects often respond as well or better to the hope of a reward (or reinforcement) than to the threat of punishment.[9] If you want to get a rat to push a lever, you can do this by rewarding the rat with food whenever the lever is pushed, or you can punish the rat by administering an electric shock whenever it does *not* push the lever. Both techniques seem to work, but rewards often appear to work better.[10] Skinnerian behaviorism is less fashionable now than it has been in the past, but we still owe to Skinner and his followers the most sustained research program on the ways in which positive as well as negative sanctions can influence behavior.

Bentham, whom we credit for the initial creation of a sanction-dependent account of the nature of law, and who was more interested in human beings than in rats,[11] also recognized that human motivation can be positive or negative. And thus he well understood the way in which rewards as well as punishment can influence behavior. Yet even though Bentham recognized the inducement power of the positive, he nonetheless often (but not always[12]) resisted including positive governmental inducements within the domain of law and legislation. Part of this resistance was simply a curious definitional fiat: "I say nothing in this place of reward; because it is only in a few extraordinary cases that it can be applied, and because even where it is applied, it may be doubted, perhaps, whether the application of it can, properly speaking, be termed an act of legislation."[13] But as the reference to "only in a few extraordinary cases" suggests, Bentham downplayed the importance of what he later called the "alluring motives,"[14] in part because he believed that "any man can at any time be much surer of administering pain than pleasure,"[15] and even more because the role of the state as the supplier of benefits was vastly less important in the late eighteenth century than it is in the early twenty-first. Thus he said, "So great, indeed, is the use that is made of [punishment], and so little in comparison is that which is made of reward, that the only names which are in current use for expressing the different aspects of which a will is susceptible are such as suppose punishment to be the motive. Command, prohibition, and permission [all] point at punishment."[16] And, he continued, with characteristic Benthamite hyperbole, "By reward alone, it is most certain that no material part of [the] business [of government] could be carried on for half an hour."[17] For Bentham such conclusions were empirically sound. The state that he knew best was a state that possessed and often used the power to punish, but only rarely was it one that supplied benefits. Welfare, pensions, social security, state-supported education and healthcare, and even extensive government employment were still a long way in the future, and thus it is hard to fault Bentham very much for stressing the state's power to punish and for not believing that much of importance was implicated by the state's power to provide.[18] Bentham's exclusion of rewards from the incentives to legal compliance and consequently from an incentive-based account of law itself was thus in part definitional, but the definitional exclusion seems itself to have been driven substantially by the empirical rarity of the government-provided benefits whose potential behavior-shifting use Bentham excluded from the idea of legislation, and thus (for him) of law.

When John Austin further developed the framework and details of Bentham's command theory of law, the role of rewards found itself pushed even further off to the side. Austin explicitly rejected applying the term *sanction* "to conditional good as well as to conditional evil: to reward as well as to punishment."[19] He believed that such an extension would be too much a departure from the established meaning of terms such as *sanction, duty, obligation,* and *obedience,* and certainly from what he understood to be the meaning of *command.*[20] Thus,

If *you* expressed a desire that *I* should render a service, and if you proffered a reward as the motive or inducement to render it, *you* would scarcely be said to *command* the service, nor should *I*, in ordinary language, be *obliged* to render it. In ordinary language, *you* would *promise* me a reward, on condition of my rendering a service, whilst *I* might be *incited* or *persuaded* to render it by the hope of obtaining a reward. . . . If we [thus] put *reward* into the import of the term *sanction*, we must engage in a toilsome struggle with the current of ordinary speech.[21]

Whether Austin was correct in his understanding of the ordinary language of 1832, when these words were first written, is a matter best left to the historical linguists. But Austin, unfortunately, offers little else by way of argument for why rewards as well as punishments should be excluded from the domain of sanctions, and thus from the ambit of an inquiry into how the state can motivate compliance with its legal directives. Austin's modern biographer W. L. Morison attributes Austin's exclusion of rewards largely to Austin's desire for "tidiness,"[22] and thus as part of what was essentially a definitional or naming exercise. But even if we are (as we should be) sympathetic to definitional exercises, at least when they are pursued in the service of clear thinking and analytic precision, this particular definitional maneuver seems odd. There may well be psychological, even if not economic, differences between the state telling me that I will be fined $10,000 if I do not do something and the state telling me that it will give me $10,000 if I do,[23] but importing those contingent and variable psychological questions into a definition of law or a definition of legal coercion should strike us as a mistake. After all, if what the state labels a reward is in actuality a necessity for a successful life, then losing the reward will seem very much like a punishment. And if what the state labels as a punishment is seen as merely a cost of doing business, as it often is in many contexts, then many people will consider the state withholding punishment almost the same as it offering a reward for complying with its wishes, a conditional reward that the subject may well be free to accept or reject.

At this point, it is clear that these issues cannot be determined by definitional edict. There may well be circumstances in which coercion by what Austin called the threat of "evil" is different from inducement by reward, but we cannot identify those circumstances at the level of definitional ipse dixit. Rather, we must explore more carefully the nature of positive and negative incentives. In doing so, we can nod at the substantial work done by economists on the question,[24] as well as the considerable quantity of psychological research on the topic,[25] but the goal here will be less to describe or evaluate that research than to connect the general question of rewards versus punishments—positive or negative incentives— with the themes that pervade this book.

8.2 Two Kinds of Benefits

Vastly more now than in Bentham's day, the state is the provider of benefits in countless varieties. And in its capacity as provider (and thus as potential withholder) of benefits, the state has the ability to influence behavior in ways that a less positively active state could not.[26] The more the citizen is dependent on the state for many of the necessities, or even the luxuries, of life, the more that the power to grant or withhold such benefits can serve as an inducement for legal compliance. Most modern developed countries, for example, provide pensions, medical care, housing, education, employment, welfare for low-income citizens, and benefits for military veterans and others who have served the state. Many of these benefits, however, are not offered for the purpose of inducing a desired form of behavior. Yes, the state would prefer that those to whom it provides medical benefits not smoke, in part because not smoking reduces the state's medical costs.[27] But because the state does not condition medical benefits on the recipients' engaging in certain forms of health-beneficial behavior, the benefit cannot plausibly be understood to be aimed at controlling citizen behavior. And much the same can be said about many of the other benefits that the modern industrial state provides. At least in their central cases, most government pension plans, public housing, welfare benefits, state-based education, and government employment are not conditional, in the sense that the receipt of such benefits is not dependent on the recipients performing or refraining from the specific behaviors that the state might wish to encourage or discourage.

There are, however, other governmental benefits that are provided conditional upon the recipient engaging in a certain form of desired behavior. And because the benefits are conditional in just this way, they more closely fit the category that Bentham and Austin described as rewards. These benefits are rewards for desired behavior—in some cases engaging in certain activities and in others in refraining from certain activities. If the state, desirous of limiting smoking, were to provide cash benefits to nonsmokers rather than or in addition to penalizing smoking, we could properly consider this a reward. Indeed, although modern states do not provide such benefits for nonsmokers, insurance companies do just that, offering lower rates for those who refrain from smoking. Even if more commonly practiced by insurance companies than by the government, therefore, the idea of inducing a desired behavior by financial benefits is hardly alien to modern culture. And among the most common of behavior-modifying rewards is, in many countries, the tax deduction. In the United States, for example, people are rewarded for buying houses insofar as the interest on a mortgage is tax deductible, whereas the interest on an automobile loan is not. And taxpayers are rewarded for giving to charity, because such donations are tax deductible even though donations to political parties and family members are, in general, not.

Rewards for engaging in governmentally desired behavior are even more common in intergovernmental contexts. The U.S. federal government, for example, often seeks to have the states, which have primary control over roads and highways, impose various safety-related or energy conservation–related driving restrictions, such as speed limits and seat belt requirements.[28] For various reasons, some of which relate to constitutional limits on federal power that are not germane here,[29] the typical method of the federal government's preferences in this area is not to mandate that the states impose these federally desired restrictions but instead to condition the receipt of federal highway funds on a state's willingness to impose the restrictions. The states could refuse the federal funds and thus legally refuse to impose the restrictions, but in practice the amounts are so substantial that policy making by conditional reward turns out be as effective, or maybe even more so, than a direct mandate coupled with a punishment for disobedience.

There is, however, an important distinction between two types of conditional rewards. One type is best understood as a direct subsidy for state-desired behavior, and *subsidy* may in this context be a better word than *reward*. If the state wishes to reduce pollution, it may simply punish polluters. But it may also or instead provide a subsidy to companies for the purpose of purchasing pollution-control equipment. Indeed, rather than provide funds to purchase the equipment, the state might just give the equipment to a company. Similarly, instead of giving nonsmokers monetary rewards, the state might provide smoking cessation medication or treatment (or electronic cigarettes) for free or at subsidized rates. Such programs are in some sense rewards, but they are different from the situation, to use the same examples, in which the state provides a cash reward for any company using a certain kind of pollution control device, provides a monetary reward for any company that reduces its pollution rate below a certain level, or gives a cash payment to nonsmokers. It is true that under certain conditions such subsidies are economically equivalent to straight rewards (and also to fines or penalties for engaging in the disapproved behavior), but there is nevertheless a difference between a direct subsidy for a specific purpose and a reward simply for engaging in the preferred behavior. At the very least, the latter is likely to give the subjects of the reward scheme more choice and thus may under some conditions be more effective. A state (or, more realistically, a school or a professional sports team) could deal with habitual drug users by subsidizing entrance into a rehabilitation facility or instead by giving a cash reward to anyone who was determined by testing to have been drug-free for a certain period of time. One or the other of these approaches may be more effective under some conditions, but it is at least useful to recognize the distinction between the two, and the occasionally important distinction between a general reward and a far more specific subsidy.

8.3 The Politics of Rewards

Although conditional rewards are thus a plausible alternative to governmental punishment, Bentham may not have been very far off in observing that in fact governments make little use of rewards as a device for controlling the behavior of errant citizens. Not only in Bentham's day but even now, and despite the vastly wider scope of governmental payments and other benefits in general, using rewards as a method of inducing desired conduct and discouraging undesired acts remains quite rare, at least in the context of individual behavior. Insurance companies reward good drivers and nonsmokers, but governments do not. And although parents and schoolteachers often reward obedient children with prizes and various more tangible benefits, few governments bother to reward good citizens. Indeed, although American prisons often give prisoners time off from a sentence for good behavior, they also, and even more often, add time for bad behavior.

The most obvious explanation for the relative paucity of reward-based behavioral control even in a world of increasing government benefits is that often rewards simply do not work. There are numerous positive incentives for not smoking, for example, including better insurance rates and various other forms of positive reinforcement for the non-smoker, but the rate of smoking still remains dangerously high.[30] Prisons add time for misbehavior or escape attempts because the allure of a reduced sentence for exemplary conduct appears to provide insufficient incentives to forestall such acts.[31] And implicit in the reluctance of the state's Division of Motor Vehicles to reward good drivers with shorter lines at the registry, easier renewal procedures, or special lanes at toll booths is the assumption that none of these practices would have much effect on the incidence of dangerous or otherwise unlawful driving habits.

Some of this preference for punishment over rewards can be explained by the research confirming Bentham's unscientific but seemingly sound assumption that negatives are often more powerful than positives in affecting behavior.[32] But perhaps a better and more pervasive explanation for the widespread use of negative rather than positive inducements—for the fact that rewards are employed more by parents and teachers than by governments—lies in the domain of political economy. So consider an example from Bentham regarding the possibility—one that Bentham favored even though it was not the law of England at the time he was writing, or even now—that citizens would have an affirmative obligation to report crimes of which they were aware, even if the obligated citizens were in no way involved in committing, aiding, abetting, or actively concealing the crime. With respect to this proposed legal obligation, Bentham says, as an example, "[w]hoever comes to know that a robbery has been committed, let him declare it to the judge: if he declares it accordingly, he shall receive such and such a reward: if he fails to declare it, he shall suffer such or such a punishment."[33]

But now consider the costs of the two sanctions that Bentham proposes. Assuming, quite plausibly, that there are a considerable number of robberies, we can expect, if the reward amount is high enough, that there will also be a considerable number of citizens who will report robberies and earn the reward. This will require substantial outlays from state funds, as well as an additional bureaucracy to administer the reward scheme. But the punishment for failing to report a robbery—and presumably Bentham is imagining reporting of the identity of the perpetrator—will seem, especially in the short run, costless. If the threatened punishment is great enough, it will rarely need to be actually administered, and thus the additional law enforcement and prison costs will be minimal. And even if the obligation will require law enforcement expenditures, those expenditures, likely buried in existing law enforcement and prison budgets, will be largely invisible.

The lesson of the example should be clear. Punishment for engaging in wrongful acts or failure to perform required ones will often appear as relatively costless to legislators and their constituents and, at the margin, may actually be so, while rewards for engaging in obligatory behavior will typically seem to those same legislators as necessitating new and incremental expenditures. So consider, as another example, the relatively recent prohibitions or serious restrictions, in Europe and elsewhere, on the manufacture of raw milk cheese, on the grounds that using raw (un-pasteurized) milk in making cheese can cause listeria and other serious illnesses.[34] One way to accomplish the goals behind these regulations would simply be to prohibit the manufacture of cheese with raw milk and attach a penalty for violation. Such an approach would likely not involve short-term additional governmental expenditures, especially if an extensive food inspection bureaucracy were already in place. But if the cheese makers were promised a reward or bounty for developing and using alternative production methods, the reward would require an immediate outlay of public funds and might well be resisted on those grounds alone. This is not to deny that there might be hidden costs in the punishment approach. Over time, law enforcement expenditures can be expected to grow as the numbers of potential violators and violations increase. And in some cases, of which cheese might be a good example, some of the costs of new prohibitions will be borne by those who are regulated rather than by the public purse, which does not mean that such costs are not still social costs. If the cheese makers have to spend money on alternative production methods, or if they lose the customers who desire raw milk cheese, there is indeed a cost. It is just that these costs may be long term and not short term, and be initially borne in the private sector rather than by the government. As a result, prohibitions will often appear less costly for the government, even when their costs to society as a whole are as great. So if we think of this as a question of political economy and not economics—that is, of the incentives that drive political actors and not the actual underlying economics—we can understand why it is so often the case that rewards will be resisted on the grounds that they require incremental expenditures but that punishment, which will appear relatively costless even though it is not, will wind up as the preferred option in the legislative process.

In addition to issues of political economy, there are actual economic concerns that may explain the historical and continuing preference for punishment. Specifically, in many contexts implementation costs for reward schemes may actually be greater than for punishments. As a strictly logical matter, requiring people to wear seat belts and prohibiting them from not wearing them may be identical, but logic may not do all of the work here. It would, after all, be far easier to apprehend and punish violators of a prohibition, especially because violations are easily visible by the authorities, than it would be establish a system by which seat belt wearers received a reward for their good behavior. Here and elsewhere, the institutions required for the reporting and monitoring of compliant behavior seem more cumbersome, expensive, and inefficient than a simple system of apprehending and punishing violators. And this is especially true with a prohibition system in which the penalties are sufficiently high as to generate serious deterrence and thus require little by way of actual enforcement and actual enforcement costs. And it is hard even to imagine a system by which people who did not commit robbery, or did not have unsafe workplaces, or did not discriminate in employment, received rewards for their law-abiding behavior. And so, although tax deductions and various other reward schemes are plausible alternatives to punishment or other negative sanctions in some narrow contexts, it is understandable why the law can be expected to continue to make far more use of sticks than it does of carrots.

8.4 Rewards and the Nature of Law— Perhaps Austin Was Right After All

When we consider the difficulty and expense of administering a system of rewards for engaging in advantageous behaviors and not engaging in disadvantageous behaviors, we can better appreciate Bentham's and especially Austin's exclusion of rewards from the domain of law. It is true that government has the ability to use carrots as well as sticks to create the incentives for socially desirable behavior, whether that behavior involves acting or refraining from acting. And it is also true that the use of carrots—rewards—is becoming increasingly common in the modern world, even if, as we have just seen, it remains less common as a method of governance than it is as a method for classroom instruction or effective parenting. Yet, even to the extent that rewards are employed, the question remains—Austin's question even more than Bentham's—whether we ought to understand such reward mechanisms as law.

Consider two alternative approaches to enforcing the proposed legal requirement in the United States that commercial woodworking businesses use a particular kind of table saw, one that has a remarkable device that will stop the blade within five-thousandths of a second after it contacts human flesh, thus converting what had in the past been finger-losing injuries into minor nicks.[35] One enforcement possibility, at least in the context of commercial businesses, would be consistent with existing workplace safety enforcement procedures, according to which inspectors from the Occupational Safety and Health Administration make random unannounced checks on covered businesses, with the power to impose fines for violations. Accordingly, using a saw without the device in a commercial establishment would be a violation, enforced by the just-noted random inspections. But another way of implementing the requirement would be by way of a system in which everyone who purchased and installed the device would receive a cash reward, somewhat akin to a store rebate, and with more or less a similar system for verifying purchases.

Even if we assume (perhaps counterfactually) equivalent governmental cost, and even if we assume (again probably counterfactually) equivalent enforcement effectiveness, it would not be implausible to imagine that the punishment system would more often use the legal system's traditional devices and personnel, including lawyer-drafted regulations, courts, appeals, and lawyer-dominated adversary proceedings. By contrast, we might suppose that the reward system could be managed largely, even if not completely, outside of the formal legal system, and would make less use of lawyers, formal procedures, and courts. And to the extent that such differential use of formal legal institutions existed, we may find ourselves with a new perspective on the relationship of rewards to law. That is, the question about rewards and punishments may not only be about which approach is more efficient in which context or about which approach would produce greater levels of compliance with legal obligations but about which approach would exist within or closer to the various procedures and institutions that have traditionally pervaded and characterized the legal system. And thus when Austin excluded rewards from his definition of law, and Bentham at times seemed close to doing the same thing, they might have implicitly been adopting what we might call a sociological or procedural definition of law, an issue to which we shall return in Chapter 11. Rather than defining law in terms of the nature of its norms or the nature of its sources, we might instead think of law simply as the activity engaged in by courts, lawyers, and the sociologically defined array of institutions that surround them. Just as at least one definition of *art* is simply what artists and the culture and business of art do,[36] and just as Ronald Dworkin's definition of *law* has sometimes seemed close to defining law as just what courts and lawyers do,[37] one definition of law might be parasitic on the activities of courts, judges, lawyers, and associated institutions. Seeing the issue in this way is probably not what Bentham had in mind, and it is certainly not what Austin had in mind. Still, such a way of perceiving the differential connection between rewards and law, and punishment and law would provide some support for an understanding of law (better than a definition for some purposes) that distinguished rewards from punishment not on the basis of some attribute intrinsic to one or the other but largely on the basis of the way in which the latter much more than the former would use the traditional apparatus and institutions we (sociologically) know as the legal system.

A sociological or institutional approach to understanding more sympathetically Austin's and Bentham's exclusion of rewards from *their* definitions of law is open to the charge that it is question-begging. After all, why should we understand courts and judges and lawyers as central to law but various bureaucratic and administrative procedures and institutions as something else? Asking the question in this way in turn leads to an even larger question, and one to which we return in Chapter 11. Just what are the features of law that we wish to explain? Or, what are the features of law that any successful account of the nature of law *must* explain? If we wish only explain a system of norms or an institution of social organization whose purpose is to achieve desirable aims and to use governmental resources in the service of those aims, then the reward system just described would certainly qualify. But we would then have arguably dragged under the umbrella of law the entire system of policy making and policy enforcement. That understanding of the compass of law may or may not be a good thing to do, and it may or may not be useful for some practical or theoretical purposes, but it fails to explain what seems to be at the very least a sociological difference between courts and other public institutions, between lawyers and other policy professionals, and between the legal apparatus and numerous other devices of public policy.[38]

In failing to explain an obvious and seemingly important fact about how law and legal systems exist in most modern societies, any approach that collapses the seemingly important sociological fact of the differentiation of law from other norms systems and from other governmental and policy institutions could be thought to fail for exactly this reason. And, conversely, an approach that recognizes the difference between law and administration, between law and policy, and between law and politics, even as it recognizes that these are overlapping systems with fuzzy boundaries and vague demarcations, will be an approach that does not assume that every implementation of public policy is best understood as law. And if this is so, then perhaps we can glimpse what Bentham and Austin were trying to get at and what might have led them, not necessarily correctly but hardly obviously incorrectly, to think of a system of rewards as, generally, less a part of law and legal system than other approaches might suppose. I do not offer this as a definitive or even tentative interpretation of their work but perhaps more as a useful and partial reconstruction. For although Bentham did write *Of the Limits of the Penal Branch of Jurisprudence* as a continuation of the far less legal system–specific *Introduction to the Principles of Morals and Legislation*, he also, as discussed in Chapter 2, maintained an abiding contempt for almost all aspects of the legal system he knew best. This contempt was at times focused on the methods of the common law, but it was even more commonly and vehemently applied to judges, lawyers, and the functionaries of the courts. And thus, Bentham's contempt for the law was a contempt focused far more sociologically than philosophically. He saw a group of people—or, perhaps more accurately, a conspiracy— who were working together to undermine the common good in order to maximize their own wealth and power. One does not have to agree with Bentham about the conspiratorial aspects of this agglomeration of individuals and institutions, or even about its pernicious tendencies, to recognize the target of his ire—lawyers and judges—as substantially demarcated in sociological rather than philosophical ways. Looking at the distinction between reward and punishment may thus have provided a window into just what we are doing when we seek to understand the phenomenon of law. The phenomenon of law has numerous normative, philosophical, and political dimensions, among others, but it also has, especially in the modern world, sociological ones. And thus if we are trying to understand what differentiates law from other social systems, we may be assisted by recognizing law's partial sociological differentiation, a differentiation that is no less real and no less important than various other forms of differentiation. In saying this, however, we become now rather far removed from the narrower question of rewards and punishments. Nevertheless, there is much more to be said about the differentiation of law, including its sociological differentiation, and at least some of it will be said in Chapter 11.

9

COERCION'S ARSENAL

9.1 Beyond (or perhaps before) Threats

The threat stands at the center of the conventional picture of coercion in law. The gunman who says, "Your money or your life" is giving his victim a choice, but it is an illusory one. Few people, after all, would sacrifice their lives to save their money (which probably would not happen in this scenario anyway). Like the gunman, the law also sometimes threatens people with loss of life—capital punishment—if they do not comply with law's demands. Typically, however, what the law threatens is at least a bit milder: jail, fines, loss of benefits of some kind, flogging in earlier times and in some countries now, and loss of various privileges particular to citizenship, such as voting. But although there are differences between the threats of the law and those of the gunman, the threat of unpleasant consequences if the subject does not behave in a particular way is still the principal weapon in law's coercive arsenal. "Speed Limit 65" is coercive just because, and to the extent that, people would prefer to drive more slowly than appear in court, pay a fine, and possibly have their driving privileges curtailed. The deterrent aspect of serious criminal punishment operates similarly, on the assumption that the threat of after-the-act penalties will deter people from engaging in prohibited acts in the first place.[1] And much the same applies to the deterrent dimensions of private law, tort law most commonly, but also various others noncriminal forms of after-the-act liability.

Yet however ubiquitous the threat of after-the act sanctions may be, it is important to recognize that coercion may be applied even more directly than the threat and may give even less choice to the potential law violator. Consider, for example, the use of engine immobilizers as a method of deterring car theft.[2] The traditional approach to minimizing car theft is to threaten thieves with substantial punishment in the event of apprehension and conviction. The theory, trivially obvious, is that the prospects of imprisonment will deter people otherwise inclined to steal cars from actually doing so.

But we know, of course, that the threat of unpleasant sanctions is not perfectly effective. People steal cars anyway. And that is why cars have locks. An engine immobilizer is in effect a more sophisticated lock. It locks the car's engine unless the car recognizes the owner, whether by an actual physical key, a code that only the owner knows, or, in more sophisticated versions, by recognizing the owner's fingerprints, retinal pattern, facial features, voice, or something of that variety. Without the immobilizer's recognition of the owner, the car will not move.

Immobilization is a form of incapacitation, and incapacitation is a form of coercion. I can keep you out of my house by threatening to shoot you if you enter, but I can also keep you out of my house by locking the front door. I can rely on the deterrent effect of the criminal law to keep people from stealing my valuables, but I can also bury them or put them in a safe. The police can threaten disorderly people with arrest when they interfere with police officers performing their duties, or police officers can simply carry off those who are disorderly or obstructive. Similarly, a judge can coerce people to behave properly in court by threatening to hold them in contempt and thus impose fines or imprisonment, or in the alternative she can simply have the police forcibly remove those who are disruptive. And although one way of enforcing an eviction order is for the court and the sheriff to threaten fines or imprisonment for failing to leave the premises, another and quite common way is for the bailiffs to enter the premises and remove all of an evicted tenant's belongings. Immobilization, incapacitation, and removal, among other approaches, are in fact the most directly coercive implements available to the state. And thus, one way of understanding the threat of unpleasant after-the-act sanctions is as a potentially more efficient way of achieving the goals of even more direct coercion. It is expensive to pay a police officer to drag someone out of a courtroom, and we might conceive of the threat of contempt penalties as a way of shifting the cost of enforcement from the state to the potential perpetrator.

Such direct forms of coercion are more common than we might think. Speed bumps (which in Jamaica and a few other places in the world are charmingly called "sleeping policemen") coerce people into driving more slowly by making it more or less impossible to do otherwise, the inclinations of the driver notwithstanding. Locks protect houses and cars and businesses, and firewalls do much the same thing in the word of cyberspace and information technology. Although there are in that world often penalties for unauthorized access and invasion of privacy, using electronic means to keep people from seeing what *they* want to see is a form of coercion. And insofar as incapacitation is, in practice and often in theory, one of the goals of criminal punishment, we can see the imprisoned perpetrator not only as someone who has been punished in the retributive sense but also as someone who is directly prevented by walls, guards, bars, and barbed wire from doing what he otherwise would want to do, including, or so the theory of incapacitation has it, committing the crimes he would still otherwise be inclined to commit.

Such direct ways of preventing wrongs are often ignored in the theoretical literature on coercion. Or sometimes they are acknowledged but mistakenly distinguished from coercion. Yet it is important to recognize the ubiquity of such directly preventive approaches and to appreciate that by altering people's preferences and motivations, they are best understood as coercive.[3] Often such approaches are not employed by official authorities because of their expense, but even more frequently they are avoided because of their overinclusiveness. The gate that keeps out the thief also keeps out the innocent visitor, the heavy bicycle lock and chain that frustrates the thief also inconveniences the owner, and the computer firewall that makes things more difficult for the hacker also makes it more difficult for the rest of us to take full advantage of cyberspace's legitimate search capacities. And at times direct physical prevention is simply insufficient to foil the determined and resourceful criminal. Indeed, on the plausible assumptions that creative and experienced thieves can break into and drive almost any car with almost any kind of lock, and that clever hackers are usually one step ahead of even the most sophisticated attempts to block their activities, the threat of after-the-act punishment may succeed in deterring acts that are beyond the deterrent capacities of physical or electronic barriers. It is thus important not to ignore the option of direct physical enforcement of the law to prevent its violation, but it is equally important to appreciate why such measures are not always, and perhaps not even usually, the approach of first resort.

9.2 Are Sanctions Always Coercive? Does Coercion Always Involve Sanctions?

Until now we have been using the terms *force, coercion,* and *sanctions,* among others (including *compulsion*), more or less interchangeably, with the promise in Chapter 1 of later and needed clarifications and distinctions. And it is now time to make good on that promise.

The literature on coercion is vast, but it turns out that much of it is not directly relevant to the questions that dominate this book—questions about the relationship between coercion and legality and about the role of coercion in facilitating legal compliance. More specifically, much of the existing literature on coercion is situated within a range of legal doctrines and moral questions in which a legal judgment or moral conclusion follows from the presence or absence of coercion. A few examples will make this clear. Consider first the law of contract. Normally a necessary condition of a contract's legal validity is the presence of an agreement between the contracting parties. But if one of the parties is coerced into entering into the contract—if there is duress—then there is no genuine agreement, and the contract is void. As with the criminal law's general defense of duress,[4] coercion or compulsion is ordinarily a defense to contractual liability.[5] Similarly, the crime of rape requires force, and under some circumstances coercion may count as force for purposes of the law of rape.[6] And although a suspect's confession to having committed a crime can be used as evidence against him if the confession is voluntary, it is, at least in most constitutional democracies, inadmissible if obtained by duress—that is, if it is coerced.[7] And for most of these legal questions there are moral analogues. Just as contracts made under duress are not legally binding, for example, so too with the lack of any moral obligation to keep a promise secured by coercion. And just as coerced sexual conduct is often a crime, so too is it always a moral wrong.

As lawyers and philosophers consider these questions, two principal positions have emerged.[8] Each has many variations, of course, but for our purposes we need only sketch the basics of the two opposing understandings of the idea of coercion. One understanding is largely factual, maintaining that the existence or not of coercion is a factual matter conceptually independent of the normative question of what kind of coercion, or how much coercion, is necessary for a certain moral judgment or legal outcome to be reached.[9] And the opposing understanding insists that coercion is a moralized concept, such that we cannot determine whether there has been coercion without incorporating into the very idea of coercion certain morally generated normative conclusions.[10]

If, with Austin, we were to believe that the threat of "evil" was among the necessary criteria for an individual norm to have the status as law, then many of the issues raised in these debates about what is necessary for some act to qualify as coercive would be highly relevant. Because Austin believed that coercion, or the threat of sanctions, was a necessary condition for a norm being a legal one, he needed (although he may not have provided[11]) a definition of coercion and a definition of a sanction for his analysis to succeed. But as should be clear by now, the concern of this book is no longer with the essential properties of law, and certainly not with the properties necessary for an individual law to be a law properly so called. The idea that coercion is a necessary condition for a prescription to count as a law or legal rule is among those of Austin's ideas that we have wisely discarded, however much his focus on coercion in general provides a valuable if now too-often unappreciated guide to understanding the phenomenon of law generally. That coercion is a pervasive characteristic of legal systems, and that it is also an important if not logically essential component of law as we know it, however, does not entail the conclusion that a threat of coercion is an essential component of every individual prescription that we should designate as law or recognize as a component of the legal system.

Accordingly, the running claim in this book that coercion has jurisprudentially underappreciated importance in understanding and explaining the phenomenon of law does not require that we have a definition of coercion that will distinguish instances of coercion from those of voluntariness. We need only keep in mind the basic idea that law, and not just this law or that law, generally makes us do things that we do not want to do or not do things that we do want to do. How and why law does this is assuredly of great importance, but identifying the coercive dimension of each individual law is equally assuredly not.

Although it is not important for our purposes here to distinguish the coercive from the voluntary with respect to individual laws, it is useful to recognize that coercion is best understood as an attribute of the effect of law upon the decisions of particular agents and is thus valuably distinguished from the less relational idea of a *sanction*. That is, sanctions are the devices that law uses or threatens, but whether the sanctions that are applied or threatened are coercive depends on the way in which those sanctions affect the decision-making capacities of the targets of the laws. The law may well contain a sanction for those who violate the laws against burglary, for example, and it may authorize particular officials to apply those sanctions in the event of disobedience, but because these laws will not change the preferences or motivations of those with no reasons or desires to burgle, they cannot be considered coercive for such individuals.

Even within the category of sanctions, it is useful as well to distinguish the threat or actual application of physical force from various other sanctions. The loss of a driver's license, for example, is a sanction, but it is not the direct application of raw physical power. It is true that most, and perhaps even all, of law's sanctions ultimately depend on people with guns and that there is thus something important in the common observation that law depends on the state's ultimate monopoly of the legitimate use of physical force.[12] After all, the sanction of losing my driver's license depends on the fact that my driving without a license is a crime and that if I commit that crime, I will be liable to a fine or imprisonment. The effectiveness of both of these sanctions ultimately depends on the state's ability to direct people with guns and uniforms to put me in prison, where I will be kept from escaping by other people with guns and uniforms. Yet though the state's power to enforce the law may ultimately depend on the use of brute physical force, the array of sanctions available to the state is far wider in normal and nonultimate circumstances than just the use of physical force, and thus, it may be useful, questions of terminology aside, to distinguish force as physical force from the wide range of nonphysical sanctions that the modern state has at its disposal, a range whose exploration will occupy the balance of this chapter.

Thus, if we were looking for a rough distinction among the various terms that have been used up to now in this book, we might say that sanctions are what law imposes in the event of noncompliance with legal mandates; that the application of force—meaning physical force—is among law's available sanctions; that law is coercive to the extent that its sanctions provide motivations for people, because of the law, to do something other than what they would have done absent the law; and that law can be said to exercise compulsion when its coercive force actually does induce the aforesaid shift in behavior. All of these definitions are stipulative, of course, but at the very least they highlight the way in which the coerciveness of law is in fact an interrelation among a group of connected by different phenomena.

9.3 Fines, Taxes, and the Cost of Doing Business

Most railroad, tram, and subway cars have a cord or handle designed to cause the train to come to more or less an immediate halt in the event of an emergency. And it is typical for there to be a sign in the immediate vicinity of the cord or handle warning passengers not to use this device except in cases of genuine emergency, and further warning them that using the device in the absence of an emergency will subject the user to a fine. The implications of this process were not lost on P. G. Wodehouse, whose Mr. Mulliner made the following observation:

> It is a curious thing that, in spite of the railway companies' sporting willingness to let their patrons have a tug at the extremely moderate price of five pounds a go, very few people have either pulled a communication-cord or seen one pulled.[13]

Obviously the railway companies to which Wodehouse was referring considered a £5 fine (in 1927) a serious punishment and thus a substantial deterrent. Equally obviously Wodehouse's typically carefree and wealthy characters saw the amount not as a penalty but as a price, and a rather reasonable one at that, for the thrill of bringing an enormous train to an immediate halt.

Wodehouse's Mr. Mulliner puts before us the question whether there is a difference between a price and a penalty, and thus, whether the coercive aspects of any threatened penalty are entirely a function of the resources and preferences of the subject of a law. When the state says that you must pay a fine of such-and-such an amount for engaging in such-and-such behavior, is it telling you not to do something or is it just setting the price for doing it? And if it is the latter, is it the same if the penalty is imprisonment? There are, after all, many people who might be willing to exchange relatively short prison terms for great wealth. And if the former, if the penalty is merely an adjunct to the law's command, and if the law is thus not indifferent as between compliance and penalized noncompliance, does the same apply to private law? When the law awards damages for breach a contract or for committing a tort, is the law saying that one ought not to breach contracts or commit torts, or is it simply setting the price for engaging in such activities?

For Oliver Wendell Holmes, the distinction between a price (or a tax) and a penalty was largely illusory, at least in the context of private law generally and contract law in particular. Many penalties are best seen simply as taxes, he insisted, and an award of damages for breach of contract, he also believed, was simply the price of engaging in a certain form of behavior, a price that the existence of the contract had increased.[14] But once the price had been set, the law was indifferent between compliance and noncompliance.

Holmes was unwilling to apply this perspective to the criminal or regulatory law, but others have been less reluctant.[15] There are, of course, those penalties that are so small that they seem for most of us largely like taxes or prices. The penalty for overtime parking is a good example, and if the penalty is not high enough, most people think of it as simply the price for parking. But even putting such small penalties aside, we can still ask whether a substantial fine for engaging in, say, insider trading is best understood as a way of coercing people otherwise inclined toward insider trading to refrain from the practice or instead as simply a price for engaging in what is often an extremely lucrative activity.[16] From the point of view of the law, of course, it would be a mistake to say that the law is indifferent between no murders and a thousand murders with a thousand murderers behind bars. The law has a point of view, and from that point of view it would prefer that there not be any murders. Or insider trading. Or almost all of the other things that are the subjects of the criminal law.[17]

But why should we care about the law's point of view? From the citizen's point of view, the law's point of view on this or anything else matters only if the citizen takes the existence of law *qua* law as a reason for action, and one of the things we have seen is that it is hardly clear that very many citizens behave in this way. Some ignore the normative force of the law because they are philosophical anarchists, believing that the existence of a legal proscription does not change what would otherwise be the moral and prudential calculus.[18] And others ignore law's proscriptions for less deeply thought-out reasons, acting as they do only because self-interest looms so large in their practical reasoning. And thus, consistent with the conclusions in Chapter 5, it may well be that from the perspective of many, or even most, citizens, the difference between price and penalty may be only a matter of degree.

Many find such a conclusion profoundly disturbing, or simply mistaken, but their worries may be misplaced. First, the fact that law's penalties may be thought of as prices does not (or should not) change the citizen's moral calculus or the official's policy one. Just because the law attaches a high price to murder, it does not make murder morally right for the person willing to pay the price. Thinking of the law's penalty as a price only makes murder legally right, or at least not legally wrong, but murder remains morally wrong—very morally wrong. Similarly, the American official who might view the constitutional prohibition on "cruel and unusual punishments" as morally inert—the constitutional status adds nothing to the moral calculation—should not view the wrongness of cruel and unusual punishments in the same way. She could believe, correctly, that cruel and unusual punishments are morally wrong, and the fact that the Constitution repeats and reinforces the message might make no difference for the person who has already internalized that message.

In addition, the law, from its point of view, is free to set the price in a way that strongly discourages the acts that the law wishes to discourage.[19] It is true that the law is saying to citizens that from the law's point of view, this is what citizens *ought* to do, but the law is also saying that this is what the law *will* do to you if you do not do what the law tells you to do. And while it may be true that the former without the latter could still characterize a legal system, we now find ourselves back to the discussion in Chapter 3 about the difference between law's essential and typical properties. And thus, if it is true that, whether for reasons of philosophical anarchism or self-interested prudence, the fact of law, by itself, is less commonly a reason for action for most people, and even for most officials, than many commentators believe, then the fact that the law is telling people what will happen to them if they do not obey is a more salient feature of law than the fact that the law is expressing its unenforced preference about how people ought to behave. So although it is true that the law purports to create legal obligations, it is important to recognize both that the nonacceptance of legal obligations is fully consistent with the robust acceptance of moral obligations and that the conceptual existence of legal obligations *qua* legal obligations is also fully consistent with such obligations playing a small role in the practical deliberations of most citizens and most officials. And if that is so, then the distinction between a price and a penalty, holding equal the amount of the price and the size of the penalty, may turn out to be even less consequential than even Holmes believed.

9.4 Reputation Matters

In Nathaniel Hawthorne's novel *The Scarlet Letter,* part of Hester Prynne's sentence for committing adultery in seventeenth-century Puritan Boston was having to wear a scarlet "A" on her clothing at all times. Such shaming penalties are rare these days, but they are hardly unheard of. People convicted of driving while intoxicated have been forced to put bumper stickers on their cars identifying themselves as drunken drivers.[20] Those found guilty of child molestation and other sex crimes have been made to identify themselves in various public ways. A man convicted of domestic violence was forced to apologize in public to his victim and the community.[21] And corporations are occasionally made to identify themselves as polluters or perpetrators of various other legal and social wrongs.

The actual and potential uses of shaming as a method of law enforcement have been much discussed in recent decades, partly because many consider it an efficient alternative to the expense of imprisonment. Detractors, however, object to the ways shaming inflicts an often inappropriate humiliation and lack of respect for the lawbreaker's dignity.[22] This debate has important policy and deep moral implications, and it raises fundamental questions about the nature and justification of punishment. But for our purposes here, its importance lies in how shaming can be seen as just another weapon in law's coercive arsenal.

Shaming penalties may serve diverse purposes. On a Saturday night, I would like literally to steer clear of someone who has been convicted of intoxicated driving, and thus, what may be shame to the driver is a warning to me, in much the same way that public identification of child molesters may not only shame the molester but also put members of his community on alert. But even apart from the warning function, shaming may serve larger reputation-harming functions. Insofar as people value good reputations and seek to avoid bad ones, hardly a revolutionary or controversial proposition, shaming may simply be a state-promoted form of reputational harm and thus merely another form of punishment. Such official shaming may or may not be a good idea as a matter of morality or penal policy, but the mistake would be in assuming that sanctions for disobedience must only be penal or monetary or involve loss of legal privileges. As long as the penalty is something that people would normally seek to avoid, the state's ability to impose it is no different from any of the other components in the state's array of available sanctions. Once we understand sanctions as attempts by the state to provide motivations for obedience to law apart from those of content-based motivations to engage in conduct consistent with the law, and thus to coerce people into following the law just because it is the law, there is no need to think, at least for our purposes here, of shaming and various other reputation-harming penalties as different in kind from prison, fines, civil disabilities, or, for that matter, flogging.

Reputational sanctions need not only be imposed by the state. Insofar as legal violations hurt an individual's reputation, then the law's coercive powers are increased, and the state can leverage its own sanctions. But to the extent that reputational penalties are understood as the sole form of sanctions, their effectiveness depends on and brings us back to the question introduced in Chapter 4 and persisting since then: the importance of law *as law*. More specifically, we need to distinguish the reputational harm from having engaged in conduct of a certain kind from the putative reputational harm of violating the law. When people prefer not to associate with rapists or have business dealings with those who have committed fraud, a conviction (or civil judgment) for such offenses will have reputational consequences for the perpetrator independent of any fine, civil judgment, or period of incarceration. And in such cases we can imagine the state free-riding on the reputation-harming ability of the public by, for example, rendering a sanction-free judgment and saving the cost of imprisonment. In such cases, however, the reputational damage is a function of the low esteem in which people hold individuals who have committed the particular act. The law serves an informing function, but the reputational damage comes from the reputational consequences of being the kind of person who has engaged in conduct of that sort. This form of content-based reputational harm is different, however, from the reputational consequences of being known as a law violator *qua* law violator. Will the public or some relevant subset of it lower its estimation of those who violate laws with whose content the relevant reputation-creating or reputation-damaging population disagrees? Do people who disapprove of the laws against marijuana use or price-fixing lower their estimation of people who break those laws just because they have broken the law? Perhaps the answer to this question is yes. Perhaps having a reputation as law-abiding for the sake of being law-abiding is valuable in some or many contexts. But some of the lessons of Chapters 5 and 6 suggest that this may not be so always or everywhere, and that the reputational effects of law-breaking may be rather more content-based than content-independent. And when and where this is so, the role of law *qua* law may be less than is often thought. The state, after all, could simply publicize the names of those who engaged in widely scorned activities without making them illegal and would thus achieve its content-based goals without having to resort to the law at all. Such state behavior may be rare, but identifying its possibilities alerts us to the risk of assuming too quickly that the reputational consequences of breaking the law are attributable to breaking the law as opposed to having engaged in conduct that is subject to disapproval regardless of the law.

9.5 Get Out! Expulsion and Other Disabilities

Many Australians trace their roots to ancestors who were sent there as punishment for crimes committed in England. The sentence of transportation, as it was called, was typically for life, and it was thought among the harshest the English legal system had to offer, at least short of hanging. The perceived harshness of transportation was partly a function of the journey itself, which involved months of unpleasantness and the danger of disease and shipwreck. And it was partly a function of the conditions at the end of the journey, which for all practical purposes were the equivalent of prison, except with more manual labor, more flogging, and fewer possibilities of escape.[23] In this respect transportation is historically interesting but perhaps not philosophically or jurisprudentially so. New South Wales and Tasmania can be thought of simply as prisons, albeit prisons that just happened to be farther away from London than Newgate Prison.

Transportation was also understood to be an especially harsh punishment, however, just because it involved exclusion from one's residence, one's community, and one's country, and this aspect of the sanction of transportation is more theoretically interesting, at least here. But when we look at transportation from this angle, we glimpse a host of interesting issues about exclusion as punishment more generally. Part of the pain of transportation was exclusion from the community, but England, even then, was pretty large. And it is thus hard to imagine exclusion from England, apart from removal from a smaller family and social environment, as hugely consequential in itself.

When we turn from the community that was eighteenth-century England to smaller, more closely knit, and more homogeneous communities, however, we can perceive domains in which exclusion, by itself, constitutes a substantial sanction. Where exclusion is perceived as a substantial sanction and something to be avoided, the threat of it can have a significant coercive effect. Religious communities have long practiced exclusion in the form of shunning, ostracism, and excommunication. Private clubs and associations use the threat of expulsion as a way of enforcing their rules. And, of course, the typical extreme sanction for violating the law of the workplace is dismissal from one's job.

In addition, and as recounted and analyzed by Oona Hathaway and Scott Shapiro,[24] various rule-based and rule-making cooperative arrangements use expulsion (Hathaway and Shapiro called it "outcasting") as a plainly coercive approach to rule enforcement. There is no legal requirement that a nation be a member of the World Trade Organization, for example, but membership brings sufficient economic benefits for all of the members that the WTO can use the threat of expulsion as a way of enforcing its many rules.

Indeed, the WTO, as well as many religious organizations and private clubs, have many of the attributes of legal systems. They do not, to be sure, typically have the *ultimate* coercive power, because in most cases they exist within larger and more comprehensive legal environments, as with various within-state organizations. Or, like the WTO, they exist alongside of and between various nation-states and typically have no (as with the WTO) or only derivative (as with the United Nations) ability to use the coercive power of armies and other repositories of physical force. But these organizations universally have primary rules governing the conduct of their members and have secondary rules of recognition, change, and adjudication, as well as, often, elaborate institutions for interpreting the rules and judging violations. And thus, insofar as such organizations also have an effective power of coercion through their ability to expel, there may be more to be gained than lost by thinking of them simply *as* legal systems rather than merely as analogous to legal systems.[25]

The foregoing conclusion may create some discomfort. After all, there are nonstate organizations that share the attributes just described but whose goals and methods are less benign. Take the Mafia, for example. By all accounts (accounts whose verification is understandably difficult), the Mafia imposes primary rules of conduct on both its members and nonmembers whose behavior it wishes to control; it has rules of recognition, which identify the primary rules and the individuals or groups who have the power to issue the primary rules; it has other secondary rules governing the processes of rule and regime change; and it has rules about the procedures to be followed when it is suspected that the rules have been broken. And the Mafia no doubt has the power of coercive enforcement. Finally, it seems plain that the relevant Mafia officials have the appropriate internal point of view with respect to those rules. Outside of a single leader and his inner circle, most of the officials may internalize the rules more out of fear than out of full substantive acceptance, but, as we have seen, this is no bar to the existence of a legal system. And although some of these "officials" may internalize the rules of recognition out of fear of death, for many others the real fear is a fear of expulsion. For many or most, or perhaps even all, of organized crime insiders, the material advantages (including power) of membership are sufficiently great that the threat of expulsion may well be as potent a form of coercion as the threat of a gangland execution.

It is hard to see that very much is lost by acknowledging that the Mafia and such organizations are in many respects legal systems. In some dimensions, of course, they may differ from the traditional municipal legal system. For example, they may not represent the ultimate source of raw power within some physical territory. At times (but only at times) their claims of control are less comprehensive than those of most legal systems.[26] It would be hard to claim that they are the source of *legitimate* power. And if one believes, with Shapiro and Raz, for example, that it is definitional of law that the ultimate legal authority at least *claim* to give its subjects moral reasons for action, then the Mafia may not qualify. But from a more strictly positivist perspective, one that is as unconcerned with the moral goals of a system as with its ultimate moral worth, then in many respects we might just say, without losing very much, that the Mafia is simply a legal system, even if a nonstate one. Especially once we realize that systems that are more obviously legal ones are more than occasionally built around the entirely self-serving goals of a small number of power-wielding despots—The Philippines under Marcos, for example, or Zaire under Mobutu, or any of some number of countries, past and present, that rarely even bother to claim high-sounding goals but just operate for the benefit of the wealth and power of a ruling elite—the compatibility between the lack of moral pretensions and existence of law commonly so called is more apparent. Yes, it is worthwhile to understand the differences between the law in despotic nation-states and nonstate despotic law, but as nonstate organizations proliferate in number and power, and as such organizations become ever more procedurally elaborate, it may be increasingly important simply to see them not as similar to legal systems and not as analogous to legal systems but rather just as legal systems, albeit of a somewhat less historically conventional variety.

9.6 Coercion and the Role of Private Law

Not only is it useful to see exclusion and its analogues as often an effective means of law enforcement, but it is also important to recognize that the criminal law is hardly the only overtly coercive facet of most legal systems. As we saw in Chapter 4, even the forms of law we see as primarily empowering rather than coercive—the law of contracts, wills, corporations, and even family law, for example—have their channeling and thus coercive dimensions, even if we acknowledge that the nullity of a transaction may not always be coercive, and even if nullity may not fully capture all that is important about law's empowering and constitutive aspects. But even less controversially and more overtly, various aspects of so-called private law still serve important functions in enforcing a polity's collective norms.

Understanding private law as serving functions similar to those we normally associate with the criminal law is most obvious when criminal law itself is embedded in various aspects of private law. In the United States, for example, many aspects of criminal antitrust and securities law have their civil counterparts, often with the express goal of thereby empowering so-called private attorneys general to bring private law actions in which the goals of public law will be served. When such actions allow for multiplied damages, as with the antitrust laws, or generous attorney's fees, as with much of consumer and antidiscrimination law, or class actions in which attorneys are again more than amply compensated, the incentives are in place for private law to take on much of public law's coercive aspect. Indeed, once we understand that the extent to which the behavior of tobacco companies, manufacturers of dangerous consumer products, and industries with environmentally dangerous methods or by-products is influenced far more by the threat of lawsuits than by the threat of criminal or regulatory law, we can appreciate the coercive aspects of private enforcement of public norms.

The foregoing is most obvious, of course, with respect to the law of torts. Although tort law has important compensatory functions, the fear of tort liability also deters and consequently shapes the conduct of putative tortfeasors. Just as speed limits compel many people to drive more slowly than they otherwise would, so too does the fear of liability. Thus, when newspapers refrain from publishing what in their best journalistic judgment is publishable, even taking into account the risk of falsity, they typically do so because of fear of libel judgments. Indeed, libel may be a particularly good example of private law in general and tort law in particular serving the function of coercively enforcing public norms. Insofar as libel law typically, at least in most common-law countries, enforces norms of accuracy that most journalists believe to be excessive in a world of uncertainty, the idea that the journalists, editors, and publishers who are the primary targets of libel law occupy the position of Hart's puzzled man seems laughable. Journalists adopt more risk-averse attitudes toward truth and falsity than they might have otherwise not because they think such an approach is wise and not because the law simply tells them to do so, but because the law tells them what will happen to them if they do not. Here, as elsewhere in most of tort law and much of private law more generally, the public often demands standards of behavior that depart from the standards that those who engage in that behavior would otherwise have selected. As we have seen throughout this book, it is precisely here where the coercive force of law is most important and where the prospect of individuals or businesses internalizing the law just because it is law is least likely. Tort law may perhaps serve a less direct causal function in creating the social norms that will become widely adopted and thus need to be coercively enforced only against outliers, but countless examples all around us indicate that the norms of tort law are more important and more effective in enforcing desirable norms against those whose personal and financial incentives are to the contrary than in changing those norms in the first place. And as long as that is the case, and where it is the case, private law as well as public law generally and criminal law particularly may occupy an important place in the coercive functions of law.

10

AWASH IN A SEA OF NORMS

10.1 Of Legal and Nonlegal Norms

We steer our lives through an obstacle course of rules. With great frequency, rules constrain our behavior. They dictate that we do things we would prefer to avoid and that we not do things we would prefer to do. But not all of the rules that constrain us are legal rules. Indeed, it is likely that most of them are not. Many of the rules that constrain us come not from law but from our communities, and theorists often call these rules *norms*—the external rule-based constraints on individual preferences that are not imposed by formal, official, governmental law.[1] Even more specifically, in the contemporary conception of norms, norms are the prescriptive rules (or understandings, if you will) about human behavior that are not written down in canonical form, but which arise largely from our social existence. Rather than being imposed from above, they seem often to percolate from below, emerging out of social practice and becoming normative over time as those social practices are perceived as appropriate. And because norms, by this modern definition, are not part of the official legal system, the sanctions for violating them typically involve censure, disapproval, shaming, revenge,[2] exclusion, and various other interpersonal or group sanctions, especially reputational sanctions,[3] but not the formal sanctions of state law.

A few examples will make the idea of a norm, and its distinction from what we normally think of as law, clearer. First, however, it is important to understand that we are not referring to mere habits or normatively inert behavioral regularities.[4] That I routinely sleep on my side, have coffee with my breakfast, and put both socks on before putting on my shoes[5] are habits—they are things I do regularly—but I have done nothing wrong by behaving otherwise and can hardly imagine being criticized for failing to engage in such behavior or even for departing from my own habit on some particular occasion. Norms, by contrast, are prescriptive. They purport to tell us what we ought to do and not merely to describe what we routinely and regularly do. Such prescriptive norms are socially pervasive, but they do not emanate from anything ordinarily thought of as law, nor are they enforced by anything commonly understood as law. Yet although such prescriptive norms have neither legal origin nor legal status, they are understood by the public, or at least most of the public, and in some cases only some relevant subset of it, in a plainly normative way. People believe that contravening such norms is wrongful, or at least they believe that other people believe such contravention is wrongful, and thus contravention often can be the basis of criticism. Examples of such norms would include many of the rules of grammar and language—don't say "ain't," and never end a sentence with a preposition—and most of the rules of etiquette—don't chew with your mouth open, and write thank-you notes after kindnesses—as well as the rules of civility—don't use certain offensive expressions, and give up your seat on the subway to the aged and the disabled. And of course many of the complex rules of queuing are of this variety. It is a norm in most places that you stand in a queue rather than push your way to the front, and it is now a norm in many places that the next person in a bank ATM queue does not stand too close to the person using the machine. And so it is, at least for some people, with the norms of fashion. The law did not tell people to wear bell-bottom trousers in the 1970s, but many people did so precisely because of what they perceived to be a norm to that effect in the circles in which they traveled. All of these norms are prescriptive, and they are sufficiently widely accepted within a population or within a relevant segment of it such that we can call them social or cultural norms. It is true, of course, that such norms can and do change. It was formerly the norm in many Western cultures for men to open the car door for women and to include women in the category of people to whom one should relinquish one's seat on the subway, but these norms have largely disappeared. And there exists now in certain social circles a norm against smoking in another's home, or even in another's presence, but such a norm was nonexistent a generation ago. Similarly, it is now the norm among even the most serious cyclists to wear a helmet while riding, but the norm was just the opposite—if you wore a helmet you were thought of as a sissy—twenty-five years ago. And this is despite the fact that, unlike the internationally widespread (but not universal) requirement of wearing a helmet while riding a motorcycle, it is rarely illegal to ride a bicycle while not wearing a helmet.

Even more pervasive, and certainly more written about, are those norms that are specific to certain specialized professional environments or social subcultures, especially those that are relatively small, close-knit, and involve repeat players. A good example is the one documented by Robert Ellickson in writing about the rise and use of norms among the New England whalers of the nineteenth century and California ranchers in the twentieth.[6] Among whalers, for example, it was widely accepted that a killed whale belonged to the ship whose harpoon first struck and remained in the whale, even if subsequent harpoons from other ships were the ones that finally subdued the creature. And Lisa Bernstein has offered a similar historical and analytical account of the norms of segments of the diamond, grain, and cotton industries.[7] Indeed, it is common in many industries for norms to develop bottom up, as it were, rather than top down, and for those norms to be enforced not by formal law but only with the sanctions of censure, shaming, and exclusion, among others. Nor is the phenomenon limited to traditional industries. In many locales, for example, the gang culture has adopted a norm against offering assistance to the police, including the refusal to answer what others would think of as legitimate law enforcement questions about criminal activity.[8] Similarly, it was formerly the case that tournament tennis players who felt that they were the beneficiaries of a mistaken line call by the referee would intentionally lose the succeeding point. And in many domains that are part business and part something else, we see norms about the use of names and images. It is perhaps not surprising that tattoo artists have norms about originality and the impropriety of the use of others' designs,[9] just as comedians have developed and enforced quite similar norms about jokes and comedy routines.[10]

Entire books could be written about just these kinds of norms. In fact, they have been.[11] But one of the things that an account, or even a theory, of law must explain is the widely accepted fact that the systems of social norms on the one hand and of law on the other are understood to be different. Perhaps it is a mistake to think of them as different, and perhaps the common understanding is in error. But at least at the outset, we might take the widespread perception of an important difference between law in the strict sense and a system of social norms as a useful starting point. The two obviously share much in common, especially in being a collection of prescriptions that often impose second-order constraints on first-order preferences and judgments and in being prescriptions whose violation will commonly occasion justified disapproval or more overt forms of censure. But social norms, even when large numbers of them are addressed to the same domain of human life, are not systematic in the way that law is. Collections of norms tend to be just that—collections—and it is thus not surprising that few of such collections contain secondary as well as primary rules, and, more specifically, that few of them contain rules of recognition, rules of change, and rules of adjudication. As we observed in Chapter 9, such secondary rules and their accompanying systemic character is often present for nonstate rule systems, and thus, we can, without much loss, classify such systems as legal, even if those systems are not part of the political state.

But even collections of norms are different from genuine *systems* of norms. Mere collections of norms may govern behavior and support censure, and it is well established that various forms of sanctions, of which censure is only one, are necessary to ensure that the norms of cooperative behavior will endure over time against members' desire to defect, even if the original emergence of the norm was sanction-independent.[12] Yet even though social norms govern behavior and typically need sanctions to persist after their original iteration,[13] their lack of systemic character, including the lack of a canonical formulation, makes social norms appear rather different from law, even from nonstate law. Indeed, to put the point more strongly, little is lost if we talk about the law of the Catholic Church, the law of the American Contract Bridge League, the law of the New York diamond dealers, or even the law of the Mafia, as long as we understand that we are not talking about the state. But labeling the messy and unsystematic rules of language, etiquette, fashion, and much else as law appears to be a gross distortion of our everyday and even deeper understanding of law. Whatever else a person may have done by riding a bicycle without a helmet, blowing his nose at the dinner table, or (in certain circles) wearing last year's styles, we would not say that he or she has broken the law. In fact, it may be important not to say of such people that they have broken the law unless they have violated a norm of a certain kind and emanating from a certain source. And this, as the title of this book is meant to stress, is the entire point in some contexts of emphasizing that a certain rule, norm, or prescription has "the force of law." To say that something has the force of law is to contrast it with something that is similar but does not have the force of law, and the something to which the contrast is usually being drawn is a social norm or collection of social norms.

Yet although norms are commonly thought to be different from law, the two intersect in multiple ways. One of these intersections is peculiar to common-law systems and is the way in which norms—customs—come to be part of law and are enforced as such. In one of the more famous examples, it was at one time the norm among fishermen in the town of Walmer on the coast of England to dry their nets at certain nominally private places on the beach, and with no objections from the landowners. When one landowner finally decided to build structures where the fishermen had been drying their nets, the fishermen sued and won, securing official recognition of their legal right to continue their past practices despite the objections of the landowner. The court determined that the long-standing normative custom (normative and not just a practice, in that the custom had come to be understood as a matter of right and interference with it wrong[14]) had in fact become part of the common law.[15]

Had the norms (or customs) of the Walmer fishermen been sufficiently well accepted by the larger community to deter the claims of the landowner, the fishermen would plainly have had no reason to go to law. But when the informal enforcement measures of censure, gossip, shaming, and, at times, exclusion, are insufficient to enforce the norms against outliers, we see the common phenomenon whereby the law is summoned into service. Sometimes the mechanism for law's enforcement of nonlegal norms is as it was for the Walmer fishermen: where law is called upon to enforce a preexisting norm in ways that are not totally dissimilar to the way in which law is often called upon to enforce the preexisting promises that we call contracts. More often, however, law arises precisely at the point where a norm's informal methods of enforcement turn out to be insufficient. We explored the "occasions of law" briefly in Chapter 7, and the imperfect enforcement of social norms gives us another example. Thus, law is frequently called into action when a norm is sufficiently well regarded that it is thought important to keep its normative behavioral consequences alive, but which is disregarded often enough that it is also considered important to supplement the social pressure supporting the norm with the more systematic, and ordinarily more consequentially coercive, powers of the legal system. If, as we have stressed from the outset, coercion is law's comparative advantage even if not its logically defining characteristic, then we should not be surprised at the frequency with which law is called upon to supply the coercive power that other social mechanisms may sometimes lack.

The relationship between law and social norms, however, is even more complex. We might ask (and are about to ask) about the causal effect of law on the content of norms and about the causal effect of norms on the content of law. These are important but importantly different topics, and they are addressed in the ensuing two sections.

10.2 The Effect of Law on Norms

It is often said, especially by those who are committed to a belief in the importance of law,[16] that law can often do the greatest good not by directly coercing its subjects into socially desirable behavior but instead by creating or reinforcing the social norms that will then more directly influence behavior.[17] If the law can signal the unacceptability of a certain practice, it is said, previously absent norms against that practice may develop, and previously weak norms may be strengthened. In this way, so the argument goes, law can have an effect on behavior apart from or in addition to its more obvious direct coercive power. Thus we see arguments about the role that law can play in promoting social norms against, for example, pollution[18] and smoking in public places.[19]

The claim that law can have a causal effect on the development, enforcement, internalization, and reinforcement of norms is a component of a larger set of issues, touched on in earlier chapters, about the effect of law on moral values generally. But to consider the claim carefully, we need to draw two different distinctions. First is the distinction between the effect of law on the public's internalization of certain values and the effect of law on the development of social norms. Consider, for example, the often-discussed case of laws requiring that people pick up their dog's waste—the so-called pooper-scooper laws.[20] Let us assume, realistically, that prior to and in the absence of a law requiring "scooping," people had been disinclined to clean up after their pets either because they saw nothing wrong with not cleaning up the dog waste or because they just could not be bothered. And then suppose a law is passed requiring people to clean up after their dog , with a penalty of, say, a $50 fine for each violation.

One hypothesis about the effect of the new pooper-scooper law would be that the law itself would transmit the signal that not cleaning up after your dog is selfish and wrong. This is, of course, a minor immorality in the larger scheme of things, but it is an immorality nevertheless. And under this hypothesis, the fact of a legal prohibition, especially a new one, would alert people who were previously unaware of the wrongfulness of the practice to its negative moral dimensions. And thus it is possible—remember, we are still talking only about hypotheses and not conclusions—that the very fact of making unlawful the practice of not cleaning up dog waste will alert or convince people of the wrongfulness of the behavior, and they will change their behavior accordingly, at least assuming they possess some degree of generalized or inchoate moral sensibility.[21]

An alternative (or additional) hypothesis would posit that the existence of the law would have little or no direct effect on people's internalization of certain values, but might help to create or reinforce a social norm, such that members of the public who would have been disinclined, even after enactment of the law, to change their views would nevertheless respond to a new social norm. And there is some evidence that this was the mechanism that actually operated in some locales with reference to pooper-scooper laws. The very existence of the law, it has been argued, empowered critical reactions in ways that were less possible or less frequent before enactment. After enactment, however, people felt more empowered to scold the nonscoopers and in doing so helped to create a social norm, which then had an effect on behavior without the necessity of formal legal enforcement.

Thus, it is important to distinguish law's direct effect on value internalization from law's norm-mediated effect on behavior by helping to create a social norm which will then influence behavior in a law-independent way. But within each of these causal pathways there is a further distinction to be drawn among, first, law's indicative power; second, law's behavior-modifying power; and third, law's reason-giving power. With respect to the first, which we might also label as law's epistemic power, the very fact of a law's existence provides people with information they previously did not have.[22] This information might be normative in the sense that the law informs or reminds people of a moral or other normative argument of which they were previously unaware, which they then proceed to adopt.[23] More likely, the information is factual. So although it is unlikely that people would be unaware of the annoyance of dog waste on sidewalks, the fact of legal prohibition might signal to the previously unaware the fact that the practice of not picking up after one's dog has negative environmental and health consequences. Similarly, if people were to discover that there was a law prohibiting the sale of model airplane glue to minors (as there now is in many places), the fact of the law would provide them with information they previously did not possess about the way in which the product might be used—or misused. In such cases the fact of legal prohibition does not give people new reasons to engage in the now-prohibited practice but instead provides information allowing them to apply the reasons they already possessed to a particular form of behavior.

At times, however, the law may not serve merely to remind or inform people of a pre-existing norm, but may have a more overt behavior-modifying power. That is, the very fact of legal enforcement might alter people's behavior in a more direct and sanction-influenced way. And as a consequence, the behavioral change induced by the threat of sanctions might in turn have a causal effect on people's longer-term sanction-independent behavioral inclinations. If people were inclined to avoid other people just because of their race, for example, and if the law compelled people to interact with those of different races more than they would otherwise have preferred, they might very well discover that the forced contact had more positive and fewer negative consequences than they previously had supposed. Indeed, there is some indication that this was the mechanism that had at least some effect in the context of desegregation of American public schools in the 1950s and 1960s. Although integration in almost all previously segregated schools was overwhelmingly court-enforced (and in some cases militarily enforced[24]) and thus involuntary, some evidence suggests that being in a school with African-Americans (or having one's children in a school with African-Americans) had a positive effect on genuinely internalized racial tolerance, even if the initial effect of the law was entirely directly coercive.[25]

Relatedly, the effect of law on attitudes might be a function of the well-supported psychological conclusion that people's preferences often change as a consequence of forced choice.[26] Insofar as the law (or something else) compels people into a behavior inconsistent with their prior preferences, some number of mechanisms, of which the most prominent is the desire to reduce cognitive dissonance, may well lead people to adapt their preferences to what the law requires. We might call this process simply one of persuasion, but the idea of adaptation seems closer to what is transpiring. But regardless of the label and regardless of the mechanism, legal coercion might produce preference change in just this way, making subsequent coercion, at least for those whose attitudes have been so changed, somewhat less necessary.

The final member of this trilogy of causal pathways is the one most discussed in the jurisprudential literature: the possibility that the very fact of legal prohibition would give people a new reason to engage, without coercion, in legally mandated behavior. But although this is the pathway most commonly discussed and, indeed, most commonly assumed,[27] it is important to recognize that this pathway to legal effect is parasitic on people taking the fact of law as itself a nonindicative reason for action. If people do not believe that law provides a reason for action by virtue of its being law, then there is no reason to believe that law will have the consequence of changing their reasons and thus of changing their sanction-independent behavioral inclinations. If you do not believe you have a moral or other reason to clean up after your dog, and then if the practice becomes illegal, your array of reasons will change if and only if you believe that the very fact of law provides a moral or other reason for action.[28] In other words, your reasons will change as a consequence of a change in the law only if you have an antecedent belief that the fact of law, as law, is a reason for action. Again, it comes back to the puzzled man. The puzzled man, in Hart's sense of someone who will obey the law just because it is the law and without reference to possible sanctions,[29] will clean up after his dog, or will at least have a reason to clean up after his dog, simply by virtue of its being a legal requirement. But if, as we have seen, puzzled men are thinner on the ground than Hart and his followers have supposed, then this third pathway to the effect of law on moral views or social norms will be of little practical consequence.

This is not to deny that law can affect behavior other than by its direct coercive force. But insofar as the effect is produced by way of triggering the coercive force of social norms, then coercion still occupies center stage in explaining how law affects behavior, although in this context we might think of law as simply outsourcing its coercive power to private actors. And insofar as law's effect is produced either by giving people new reasons for action or by spurring the creation of new social norms that will then directly affect behavior, such mechanisms again presuppose the ability of law *qua* law to make a difference in people's nonprudential calculations. That law can do so is not the issue—at least if we accept that law's ability to do so is a function of people internalizing a moral obligation to obey the law as opposed to some more mysterious nonmoral normativity of law. But that law actually does activate in people what they understand to be a moral reason to obey the law turns out to be a claim with far less empirical support than the conventional wisdom in both jurisprudence and the literature on norms has typically assumed.

10.3 The Effect of Norms on Law

As noted above, law is sometimes called upon to provide the coercive supplement to the often mild coercive powers of social norms themselves. That law is more coercive than the social pressure of a social norm is, of course, hardly a universal truth. Some forms of legal coercion are relatively toothless, especially when there are low penalties or low levels of enforcement. Conversely, some of the social sanctions that support social norms will appear far more consequential to their targets than anything that the formal law can do to them, especially in small and close-knit communities dominated by repeat players.[30] In certain circles, for example, being known as a person who does not pay his gambling debts was, and perhaps remains, a far worse penalty than a mere monetary fine or civil judgment. And, depending on the setting and the audience, a public reprimand for violating a social convention may cut to the quick far more than a quieter legal sanction.

In the context of what he called the liberty of thought and discussion, John Stuart Mill observed this phenomenon in the middle of the nineteenth century in his essay *On Liberty*.[31] Although chapter 2 of *On Liberty* is now best known for its defense of freedom of speech against governmental censorship, Mill took pains to emphasize that what he called "social intolerance" could be far more stifling of individual expression and thus far more dangerous to what we now call the "free market in ideas." Insofar as people are reluctant to be criticized, marginalized, shamed, mocked, or ostracized, for example, the weight of public opinion can often be every bit as coercive as the state's control of the formal machinery of compulsion.

Yet although society can sometimes enforce its norms without the state's assistance, quite often it cannot. And thus, we frequently see prevailing norms buttressed by legal sanctions in order to coerce those for whom the sanctions of social disapproval, shaming, exclusion, and the like are inadequate. Sometimes the fact of illegality may, in some places and on some subjects, empower social condemnation, as it appeared to have done in the example of pooper-scooper laws. More often, however, norms *produce* law. When it is believed that norm violation will attract too little condemnation or other social pressure to align the level of compliance with the level of most of society's commitment to the norm, laws will be enacted that convert a mere social norm into a norm with the force of law. And in such cases we see the use of law's direct and coercive power to enforce a norm that attracts some but not enough coercion through nonlegal sanctions. The law's sanctions against public nudity, for example, are adopted not because of a feared epidemic of the practice but because those who would be inclined to engage in the practice may be those who would be especially likely to flout the not insubstantial social sanctions against it.

Although law is thus used with great frequency to protect established social norms against outliers—the laws against murder, rape, armed robbery, and other violent crimes can be so characterized, as can the laws against fraud and other forms of blatant dishonesty—law is also employed when there is at most a weak social norm against a practice that in fact has socially detrimental consequences. That is, there may be laws that are objectively desirable but whose desirability is unrecognized by the public at large and is unrecognized or consciously ignored by the most immediate esteem-granting group within which the perpetrators principally exist. The laws against price-fixing and insider trading may fit this mold, partly because the professional subculture in which price-fixers or inside-traders are typically located is often a subculture that tolerates or even encourages the practice.[32] In this case, the embarrassment is in getting caught, not in engaging in the practice. This is true in part because most people do not know what these activities are, and even when they are informed, they do not think there is very much wrong with these practices. And thus, if there really is something wrong with the practice, there is little reason to believe that either internalization of the act's wrongfulness or the pressure of social norms will be either likely or effective. And it is just at this point that the law's coercive dimensions are most needed and thus most important.

It is thus useful to distinguish the instances in which law protects largely self-enforcing social norms against outliers from those in which law seeks to achieve substantive first-order goals that are widely rejected, that are frequently unappreciated or underappreciated, or that incorporate values that may be accepted in the abstract but whose acceptance is typically weaker than the countervailing pull of potential gains. Even if people believe there are moral reasons to pay taxes,[33] for example, the gains from not doing so are sufficiently great that law is needed to align the private incentives with the public good. The idea of using sanctions to adjust citizens' sanction-independent array of motivations was Bentham's basic impulse, for although he understood, common caricatures of his beliefs notwithstanding, that people could and did have altruistic or common good motivations, he understood the relatively small weight that those motivations typically carried when compared to the motivations of self-interest. For Bentham, therefore, law's sanctions were motivational supplements, and there is little in modern practice to indicate that he was mistaken. Tax avoidance, after all, is unlawful, and just the fact that the Internal Revenue Service in the United States takes pains to induce the taxpaying public to believe that the risks of sanctions are much greater than they actually are[34] is evidence that sanctions are typically necessary to enforce even those laws that the public tends to view as fundamentally sound.

10.4 Is There a Norm of Law?

One way of understanding some of the conclusions in Chapters 5 and 6, which had a skeptical cast about the extent to which law *qua* law exerts much of a hold on human motivation, is as hypothesizing the existence of what we might label a *norm of law,* but concluding that, empirically, such a norm was a weak one, at least in the United States. H. L. A. Hart observed, correctly, that internalization of a rule—or social norm, we can now add—can take place absent coercion. And he also observed, again correctly, that when a rule or norm was internalized, its violation could be the cause for criticism even if no other sanction was in the offing.[35] And so now we can ask whether there actually exists a norm of obedience to law just because it is law. If people respect queues in part because not doing so will incur social disapproval, if nothing else, then does respect for the law have the same status? Is breaking the law itself, and for that reason, an occasion for criticism? Is there a content-independent social norm of respect for law?

This question is plainly nothing more than a recasting in the language of social norms the basic analytical point in Chapter 4 about what it is to obey the law because it is the law. Does law-breaking *qua* law-breaking—and divorced from the first-order or content-based or substantive wrong of the law-breaking behavior—itself violate a social norm in the same way that eating with your mouth full, not cleaning up after your dog, wearing a white suit in winter, or speaking to the Queen before she speaks to you does? And as we saw in Chapters 5 and 6, the answer to this question is not self-evidently in the affirmative. Although these chapters had a patently contemporary American focus that makes it impossible to generalize to other countries or other times, the lesson to be drawn is that, at least in the contemporary United States, a norm of law may well not exist.[36] And perhaps that fact is neither totally surprising nor necessarily to be lamented. Henry David Thoreau may have put it best. Writing in justification of his own civil disobedience and arguing for the frequent wisdom of the practice, he observed that it is "not desirable to cultivate a respect for the law, so much as for the right."[37] In saying this, Thoreau was not making a descriptive sociological point, but a normative one. More than a century and a half-later, however, it is plausible to suspect that, at least in his own country, what Thoreau wished to happen may have transpired more than he might have predicted, and more than people believe is actually the case.

If Thoreau turns out to have been so prescient that his normative claim is now descriptively accurate, and if therefore there actually exists in the population much more of a norm of right than of law, and if in addition there thus is a more powerful norm of right than of law in many of the cases in which two clash, then the necessity of law's coercive force becomes even more understandable. When people have a strong taste for the right but not much of a taste for the law just because it is the law, then it should come as no surprise that they will prefer the right to the legal. But if people's taste for the right is often mistaken, and if in preferring the right they often prefer the wrong, whether because they confuse what is good for themselves with what is good simpliciter or whether because they are simply morally or factually mistaken, then the unfortunate consequences of a tendency to prefer the right to the law are obvious. And if those unfortunate consequences are to be avoided, then people's preferences for what they wrongly think is right will need to be better aligned with what is actually right. Law is vital precisely because of the frequent necessity of persuading people to set aside their own judgments of right on the grounds that those judgments may be wrong more often than those who hold them are likely to believe. A norm of law, if it is in fact internalized, will perform this judgment-suppressing function with little need for sanctions or coercion. And there may be places where just this internalization of a norm of law exists. How else, after all, can we explain the phenomenon of Finns standing obediently on the curb in the face of a "Don't Walk" sign even though there are no vehicles or police officers anywhere in sight? But the obedient Finns may not be representative.[38] And thus, when there is no norm of law, or merely a weak one, as seems so often to be the case, then law *qua* law needs the assistance that only an organized system of coercive sanctions can provide.

11

THE DIFFERENTIATION OF LAW

11.1 A Bundle of Differences

Law is different. That much seems obvious, at least on the surface. But although saying that law is different is stating the obvious, sometimes the obvious needs stating. What is taught in law school, for example, is strikingly different from what is taught in medical schools, graduate schools of business, or even schools of public policy. The examination that one must pass to qualify as a lawyer tests different skills from the examinations necessary to practice as an accountant, a social worker, a psychiatrist, or an auto mechanic. And the books that line the shelves of a law library hardly resemble those in any other library.[1] Moreover, what lawyers actually do seems different as well. People engaged in disputes typically know to consult a lawyer and not an accountant, and companies seeking to broaden the market for their products will go to an advertising agency rather than a law firm. And although one way to settle a dispute is to go to court, another is for the disputants to sit down over a few drinks and resolve their differences. One needs a lawyer for the former, but typically one needs to keep the lawyers away for the latter.

Such differences are part of the data that any satisfactory account of the phenomenon of law, and thus of law's typical features, needs to explain. Indeed, even (and perhaps especially) those who believe that the search for the nature of law is a search for law's essential properties accept, sometimes explicitly but usually implicitly, that law is in some important way different from other social institutions.[2] The law, or the legal system,[3] is different from the military, from medicine, and, perhaps more controversially, from finance and from politics and from public policy. But whatever law is different from, it is plainly different from many things, and from many social institutions, and explaining the source and nature of those differences is an important task of legal theory.

Law's differences present themselves across many dimensions. In some respects the differences are sociological. The existence of separate schools, separate associations, separate career paths, somewhat of a separate language, and some number of other loose and overlapping but nonetheless real separations between law and other social institutions and groupings bespeaks of what the social theorist Niklas Luhmann has called "social differentiation."[4] We thus observe what we will label law's *sociological differentiation*. Even were law largely similar in its methods (which it is not) and sources (which it is not) to other professions and other institutions, the very fact that lawyers and judges group themselves both with each other and somewhat apart from the members of other segments of society not only exemplifies the differentiation but also reinforces and increases it.[5] To repeat, it is theoretically possible that such social differentiation could exist alongside an undifferentiated set of methods, procedures, and sources, but this theoretical possibility is unrepresented in the actual world. Realistically, the very fact of the social differentiation of law is both the cause and consequence of the differentiation of law across a number of other dimensions as well.

Prominent among these other dimensions is what we can call *procedural differentiation*. Law's processes appear, at least in most legal systems, to be procedurally unlike the decision-making procedures employed in other social and public institutions. Whether it be the definitive resolution of disputes, the rendering of judgments with opinions whose law-making effect extends beyond particular disputes between particular parties, the requirement of reason-giving for many of the law's most important decisions, or the centrality of the adversary proceeding with its requirement of notice and its typical two-party organization, the procedural setting for legal argument, legal judgment, and legal decision making is at least somewhat different from that used in other social, political, and policy making settings. Thus, although modern litigation offers numerous variations on and complications of the basic adversary model, we should not forget that litigation is the archetypal procedural device of the law and that in litigation the typical number of parties is two, the typical verdict has a winner and a loser, the typical judge is in theory disinterested in the outcome, the typical decision requires notice to and hearing of all parties, and the typical assumption would be that it is inappropriate for judges to find for plaintiffs on the grounds that they had found against the same plaintiffs in the last three lawsuits and fairness required that this plaintiff won every once in a while. None of these characteristics of the decision-making process is universal, and there are legitimate public and private decision-making institutions and environments that employ none or only some of them. And thus the processes of the legal system, whether it be in finding the facts or applying the law to them, differ in important respects from the decision-making procedures of the political world, of much of administrative and bureaucratic regulation, of the world of scientific and also of police investigation, and of military commanders deciding on strategy and tactics. If a scientist wishes to determine whether drinking alcohol increases the likelihood of heart disease, she does not hold an adversary proceeding in which representatives of the liquor industry and the Temperance League each present their best case to her. In fact, the very absurdity of the idea of such a proceeding within science, one that seems entirely normal for law,[6] illustrates the often ignored way in which law's procedures for decision making vary considerably from what we find in other decision-making domains.

Even were law not typically procedurally differentiated from other decision-making environments and institutions, it might still employ a differentiated method of thinking, reasoning, and decision making. For the sake of parallelism we can call this *methodological differentiation*. The claim of methodological differentiation builds on a venerable and still conventional wisdom according to which legal reasoning differs from the reasoning employed within other disciplines, and possibly even from reasoning *simpliciter*. Thus, in 1607, Chief Justice Sir Edward Coke, one of the icons of the common law tradition, wrote, in defense of insisting that even the King would not be permitted to sit as a judge in a legal case, that although "God had endowed His Majesty with excellent science and great endowments of nature," it was nevertheless true that "his Majesty was not learned in the laws of his realm of England, and causes which concern the life, or inheritance, or goods, or fortunes of his subjects, are not to be decided by natural reason but by the artificial reason and judgment of law, which law is an art which requires long study and experience, before that a man can attain to the cognizance of it."[7]

Coke's celebration of the "artificial reason" of the law was followed by Matthew Hale, William Blackstone, and many others who not only lauded common-law reasoning but also insisted that it was a form of reasoning different from and better than that employed in most other secular institutions of their day.[8] These days, much the same claim persists, with law schools, explicitly in the United States and often implicitly elsewhere, claiming to train their students in the differentiated art of "thinking like a lawyer."[9] Such thinking might involve the importance of rules, or the frequent reliance on precedent, or the special role of authority, or a particular care with language, for example, and there are other candidates as well. These claims of methodological differentiation, like the other possible sources of differentiation, need not be, and are not, entirely distinct spheres. Differentiation is not demarcation, and differentiation is thus best understood as a differential concentration and not as a boundary. Decisions according to rules, constraint by precedent, and the pervasive presence of authority exist and are important in some number of nonlegal decision-making domains as well as in law. And in like fashion the law employs forms of reasoning, factual investigation, and decision making that are more dominant in law than they are in various nonlegal environments. But law may nevertheless use rules, precedent, authority, and the other characteristic devices of legal argument more or with more weight than they are used elsewhere. To the extent that this is so, it may explain much of law's differentiation. The view that there is something special or better about legal reasoning has, of course, long been hotly contested,[10] but for the moment we can simply note that the claim of differentiated reasoning processes within law would be one way, if true, that law could be distinguished from numerous other public and decision-making institutions.

Although the sociological, procedural, and methodological differentiations of law are each important, much of the literature on legal theory, at least in the contemporary analytic philosophical tradition, focuses on still another possible form of differentiation: *source differentiation* – a form of differentiation influenced by analytic jurisprudence's concern for legal validity,[11] and within that tradition the legal positivist view that "in any legal system, whether a given legal norm is valid . . . depends on its sources, not its merits."[12] All people in all contexts make their decisions on the basis of some sources but not others, and thus we might say that source differentiation is endemic to social differentiation generally. Auto mechanics, after all, base their diagnoses on what they know from sources about automobiles and not (normally) from the Bible, from law books, or from plumbers' manuals. Moreover, sources need not be thought of as residing exclusively in books. Some people base their decisions, in small or large part, on what they have learned from their parents, their friends, their siblings, or in the barber shop. Indeed, it might be better to think of the full array of possible sources as *inputs*, a word which has less of a suggestion of formal or written sources. Still, *sources* is a nicer word.

Although the range of possible sources for decision is vast, in some domains certain sources of information and guidance are permissible and others are not. For scientists to consult or build on discredited research, for example, is for them to go beyond their universe of permissible sources. Yet law is different from science as well as from auto mechanics and much else in being an authority-based institution,[13] one in which the very fact that something is law is, at least for those inside the system, a reason to follow it.[14] And thus, in law but certainly not in science, the role of authority may render relevant even those conclusions that the decision maker has good reason to think erroneous.

From the premise that law is, especially even if not uniquely, an enterprise in which authority matters, it follows that determining which are legitimate legal authorities and which are not is particularly important to legal decision making. And thus for law to be differentiated in a source-based way is to say that law is a limited domain,[15] one in which sources of information and guidance that are permissible in other enterprises are impermissible in law. The question of which sources are permissible and which are not has occupied legal theorists for generations, but one way of understanding Hart's idea of the *rule of recognition* is as identifying the specially legal phenomenon in which only those sources, in the broad sense, that are *recognized* by a rule of recognition are part of the law in the first place.[16]

The question of the source-based differentiation of law is important, but it is some distance removed from the central concerns of this book. Yet although the particular idea of source-based differentiation may not be highly relevant here, the very idea of differentiation is. And so, although sociological, procedural, methodological, and source-based differentiation are all candidates for explaining the differentiation of law, so too is the idea of coercion. Thus it has long been maintained, as noted in Chapter 1, that it is coercion that characterizes law, distinguishes law, and even for Austin and others, defines law. We can then add coercion to the list of candidates for explaining law's differentiation, with awareness of the fact that none of these differentiating characteristics need be exclusive of any of the others. If, putting aside questions about concepts and natures and other such mysterious entities, we simply wish to understand the phenomenon of law as we know it and experience it, it may well be that some or all of law's coercive power, its sociological differentiation, its procedural differentiation, its methodological differentiation, and its source differentiation have a role to play in explaining just how it is that law is different from the other institutions, public and private, that define our social existence.

Thus, even if we put aside the possibility that coercion defines law or is a necessary component of law, it is counterintuitive to refuse to acknowledge that it is not ubiquitous in law. Coercion may, precisely because of its ubiquity, constitute a significant part of what differentiates law from other public institutions, from other decision-making environments, and even from other authority-based human enterprises. Once we understand, to repeat and emphasize, that differentiation is not demarcation, and that the differentiation of law is one of the facts that a satisfactory account of the nature of law must explain, the role of coercion in explaining, even only partially, the differentiation of law comes back into the picture, and it is to that possibility that we now return.

11.2 The Gunman—Again

In laying the groundwork for his attack on a coercion-centered account of the nature of law, H. L. A. Hart memorably called forth the image of the gunman who "orders his victim to hand over his purse and threatens to shoot if he refuses."[17] And then, in seeking to explain the deficiencies of Austin's and others' emphasis on force and neglect of the internal and reason-giving capacity of law, Hart argued that law cannot sensibly be understood as the "gunman writ large."[18] Indeed, so obvious did Hart think the point that he earlier had emphasized it by twice (and in the same sentence) using the word "surely," a common sign of someone believing, for whatever reason, that no actual argument or evidence is necessary: "Law surely is not the gunman situation writ large, and legal order is surely not to be thus simply identified with compulsion."[19]

But why not? Let us concede to Hart, as we should, the importance of his emphasis on the systemic character of law. And so let us add a systemic dimension to the gunman scenario. And in doing so we are no longer in the realm of imaginary hypothetical examples but very much in the real world. Consider, for example, the so-called protection racket. In the standard version, an employee (they tend to be called "henchmen" in movies and crime novels, but they are basically paid employees) of an organized crime operation goes to the owner of a small business and tells him that he must pay a certain sum of money per week in order to be protected against accidents of a particular kind. And the accidents, as is well understood, are ones that the organization soliciting the payment has a singular ability to produce. Fires, for example. Or burglaries. Or assaults on customers and employees. The basic idea is that the payment to the crime boss protects the merchant, especially from the crime boss himself. And in other variations, perhaps even more suited to our purposes here, the crime boss demands that the merchant purchase his supplies from the crime boss or his designated suppliers, again with the threat of unpleasant consequences to the merchant's business, his body, or his family in the event of noncompliance.

An interesting feature of the protection racket, and even more the "buy from me or my affiliated suppliers or else" variation, is its systemic character. We are no longer talking about a lone gunman jumping out from behind the bushes and demanding money, but instead now we have a leader promulgating a set of general rules, demanding that someone else follow them, and threatening the putative followers with "evil," to use Austin's term, in the event that they do not comply. Moreover, the employees—the henchmen—are themselves instructed to take their orders, some of which are very likely to be general and not particular, from the crime boss and no one else. And thus the "treat the general orders of the boss and no one else as authoritative" understanding within most coercive criminal enterprises functions very much like, or maybe just *is* in the relevant sense, a rule of recognition.

So if we convert the lone gunman into an organization of this type and operating in this way, is it still a "distortion," to use Hart's word,[20] to say that it is law? Perhaps the protection racket or the organized crime "family" is not law, but why not? The quick answer is that this system of rules and authority does not exist within the municipal state and that law is, by definition, a creature of the municipal state. Indeed, this much was assumed by Austin, as well as others, in connecting their conception of law with the fact and idea of sovereignty. And once again we might see that Austin's simple recounting of an obvious fact, as with his connection between law and coercion, may have contained more than a germ of truth. In many respects, after all, the law of the Mafia, as just posited, and as with the rules of the National Football League, the rules of the Marylebone Cricket Club,[21] and the rules of the World Trade Organization, contains primary and secondary rules, rules of recognition, and internalization by members and officials alike. Thus, the only thing that makes using the word *law* in these contexts metaphorical and not literal is precisely the connection with the political state.[22] There is a difference between the state and a within-state organization such as the (British) Football Association, a cross-state organization such as the WTO, or an unlawful organization such as the Mafia, but once we have noted the difference, there may be little more to say. Indeed, if we say much more, we may end up being more misleading than helpful, because in important ways what is now called nonstate law is perhaps best understood as law.[23] Period. But perhaps things are a bit more nuanced than this, and so it may be useful to address the increasingly visible topic of nonstate law.

11.3   Nonstate Law

So what does it mean to say that there is "nonstate" law? It means, in large part, that all of the features we typically or even universally see in the legal systems of modern nation-states are represented in vast numbers of associations, organizations, and institutions whose physical boundaries are not those of the nation-state and that may, sometimes but not necessarily, claim jurisdiction over only a limited number of activities. Sometimes, as just noted, these are private associations. Sometimes they are religious organizations, especially hierarchical ones like the Catholic Church. Sometimes they are corporations, which, after all, also have primary and secondary rules, rules of recognition, and officials who have the internal point of view with respect to those rules. Sometimes they are cross-border organizations *of* nation-states, as with the WTO, the United Nations, and the European Union. Sometimes they are groups that used to be nation-states, or would like to be nation-states, but now exist within the borders of and under the control of nation-states, as with the Native Indian tribes in the United States and Canada. And sometimes they are organizations, like the Mafia and Al-Qaeda, whose own law is unlawful under the laws of the nation-states within which they physically exist.

To observe that organizations such as those just listed appear to have legal systems is not to deny the importance of the very idea of the nation-state. Liechtenstein is smaller and less powerful in almost every dimension than General Motors and the World Bank and even the International Olympic Committee, but Liechtenstein's very status as a state, and the extent to which the world accepts its jurisdiction over a particular piece of the planet, is of undeniable importance. Moreover, it is widely and properly accepted that nation-states have legal systems and that the boundaries of the nation-state are coextensive with the boundaries of particular legal systems.[24] Whatever else the law of Liechtenstein is or is not, it is not the law of Uruguay, and all of the citizens and officials of both Liechtenstein and Uruguay recognize this now-obvious fact about the way in which the world is divided.

Yet although all nation-states have their own legal systems, and although some people might believe that it is part of the very definition of a nation-state that it have its own legal system, it seems a mistake to make too much of the connections between legal systems and nation-states. All of the nation-states of which we are aware have legal systems of one kind or another, but it is decidedly not a logical corollary of this fact that only nation-states have legal systems. Nonstate law is not like chess without the queen, football with nine players on a side, or a dinner party without dessert—bastard variants on an accepted central case. Or if it is, we need an explanation of why, and not simply the *ipse dixit*, being part of the government and governance of the nation-state is part of the definition of law. And so perhaps it is better simply to say that there are central and marginal cases of nation-states and central and marginal cases of legal systems, but that it is not necessarily true that what is the central case of the former must be defined in terms of the central case of the latter.

The same could be said about claims of comprehensive jurisdiction. Typically, the legal systems of nation-states purport to regulate all of the activities of their citizens. And typically, the rule systems of nonstate organizations do not. But the jurisdictional claims of the WTO, the UN, and even the EU are not universal. Indeed, nor are the jurisdictional claims of national governments within strong federal systems, such as that of the United States. Conversely, the rule systems of most religious organizations, most indigenous tribes, and many tightly knit illegal organizations, such as the Mafia, claim a wide degree of control over the lives of their members. Members of the Marylebone Cricket Club might be able to say that their private and professional employment lives are none of the MCC's business, but we suspect that things are different for the Mafia and its membership. And thus although it might be true that most of the governmental or quasi-governmental systems we typically call "law" have comprehensive jurisdictional pretension and most of the complex rule-based organizations from which we withhold the label "law" do not, it is a mistake to assume that law-ness and comprehensiveness are congruent. Accordingly, we may again learn more by observing just how much nonstate organizations betake of law, or simply *are* law, than assuming too quickly that they are not.

11.4 And Thus of Coercion

One obvious characteristic of all of the above nonstate organizations, and again recalling one of Austin's lessons, is that their existence requires the acquiescence of one or more nation-states. And because Austin talked of a sovereign whose commands are owed habitual obedience but who owed obedience to no one,[25] none of these organizations or systems would have counted as law for him. Moreover, with the exception of the UN, none of these organizations, at least the lawful ones, has an army or a police force. A hockey player who refuses to go to the penalty box after having been cited for an infraction may be expelled from the game, from his team, or even from the league, but if the referees try to use physical force to get him into the penalty box, it is they who will be guilty of assault and perhaps false imprisonment under the state's law, a law that looms over the law of the National Hockey League.

That the law of the National Hockey League is subject to the laws of Ontario and Canada, among others, but that the laws of Ontario and Canada are not subject to the laws of the National Hockey League is important in an Austinian sense. But it may not be otherwise that important. The Province of Ontario, after all, also has a police department by the grace of Canada, just as the city of Toronto has a police department by the grace of the Province of Ontario. And various private organizations have security services or even police departments authorized to use force by the political state, as with the campus police forces on many American university campuses, and as with the highly empowered private security services in South Africa and other countries. In theory, therefore, or at least in *legal* theory, there is nothing preventing Canada from allowing National Hockey League referees to carry weapons and to use physical compulsion to force recalcitrant players into the penalty box and physical restraints to keep them there.[26]

Once we acknowledge the possibility of even legitimate coercive force outside of the realm of the municipal nation-state, and now that we have already acknowledged that institutions other than nation states or their subdivisions can be organized with primary and secondary rules and the internalization of an ultimate rule of recognition, the search for the differentiating characteristics of law becomes more elusive. We could say—with Austin and, indeed, with our friend the man on the Clapham omnibus—that law is, by definition, a creature of the municipal nation-state and that considering the Mafia and American Contract Bridge League rule systems as law is a metaphorical and not a literal exercise. But if we do this, we find ourselves back to one of the traditional differentiating concepts of the law: the institution that organizes what seems to be the plain fact of the nation-state's monopoly on the legitimate use of force. That it was Max Weber who understood law in such terms is noteworthy because Weber was, after all, a sociologist.[27] If we thus attribute a sociological dimension to Weber's understanding of law, we find ourselves with a differentiation between law and other normative institutions that captures a contingent reality and a popular understanding, even if it is not one that differentiates law in terms of necessary and sufficient conditions, or even provides a crisp demarcation between law and other institutions.

That the Weberian understanding fails to demarcate law in the sense of drawing a sharp boundary between law and nonlaw should be little cause for concern. Again, differentiation is not demarcation,[28] as Edmund Burke reminded us in observing that "though no man can draw a stroke between the confines of night and day, still light and darkness are on the whole tolerably distinguishable." Philosophers continue to struggle with the Sorites paradox and seek to explain Sorites vagueness (which is not the only form of vagueness) and related phenomena, but they universally accept that the ability to draw a precise line is not fatal to the existence of a usable distinction beyond the boundaries. There is a difference between a grain and a heap, just as there is a difference between the bald and the hairy,[29] the short and the tall, the fat and the thin, and between tadpoles and frogs, even if we cannot identify the precise point of demarcation between the members of any of these pairs. That the boundaries are ineluctably fuzzy does not, as Burke noticed, cause a distinction to be lacking in value.

And so it is with the difference between law and nonlaw. That there may well be no demarcation between law and nonlaw does not mean that there is no differentiation. But that differentiation need not be along only one dimension. As noted above, law may be differentiated in terms of its methods, its procedures, its sources, and its social makeup. But it may also be differentiated because of its reliance on raw force and because being subject to that raw force may be in important ways for most people nonoptional. One can avoid the coercive dimensions of the American Contract Bridge League and the Catholic Church by simply (or, in the latter case, perhaps not so simply, depending on theological views best left far to one side here) leaving their jurisdiction. But I cannot so simply leave the coercive dimensions of the laws of the Commonwealth of Virginia or the United States of America, and even if I could do so, I would still find myself within the coercive reach of another legal system. *Terra nullius,* or at least habitable *terra nullius,* no longer exists. There is no place in the world in which one can escape the law, although its presence is felt more in some places than in others. And because of law's very inescapability, its coercive capacity is largely mandatory.[30]

The presence of unavoidable coercive power is what is typically behind the very phrase "the force of law" and behind the ordinary citizen's belief that coercion is central to the very idea of law. Like many other aspects of law as we experience it, coercion is neither necessary nor sufficient for law. But legal coercion's contingent ubiquity testifies to the fact that in many domains there are valuable goals that cannot be achieved by cooperation alone, even the kind of cooperation in which people internalize second-order reasons for suppressing their first-order desires and decisions. If we ignore this fact, we will have ignored something very important about why law exists and what functions it serves. And if we think this fact's sociological, psychological, economic, and political dimensions are reasons to neglect the importance of philosophical analysis of law's coercive dimensions, we have given up a valuable resource to better understanding. The coercive dimensions of law are not all of law, but if the task of understanding a phenomenon starts with certain features of the phenomenon whose presence any satisfactory explanation of the phenomenon must provide, then coercion must be numbered among those features. If a satisfactory account of law must, as Hart reminded us, "fit the facts," then law's coercive capacity is one of the facts that such an account must fit.

Indeed, one of the facts that an account of law must fit is the fact of human failing. It is true that the legal structures that enable us to make contracts, write wills, create corporations, preserve property, and much else display law in its empowering mode, a mode whose connection with human progress and flourishing is difficult to deny. And it is true that even a community of angels would need law to serve important organizing, planning, and coordinating functions.[31] But it is also true that law serves an important, and perhaps uniquely important, constraining role. This role, however, is not limited to the role of law in keeping bad people from doing bad things, however important that aspect of law may be. Perhaps more importantly, law keeps good people from doing what they *think* are good things for good motives. Law does so in part because we live in a complex world in which the collective good is often ill served by individuals pursuing their own interests. But, even more, we live in a world in which the good things that good people with good motives think they are doing often are not as good as they think they are. That 80 percent of drivers believe they drive with above-average skill is not about driving but about the well-documented tendency of people to have great confidence in their own skills and their own judgment, a confidence that is often unjustified.[32] One important function of law, therefore, is to restrain even the well-meaning judgments of well-meaning people. And it is in this capacity that law may most need to rely on its coercive power, because people who overestimate the soundness of their own judgments may be especially unlikely to subjugate those judgments to the unenforced dictates of the law. As Bentham might have put it, people's motivations need to be adjusted to take account of and compensate for the unjustified optimism they often have in the soundness of their own judgments.

And so we end where we started. Law makes people do things they do not want to do. A state or a community that sees itself, or even all of its institutions of governance, solely in this constraining role would no doubt be a depressing and unpleasant place in which to live. States and communities have positive and empowering roles as well as constraining ones. But although the state thus has both positive and negative roles to play, it is a mistake to assume that the goals of the law are or should be coincident with the goals of the state, or the goals of a community, or the goals of any other governmental unit or collectivity within which law exists. Just as there are different tools for different functions—it is possible but not recommended to drive a nail with a screwdriver or drive a screw with a hammer—so too are there different forms of governance and different forms of social organization, not all of which are equally good at performing all of the tasks that a community needs done.[33] Law may be better at some things than at others, and other institutions may be better at some things than law. And if one of the functions that law may perform better than other institutions is constraint, then we can understand why the man on the Clapham omnibus is not that far off the mark In seeing law's coercive dimension as especially salient.

In equating law with coercion—the threat of punishment or some other "evil"—Austin was simply wrong. Law does much else besides control, threaten, punish, and sanction, and law does not always need coercion to do what it can do. But the fact that coercion is not all of law, nor definitional of law, is not to say that it is none of law or an unimportant part of law. Relegating the coercive aspect of law to the sidelines of theoretical interest is perverse. And thus, adopting a conception of the philosophy of law that facilitates such relegation is even more so.

11.5 Coda: The Point of It All

Understanding for its own sake is valuable. Much of the enterprise of jurisprudence seeks simply to enrich our understanding of the phenomenon of law, without purporting to prescribe to those who make law, follow law, or adjudicate within it. And that is as it should be, at least as long as we take the academic enterprise itself, of which jurisprudence is a part, as a worthwhile endeavor.

That said, however, a potential but often neglected practical side effect of jurisprudential inquiry is at the level of institutional design. Law is not the entirety of political or social organization. It does some things and leaves other things to others. Law is good at some tasks and deficient in others. And thus an important job for law-informed institutional design is in determining which social roles should be filled by legal institutions and which should not.

Grasping the reality of the differentiation of law helps us to take on this task of institutional design. More specifically, at least in the context of this book, examining the close relationship between law and coercion helps us to understand what law is good at and where it is intrinsically deficient. Yes, it is theoretically possible for law to play a (public) persuasive role, for example, but persuasion is a role that that may more realistically, desirably, and effectively be performed by others. Similarly, there is a place for institutions designed around the reality of cooperation, the reality of coordination, and the reality of good faith pursuit of shared goals, but when that is implausible, law's coercive capacity may become especially important. Indeed, if a society too quickly assumes that people and officials will follow the law just because it is the law, that society may find that relying too much on an unwarranted empirical assumption of internalization of the law and relying too little on law's coercive dimension will itself produce flawed institutions poorly suited to the goals they are meant to serve.

And thus, focusing on the coercive side of law helps us to understand why and when we might need law, and why and when law can do things that other political institutions and other forms of social organization cannot. This is not a book about institutional design, and it would depart far too much from this book's purpose to explore just what functions are best served by law in its coercive capacity. But if we ignore or slight that capacity, or even think that exploring it is not part of a theoretical or philosophical enterprise, we may lose some of the understanding of law that helps us to see when using law is wise—and when it is not.

NOTES

INDEX

NOTES

1. Introduction: The Force of Law

1. Chapter 9 considers whether distinctions of importance exist among *sanctions, force, coercion, compulsion,* and the various other ideas and terms inhabiting the same conceptual neighborhood. For now these words are used more or less interchangeably, depending on the context, but with no intention yet to mark differences among them.

2. H. L. A. Hart, *The Concept of Law,* 3d ed., Penelope A. Bulloch, Joseph Raz, & Leslie Green, eds. (Oxford: Oxford University Press, 2012) (first published 1961).

3. Leslie Green, "Positivism and the Inseparability of Law and Morals," *New York University Law Review* 83 (2002), 1035–1058, *at* 1049. Similarly, in commenting on Hart's argument against those who see law as the "gunman situation writ large" (Hart, *Concept of Law,* 6–7), John Gardner describes the sanction-focused position against which Hart argues as "sadly . . . familiar." John Gardner, "How Law Claims, What Law Claims," *in* Matthias Klatt, *Institutionalized Reason: The Jurisprudence of Robert Alexy* (Oxford: Oxford University Press, 2012), 29–44, *at* 37. To the same effect, Jules Coleman, in *The Practice of Principle: In Defence of a Pragmatist Approach to Legal Theory* (Oxford: Oxford University Press, 2001), maintains that "jurisprudence is the study, in part, of how law purports to govern conduct. It is not the study of how law secures individual compliance with the rights and duties it creates by its directives" (72). And see also, in much the same vein, P. M. S. Hacker, "Sanction Theories of Duty," *in* A. W. B. Simpson, ed., *Oxford Essays in Jurisprudence (Second Series)* (Oxford: Oxford University Press, 1973), 131–170; and D. N. MacCormick, "Legal Obligation and the Imperative Fallacy," *in* Simpson, *Oxford Essays,* 100–130, the latter describing the focus on imperatives backed by the threat of force as "one of the perennial and persistent fallacies in legal philosophy" (101).

4. Law's constitutive dimension is discussed at length in Chapter 3.

5. See, for example, Scott J. Shapiro, *Legality* (Cambridge, MA: Harvard University Press, 2011). Shapiro states, "It seems to me a mistake . . . to consider sanctions to be a *necessary* feature of law. There is nothing unimaginable about a sanctionless legal system" (169). He goes on to say, "I disagree with [the] claim that the law necessarily uses force" (175–176).

6. See Frederick Schauer, "Hart's Anti-Essentialism," *in* Andrea Dolcetti, Luis Duarte d'Almeida, & James Edwards, eds., *Reading H. L. A. Hart's "The Concept of Law"* (Oxford: Hart Publishing, 2013), 237–246.

7. See Shapiro, *Legality,* where he claims that "to discover an entity's nature is in part to discover those properties that it *necessarily* has. . . . Thus, to discover the law's nature . . . would be in part to discover its necessary properties, those properties that law could not fail to have" (9).

8. Joseph Raz, *The Authority of Law: Essays on Law and Morality* (Oxford: Clarendon Press, 1979), 104–105. Similar claims can be found in Julie Dickson, *Evaluation and Legal Theory* (Oxford: Hart Publishing, 2001), 17–25.

9. See Frederick Schauer, "On the Nature of the Nature of Law," *Archiv für Rechts- und Sozialphilosophie* 98 (2012), 457–467. Also see Chapter 3.

10. That our words and concepts and even the phenomena to which they refer might be understood not in terms of essential properties but instead by reference to a cluster of properties connected by no more than a "family resemblance" is a claim notably associated with Ludwig Wittgenstein, who used the example of games to demonstrate the existence of concepts that are resistant to definition by necessary and sufficient properties. Ludwig Wittgenstein, *Philosophical Investigations,* 4th ed., G. E. M. Anscombe, P.M.S. Hacker, & Joachim Schulte, trans. (Oxford: Basil Blackwell, 2009), ¶66. Relatedly, Max Black (*Problem of Analysis* (London: Routledge & Kegan Paul, 1954, ch. 2) and then John Searle offered the related idea of a "cluster concept," one whose application is a function not of necessary or sufficient criteria but instead of a weighted list of criteria, none of which is either necessary or sufficient. John R. Searle, "Proper Names," *Mind* 67 (1958), 166–173, subsequently refined and elaborated in John R. Searle, *Intentionality: An Essay in the Philosophy of Mind* (Cambridge, UK: Cambridge University Press, 1983), 231–261, largely as a response to criticism in Saul A. Kripke, *Naming and Necessity* (Cambridge, MA: Harvard University Press, 1980). The general idea is best captured by Wittgenstein's metaphor: the components of a concept are not like the links of a chain, where each is essential in that the removal of one destroys the chain, but like the strands of a rope, which interlock and overlap, but where no single strand runs the entire length of the rope. Wittgenstein, *Philosophical Investigations,* ¶67.

The most prominent criticism of the notion of family resemblance is Bernard Suits, *The Grasshopper: Games, Life and Utopia* (Boston: David R. Godine, 1990) (first published 1978). More recently, see Colin McGinn, *Truth by Analysis: Games, Names, and Philosophy* (New York: Oxford University Press, 2011).

Among the noteworthy contemporary defenses of conceptual analysis premised on the existence of necessary and sufficient conditions is Frank Jackson, *From Metaphysics to Ethics: A Defence of Conceptual Analysis* (Oxford: Oxford University Press, 1998). Joseph Raz defends the search for law's essential properties and dismisses the focus on family resemblance as largely (and irrelevantly to jurisprudence) about semantics, in "Can There Be a Theory of Law?" *in* Martin P. Golding & William A. Edmundson, *The Blackwell Guide to the Philosophy of Law and Legal Theory* (Oxford: Blackwell, 2005), 324–342.

This is not the occasion to debate the ultimate soundness of the ideas of family resemblance, cluster concepts, and essentialist or anti-essentialist views of our words, our concepts, and the phenomena to which those words and concepts are connected. We will return to these issues in Chapter 3. It is worth noting at this point, however, that even if Wittgenstein, Searle, and the other anti-essentialists are mistaken, whether about games in particular or about language and concepts generally, understanding the nature of the social phenomenon that is law might still not be best or even well illuminated by too insistent a focus on law's necessary rather than typical properties.

11. For a strong defense of just such a (narrow) conception of philosophy, see McGinn, *Truth by Analysis*. A particularly vivid example of the claim with particular reference to the philosophy of law is the quotation above from Raz, *The Authority of Law*. That Raz's understanding of the task of philosophy is a narrow one is not necessarily a fault, but now that so much of contemporary philosophy is partly empirical, and sometimes even experimental, it is useful to recognize that Raz's conception of philosophy, while by no means idiosyncratic to him (see McGinn, *Truth by Analysis*), is hardly universally (or perhaps even substantially) accepted even by professional philosophers. See Brian Leiter, "The Demarcation Problem in Jurisprudence: A New Case for Scepticism," *Oxford Journal of Legal Studies* 31 (2011), 663–677; William Ramsey, "Protoypes and Conceptual Analysis," *in* Michael R. DePaul & William Ramsey, eds., *Rethinking Intuition: The Psychology of Intuition and Its Role in Philosophical Inquiry* (Lanham, MD: Rowman & Littlefield, 1998), 161–178.

12. Letter from Oliver Wendell Holmes Jr. to Harold J. Laski (Jan. 5, 1921), *in* Mark De Wolfe Howe, ed., *The Holmes-Laski Letters,* vol. 1 (Cambridge, MA: Harvard University Press, 1953), 300.

13. The issue comes to us through Plato, in the *Apology, Crito, Euthyphro,* and *Phaedo* (Harold North Fowler, trans., Cambridge, MA: Harvard University Press/Loeb Classical Library, 1914). Important historical and philosophical commentary includes Reginald E. Allen, *Socrates and Legal Obligation* (Minneapolis: University of Minnesota Press, 1980); Thomas C. Brickhouse & Nicholas D. Smith, *Socrates on Trial* (Princeton, NJ: Princeton University Press, 1989); I. F. Stone, *The Trial of Socrates* (Boston: Little, Brown, 1988); Robin Waterfield, *Why Socrates Died: Dispelling the Myths* (New York: W. W. Norton,

2009); A. D. Woozley, *Law and Obedience: The Arguments of Plato's Crito* (London: Duckworth, 1979).

14. See Chapter 5.

15. See Chapters 6 and 7.

16. Legal philosophers spend much time and ink on the question of law's normativity—the question whether and how the law can exercise normative force not reducible to either the moral force of law's content or a moral obligation to obey the law just because it is the law. Along with others (see Brian Bix, "Kelsen and Normativity Revisited," *in* Carlos Bernal & Marcelo Porciuncula, eds., *Festschrift for Stanley L. Paulson* (Madrid: Marcel Pons, forthcoming 2014); David Enoch, "Reason-Giving and the Law," *Oxford Studies in the Philosophy of Law,* vol. 1 (Leslie Green & Brian Leiter, eds.) (2011), 1–38; Torben Spaak, "Plans, Conventions, and Legal Normativity," *Jurisprudence* 3 (2012), 509–521), and as will be explored and explained in Chapters 4 and 5, I believe the question is often improperly conceptualized and that when properly framed and understood, the issue of law's normativity is of far less consequence than many theorists have believed.

17. These issues comprise the bulk of Chapters 5 and 6, where the empirical dimensions of the problem play a prominent role and social science research is the focus of the inquiry.

18. See Chapter 8.

19. See Joshua D. Blank & Daniel Z. Levin, "When Is Tax Enforcement Publicized?," *Virginia Tax Review* 30 (2010), 1–37.

20. See, for example, Jacques Derrida, "The Force of Law: The Mystical Foundation of Authority," *Cardozo Law Review* 11 (1990), 919–1045; Ronald Dworkin, *Law's Empire* (Cambridge, MA: Harvard University Press, 1986), 111; Ekow N. Yankah, "The Force of Law: The Role of Coercion in Legal Norms," *University of Richmond Law Review* 42 (2008), 1195–1255.Arthur Ripstein's keynote lecture in Antwerp on November 2, 2012, was delivered with the title "The Law of Force and the Force of Law."

21. Robert M. Cover, "Violence and the Word," *Yale Law Journal* 95 (1986), 1601–1629. As in Cover's case, describing law's use of force as its "violence" takes place typically from a stance of skepticism or antipathy toward law and what it does.

22. Thus, the philosopher Elizabeth Anscombe noted law's characteristic "actual or threatened violence" (G. E. M. Anscombe, "On the Source of the Authority of the State," *in* Joseph Raz, ed., *Authority* (New York: New York University Press, 1990), 142–173, *at* 148); the anthropologist E. Adamson Hoebel defined law to include its "application of physical force" (E. Adamson Hoebel, *The Law of Primitive Man: A Study in Comparative Legal Dynamics* (Cambridge, MA: Harvard University Press, 1954), 28); the sociologist Max Weber

characterized law in terms of its monopoly on the legitimate use of force (Max Weber, "Politics as a Vocation" [1919]) *in* H. H. Gerth & C. Wright Mills, eds., *From Max Weber: Essays in Sociology* (New York: Oxford University Press, 1946), 77–128); the legal philosopher Hans Kelsen described law as a "coercive order" that monopolizes "the use of force" (Hans Kelsen, "The Law as a Specific Social Technique," *in* Hans Kelsen, *What Is Justice? Justice, Law, and Politics in the Mirror of Science* (Berkeley: University of California Press, 1957), 231–256, *at* 235–244); and the legal theorist Rudolph von Ihering insisted that there can be "no law . . . without coercion," that "coercion . . . makes the State and Law," and that "law without force is an empty name" (Rudolph von Ihering, *Law as a Means to an End,* Isaac Husik, trans. (Boston: Boston Book Company, 1913), 73, 176, 190). See also M. D. A. Freeman, *Lloyd's Introduction to Jurisprudence,* 7th ed. (London: Sweet & Maxwell, 2001): "It is quite realistic to regard the policeman as the ultimate mark of the legal process" (217). And it has also been observed that a long line of philosophical greats, including Spinoza, Kant, and many others, understood law as the "ordering [of] human behavior through coercion." Huntington Cairns, *Legal Philosophy from Plato to Hegel* (Baltimore, MD: Johns Hopkins University Press, 1949), 277.

23. Thomas Hobbes, *Leviathan,* Richard Tuck, ed. (Cambridge, UK: Cambridge University Press, 1991) (1649), ch. 17.2, *at* 117.

24. James Fitzjames Stephen, *Liberty, Equality, Fraternity* (Chicago: University of Chicago Press, 1991) (first published 1873), 200.

25. See notes 2 to 5 above. The prominent exception is Ronald Dworkin, who takes law's ability to marshal coercive power as the starting point for an understanding of law that would make the exercise of that power politically and morally legitimate. "A conception of law must explain how what it takes to be law provides a general justification for the exercise of coercive power by the state." Ronald Dworkin, *Law's Empire* (Cambridge, MA: Harvard University Press, 1986), 188. To much the same effect, albeit in the context of political authority more generally, is Arthur Ripstein, "Authority and Coercion," *Philosophy and Public Affairs* 32 (2004): "[T]he state's claim to authority is inseparable from the rationale for coercion" (2).

26. In recent years a few others also have contributed to the project of attempting to reclaim coercion from the jurisprudential exile to which it has been banished. See Matthew Kramer, *In Defense of Legal Positivism: Law without Trimmings* (Oxford: Clarendon Press, 1999); Kurt Gerry, "The Role of Coercion in the Jurisprudence of Hart and Raz: A Critical Analysis," papers.ssrn.com/sol3/papers.cfm?abstract_id=1911249; Joshua Kleinfeld, "Enforcement and the Concept of Law," *Yale Law Journal Online* 121 (2011), 293–315; Grant Lamond, "Coercion and the Nature of Law," *Legal Theory* 7 (2001), 35–57; Grant Lamond, "The Coerciveness of Law," *Oxford Journal of Legal Studies* 20

(2000), 39–62; Grant Lamond, "Coercion," *in* Dennis Patterson, ed., *A Companion to Philosophy of Law and Legal Theory,* 2d ed. (Oxford: Wiley-Blackwell, 2010), 642–653; Danny Priel, "Sanction and Obligation in Hart's Theory of Law," *Ratio Juris* 21 (2008), 404–411; Nicos Stavropolous, "The Relevance of Coercion: Some Preliminaries," *Ratio Juris* 22 (2009), 339–358; Yankah, "The Force of Law." And, even earlier, Dale A. Nance, "Legal Theory and the Pivotal Role of the Concept of Coercion," *University of Colorado Law Review* 57 (1985), 1–43. My own efforts began as far back as 1994, in Frederick Schauer, "Critical Notice," *Canadian Journal of Philosophy* 24 (1994), 495–509, and thus this book can be understood as the culmination of my own two-decades-long effort, an effort that also includes Frederick Schauer, "The Best Laid Plans," *Yale Law Journal* 120 (2010), 586–621; Frederick Schauer, "Was Austin Right After All? On the Role of Sanctions in a Theory of Law," *Ratio Juris* 23 (2010), 1–21; Frederick Schauer, "On the Nature of the Nature of Law," *Archiv für Rechts- und Sozialphilosophie* 98 (2012), 457–467; Frederick Schauer, "Positivism through Thick and Thin," *in* Brian Bix, ed., *Analyzing Law: New Essays in Legal Theory* (Oxford: Clarendon Press, 1998), 65–78.

2. Bentham's Law

1. See Huntington Cairns, "Plato's Theory of Law," *Harvard Law Review* 56 (1942), 359–387; Jerome Hall, "Plato's Legal Philosophy," *Indiana Law Journal* 31 (1956), 171–206; George Klosko, "Knowledge and Law in Plato's *Laws,*" *Political Studies* 56 (2008), 456–474.

2. Aristotle's most extensive observations on law are contained in Aristotle, *Politics,* Peter L. P. Simpson, ed. (Chapel Hill: University of North Carolina Press, 1996). Useful commentary includes Richard O. Brooks & James Bernard Murphy, eds., *Aristotle and Modern Law* (Aldershot, UK: Ashgate, 2003); Max Hamburger, *Morals and Law: The Growth of Aristotle's Legal Theory* (New Haven, CT: Yale University Press, 1951); Fred D. Miller Jr., "Aristotle's Philosophy of Law," *in* Fred D. Miller Jr. & Carrie-Ann Biondi, eds., *A History of the Philosophy of Law from the Ancient Greeks to the Scholastics* (Dordrecht, Netherlands: Springer, 2007), 79–110.

3. Marcus Tullius Cicero, *De Legibus* (On the Laws), *in* Cicero, *On the Commonwealth and on the Laws,* James E. G. Zetzel, ed. (Cambridge, UK: Cambridge University Press, 1999), 105–175. See also Elizabeth Asmis, "Cicero on Natural Law and the Laws of the State," *Classical Antiquity* 27 (2008), 1–33.

4. Thomas Aquinas, *Treatise on Law: The Complete Text* (being a translation of *Summa Theologica,* questions 90–108), Alfred J. Freddoso, trans. (South Bend, IN: St. Augustine's Press, 2009). And see John Finnis, *Aquinas: Moral, Political and Legal Theory* (Oxford: Oxford University Press, 1998); Anthony J. Lisska, *Aquinas's Theory of Natural Law: An Analytic Reconstruction* (Oxford:

Oxford University Press, 1998); John Finnis, "Aquinas' Moral, Political, and Legal Philosophy," *in* Edward N. Zalta, ed., *Stanford Encyclopedia of Philosophy*, http://plato.stanford.edu.entries/aquinas-moral-political/ (2011).

5. Thomas Hobbes, *Leviathan*, Richard Tuck, ed. (Cambridge, UK: Cambridge University Press, 1991). Useful commentary can be found in David Dyzenhaus & Thomas Poole, eds., *Hobbes and the Law* (Cambridge, UK: Cambridge University Press, 2012); Claire Finkelstein, ed., *Hobbes on Law* (Aldershot, UK: Ashgate, 2005); Robert Ladenson, "In Defense of a Hobbesian Conception of Law," *Philosophy and Public Affairs* 9 (1980), 134–159.

6. A valuable overview of some of the important early contributions is Gerald J. Postema, "Legal Positivism: Early Foundations," *in* Andrei Marmor, ed., *The Routledge Companion to Philosophy of Law* (New York: Routledge, 2012), 30–47.

7. Which is not to say there is anything wrong with such enterprises. Still, they were not Bentham's.

8. On the normative moral underpinnings of Bentham's descriptive project, see David Lyons, "Founders and Foundations of Legal Positivism," *Michigan Law Review* 82 (1984), 722–739, *at* 730–733.

9. Blackstone described the common law as "the best birthright and noblest inheritance of mankind." William Blackstone, *Commentaries on the Laws of England*, vol. 1 (Oxford: Clarendon Press, 1765–1769), 436. Grant Gilmore's caricature is actually not far off from accurately encapsulating Blackstone's outlook: "Blackstone's celebration of the common law of England glorified the past: without quite knowing what we were about, he said, we have somehow achieved the perfection of reason. Let us preserve, unchanged, the estate which we have been lucky enough to inherit. Let us avoid any attempt at reform—either legislative or judicial—since the attempt to make incidental changes in an already perfect system can only lead to harm in ways which will be beyond the comprehension of even the most well-meaning and far-sighted innovators." Grant Gilmore, *The Ages of American Law* (New Haven, CT: Yale University Press, 1977), 5.

10. Sir Edward Coke, *Prohibitions del Roy* (1607), 12 Co. Rep. 63. For a modern elaboration, see Charles Fried, "The Artificial Reason of the Law or: What Lawyers Know," *Texas Law Review* 60 (1981), 35–58.

11. There are multiple forms and sources of legal indeterminacy, but Bentham was particularly enraged by the inductive methods of the common law, believing that the pretense of extracting general and publicly known legal rules from a series of common-law decisions was simply a smokescreen for individual (and thus not "common") inference and thus judicial lawmaking: "As a System of general rules, Common Law is a thing merely imaginary." Jeremy Bentham, *Comment on the Commentaries and a Fragment on Government*, J. H. Burns & H. L. A. Hart, eds. (Oxford: Clarendon Press, 2008), 119. And see Postema, "Legal Positivism," 36–40. On the possibility that Bentham might have been right,

see Frederick Schauer, "Is the Common Law Law?" *California Law Review* 77 (1989), 455–471, and, less directly, Frederick Schauer, "Do Cases Make Bad Law?," *University of Chicago Law Review* 73 (2006), 883–918.

12. Jeremy Bentham, "Scotch Reform," *in* James Bowring, ed., *The Works of Jeremy Bentham* (Edinburgh: William Tait, 1838), 1–53 (originally published 1808).

13. Jeremy Bentham, *in* J. H. Burns & H. L. A. Hart, eds., *A Comment on the Commentaries and a Fragment on Government* (London: Athlone Press, 1977), 411.

14. Jeremy Bentham, "Elements of the Art of Packing as Applied to Special Juries, Particularly in Cases of Libel," *in* John Bowring, ed., *The Works of Jeremy Bentham* vol. 5 (Edinburgh: William Tait, 1838), 61–186, *at* 92.

15. On the relationship between Bentham's theory of law and his reformist goals, see Nancy L. Rosenblum, *Bentham's Theory of the Modern State* (Cambridge, MA: Harvard University Press, 1978), 88–89. And on the contrast between theories of law that operate sympathetically within an existing legal regime and those that explicitly seek an external and distancing perspective, see Frederick Schauer, "Fuller's Internal Point of View," *Law and Philosophy* 12 (1994), 285–312. See also Michelle Madden Dempsey, "On Finnis's Way In," *Villanova Law Review* 57 (2012), 827–843, *at* 842, urging that we consider the nature of law from the perspective of the law reformer—one who recognizes law's "potential for empowerment," but sees law's potential and risk of "oppression" as well.

16. On the normative goals undergirding Bentham's descriptive project, see Frederick Schauer, "Positivism Before Hart," *Canadian Journal of Law and Jurisprudence* 24 (2011), 455–471, and also in Michael Freeman & Patricia Mindus, eds., *The Legacy of John Austin's Jurisprudence* (Dordrecht, Netherlands: Springer, 2013), 271–290.

17. This is hardly the place for a full or even not-so-full bibliography of the voluminous contemporary scholarship in the legal positivist tradition. Still, a good start within the English-language literature (which excludes work by and about Hans Kelsen, generally taken outside of the English-speaking world as the most important twentieth-century legal positivist) would include, of course, H. L. A. Hart, *The Concept of Law,* 3d ed., Penelope A. Bulloch, Joseph Raz, & Leslie Green, eds. (Oxford: Oxford University Press, 2012), as well as, within the positivist tradition but excluding critiques of it (and also running the risk of insult by exclusion), Tom Campbell, *The Legal Theory of Ethical Positivism* (Aldershot, UK: Dartmouth Publishing, 1996); Jules Coleman, ed., *Hart's Postscript: Essays on the Postscript to the Concept of Law* (Oxford: Oxford University Press, 2001); Jules Coleman, *The Practice of Principle: In Defense of a Pragmatist Approach to Legal Theory* (Oxford: Oxford University Press, 2001); Julie Dickson, *Evaluation and Legal Theory* (Oxford: Hart Publishing, 2001); Robert P. George, ed., *The Autonomy of Law: Essays on Legal Positivism* (Ox-

ford: Clarendon Press, 1999); Matthew Kramer, *In Defense of Legal Positivism: Law without Trimmings* (Oxford: Clarendon Press, 1999); David Lyons, *Ethics and the Rule of Law* (Cambridge, UK: Cambridge University Press, 1984); Andrei Marmor, *Positive Law and Objective Values* (Oxford: Oxford University Press, 2001); Joseph Raz, *The Morality of Freedom* (Oxford: Clarendon Press, 1986); Joseph Raz, *The Authority of Law: Essays on Law and Morality* (Oxford: Clarendon Press, 1979); Scott J. Shapiro, *Legality* (Cambridge, MA: Harvard University Press, 2011); Wil J. Waluchow, *Inclusive Legal Positivism* (Oxford: Clarendon Press, 1994); John Gardner, "Legal Positivism: 5½ Myths," *American Journal of Jurisprudence* 46 (2001), 199–227; Kenneth Einar Himma, "Inclusive Legal Positivism," *in* Jules Coleman & Scott Shapiro, eds., *The Oxford Handbook of Jurisprudence and Legal Philosophy* (Oxford, UK: Oxford University Press, 2002), 125–165; Leslie Green, "Positivism and the Inseparability of Law and Morals," *New York University Law Review* 83 (2008), 1035–1058.

Some readers may be tempted to place the present book, especially its earlier chapters, within the positivist tradition, but the word *positivism* will rarely appear. More than forty years ago, Robert Summers urged that the term "positivism" be discarded because it had become hopelessly mired in multiple and conflicting definitions. Robert Summers, "Legal Philosophy Today—An Introduction," *in* Robert S. Summers, ed., *Essays in Legal Philosophy* (Oxford: Blackwell, 1968), 1–16, *at* 15–16. More recently, Joseph Raz has advocated much the same thing, believing that attempts to characterize this or that perspective on law as positivist or not have obscured efforts to achieve greater understanding of the phenomenon of law. Joseph Raz, "The Argument from Justice; or How Not to Reply to Legal Positivism," *in* George Pavlakos, ed., *Law, Rights, Discourse: The Legal Philosophy of Robert Alexy* (Oxford: Hart Publishing, 2007), 17–36. To the same effect, see John Finnis, "What Is the Philosophy of Law?," *Rivista di Filosofia del Diritto,* vol. 1 (2012), 67–78, *at* 73. I believe that Summers, Raz, and Finnis are largely correct, not only because attempts to characterize positivism often degenerate into caricature but also because excess dichotomization of perspectives into positivist and nonpositivist (or antipositivist), as if they were the two sides in the World Cup finals, makes it difficult to see the value, even if only partial, to be found in the individual members of an array of diverse perspectives and analyses.

18. A contemporary effort to justify the classical claim is Philip Soper, "In Defense of Classical Natural Law in Legal Theory: Why Unjust Law Is No Law at All," *Canadian Journal of Law and Jurisprudence* 20 (2007), 201–223. A contemporary contrasting view is Julie Dickson, "Is Bad Law Still Law? Is Bad Law Really Law?," *in* Maksymilian Del Mar & Zenon Bankowski eds., *Law as Institutional Normative Order* (Farnham, Surrey, UK: Ashgate Publishing, 2009), 161–183.

19. See especially, John Finnis, *Natural Law and Natural Rights* (Oxford: Clarendon Press, 1980), 3–20, elaborating a "central cases" method in which

there are central cases of the concepts of social theory (such as law), such that the noncentral cases are still law but in some way deficient or defective as law. To the same effect, see Mark C. Murphy, "Natural Law Jurisprudence," *Legal Theory* 9 (2003), 241–267. A good overview of modern natural law theory is Brian Bix, "Natural Law Theory: The Modern Tradition," *in* Jules L. Coleman & Scott J. Shapiro, eds., *Oxford Handbook of Jurisprudence and Philosophy of Law* (New York: Oxford University Press, 2002), 61–103.

20. In *Of the Limits of the Penal Branch of Jurisprudence*, Philip Schofield, ed. (Oxford: Clarendon Press, 2010), Bentham says, "A book of jurisprudence can have but one or the other of two objects: 1. To ascertain what the *law* is: 2. To ascertain what it ought to be. In the former case it may be stiled a book of *expository* jurisprudence; in the latter, a book of *censorial* jurisprudence; or, on other words, a book on the *art of legislation*" (16).

21. For examples of the caricature, and a rebuttal, see Frederick Schauer, "Positivism as Pariah," *in* Robert P. George, ed., *The Autonomy of Law*, 31–56. The caricature is also described and challenged in Anthony Sebok, *Legal Positivism in American Jurisprudence* (New York: Cambridge University Press, 1998), 2, 20, 39.

22. On the possibility (but not the necessity) of understanding the conceptual separation of law and morality as itself being in the service of moral goals, see Liam Murphy, "Better to See Law This Way," *New York University Law Review* 83 (2008), 1088–1108; Neil MacCormick, "A Moralistic Case for A-Moralistic Law," *Valparaiso University Law Review* 20 (1985), 1–41; Frederick Schauer, "The Social Construction of the Concept of Law: A Reply to Julie Dickson," *Oxford Journal of Legal Studies* 25 (2005), 493–501. More controversially, this seems to be the position in H. L. A. Hart, "Positivism and the Separation of Law and Morals," *Harvard Law Review* 71 (1958), 593–629, and in Hart, *The Concept of Law*, 207–212.

23. Bentham, *Of the Limits of the Penal Branch of Jurisprudence*. The book, earlier published as *Of Laws in General* (H. L. A. Hart, ed., London: Athlone Press, 1970), was originally written around 1780 and intended to be part of Bentham's magisterial *An Introduction to the Principles of Morals and Legislation* (J. H. Burns & H. L. A. Hart, eds., London: Athlone Press, 1970).

24. Thus, Bentham asks, rhetorically, "What is it that law can be employed in doing, besides prohibiting and commanding?" Bentham, *Of the Limits of the Penal Branch of Jurisprudence*, 3.

25. In *Of the Limits of the Penal Branch of Jurisprudence*, Bentham says, "A law by which nobody is bound, a law by which nobody is coerced, a law by which nobody's liberty is curtailed, all these phrases, which come to the same thing, would be so many contradictions in terms" (75–76). And by way of introducing the possibility that rewards as well as punishments might be sufficient to support those commands of the sovereign that would properly be understood as laws, Bentham notes that "the idea of coercion shall [in the sense of mankind]

have become inseparably connected with that of a law" (145). Note also that Bentham's cumbersome definition of a law includes the "means" of "bringing to pass" the lawmaker's desired state of affairs, and the way in which the law would supply "a motive upon those whose conduct is in question" (24–25).

26. Jeremy Bentham, *Constitutional Code*, in *The Works of Jeremy Bentham* (Edinburgh, 1842), 192.

27. Ibid.

28. See especially, Bentham's discussion of "Force of a Law," in *Of the Limits of the Penal Branch of Jurisprudence*, 142–160.

29. For example, Bentham seems to have taken the threat of punishment as a necessary condition for the bindingness of law in saying, "If [a person] is bound [by law], . . . he is at any rate in the first instance exposed to suffer." *Of the Limits of the Penal Branch of Jurisprudence*, 78.

30. My understanding of the relationship between Bentham's psychological views and his emphasis on law's coercive side has been aided by the meticulous and perceptive analysis in Gerald J. Postema, *Bentham and the Common Law Tradition* (Oxford: Clarendon Press, 1986), 376–402.

31. See *Of the Limits of the Penal Branch of Jurisprudence*, 142–160.

32. Thus, H. L. A. Hart has observed that "[h]ad [*Of Laws in General*] been published in [Bentham's] lifetime, it, rather than John Austin's later and obviously derivative work, would have dominated English jurisprudence." H. L. A. Hart, "Bentham's 'Of Laws in General,' " *Rechtstheorie*, vol. 2 (1971), 55–66 *at* 55, reprinted in H. L. A. Hart, *Essays on Bentham* (Oxford: Clarendon Press, 1982), 105–126.

33. Some of the material had, however, been translated into French and published while Bentham was still living. See "Editorial Introduction" to *Of the Limits of the Penal Branch of Jurisprudence*, xii n.2.

34. Jeremy Bentham, *The Limits of Jurisprudence Defined*. Charles Warren Everett, ed., (New York: Columbia University Press, 1945).

35. On Austin, see W. L. Morison, *John Austin* (Stanford, CA: Stanford University Press, 1982); Wilfrid E. Rumble, *The Thought of John Austin* (London: Athlone Press, 1985); Wilfrid E. Rumble, *Doing Austin Justice: The Reception of John Austin's Philosophy of Law in Nineteenth-Century England* (London: Continuum, 2005); Brian Bix, "John Austin," in *Stanford Encyclopedia of Philosophy*, http://plato.stanford.edu/entries/austin-john/ (2010). The personal side of Austin's life and its effect on his professional accomplishments is the focus of Joseph Hamburger & Lotte Hamburger, *Troubled Lives: John and Sarah Austin* (Toronto: University of Toronto Press, 1985).

36. John Austin, *The Province of Jurisprudence Defined*, Wilfrid E. Rumble, ed.(Cambridge, UK: Cambridge University Press, 1995) (1st ed. 1832); John Austin, *Lectures on Jurisprudence or the Philosophy of Positive Law*, 5th ed., R. Campbell, ed., (London: John Murray, 1885) (1st ed. 1861).

37. Austin, in *Province of Jurisprudence,* 157.

38. Ibid., 21.

39. Ibid., 21–22.

40. Recent commentary includes Michael Rodney, "What Is in a Habit,?" *in* Michael Freeman & Patricia Mindus, eds., *The Legacy of John Austin's Jurisprudence* (Dordrecht, Netherlands: Springer, 2013), 185–214; Lars Vinx, "Austin, Kelsen, and the Model of Sovereignty: Notes on the History of Modern Legal Positivism," *in* Freeman & Mindus, *The Legacy,* 51–72.

41. A widespread view holds Austin's understanding of law to be "pedestrian." Postema, "Legal Positivism," 36. Although that charge may have a ring of truth when Austin is compared to Bentham in the latter's full glory and full fury, in general it relies too much on subsequent caricatures (perhaps especially Hart's), many of which do not stand up to a close and charitable reading of Austin's writings. And on the possibility (indeed, the probability) that Austin's omissions were no greater than those of his critics, see Brian Bix, "John Austin and Constructing Theories of Law," *in* Freeman & Mindus, *The Legacy,* 1–14.

42. Austin, *Province of Jurisprudence,* 24.

43. Ibid., 31–32, 156–157, 269–277.

44. Ibid., 28–37.

45. Ibid., 158.

46. Thus, Blackstone famously stated that if a decision were "manifestly absurd or unjust," it is not that it was "bad law" but that "it was not law." Blackstone, *Commentaries,* vol. 1, 70.

47. See notes 17 and 18.

48. Cicero, *De Legibus,* I, vi, 18–19.

49. Lon L. Fuller, "Positivism and Fidelity to Law—A Reply to Professor Hart," *Harvard Law Review* 71 (1958), 630–672.

50. Austin, *Province of Jurisprudence,* 163. Austin's acknowledgment and acceptance of judicial legislation, and his departure from Bentham in this regard, is discussed in David Dyzenhaus, "The Genealogy of Legal Positivism," *Oxford Journal of Legal Studies* 24 (2004), 39–67, *at* 47; Andrew Halpin, "Austin's Methodology? His Bequest to Jurisprudence," *Cambridge Law Journal* 70 (2011), 175–202, *at* 197–198.

51. A. W. B. Simpson, "The Common Law and Legal Theory," *in* A. W. B. Simpson, ed., *Oxford Essays in Jurisprudence (2nd Series)* (Oxford: Oxford University Press, 1973), 77–99.

52. On Austin's late-life political conservatism and apologetics for the then-existing hierarchies of English political and legal life, see Wilfrid E. Rumble, "Did Austin Remain an Austinian?," *in* Freeman & Mindus, *The Legacy,* 131–154.

53. Austin had some modest law reform goals, but being less the reformer than Bentham, he was more inclined to take the analytic task as an end in itself. See Frederick Schauer, "Positivism Before Hart," *Canadian Journal of Law and Jurisprudence* 24 (2011), 455–471.

54. See Sean Coyle, "Thomas Hobbes and the Intellectual Origins of Legal Positivism," *Canadian Journal of Law and Jurisprudence* 16 (2003), 243–270; Mark Murphy, "Was Hobbes a Legal Positivist?," *Ethics* 105 (1995), 846–873.

55. Thomas Erskine Holland, *The Elements of Jurisprudence* (Oxford: Clarendon Press, 1880).

56. See, for example, W. Jethro Brown, *The Austinian Theory of Law* (London: J. Murray, 1906); E. C. Clark, *Practical Jurisprudence: A Comment on Austin* (Cambridge, UK: Cambridge University Press, 1883); R. A. Eastwood & G. W. Keeton, *The Austinian Theories of Law and Sovereignty* (London: Sweet & Maxwell, 1929). The reception of Austinian views during this period is thoroughly recounted in Neil Duxbury, "English Jurisprudence between Austin and Hart," *Virginia Law Review* 91 (2005), 1–91.

57. Henry Sumner Maine, *Lectures on the Early History of Institutions* (London: Murray, 1875), 359–60.

58. W. W. Buckland, *Some Reflections on Jurisprudence* (Cambridge, UK: Cambridge University Press, 1945), 28.

59. "But if we take the view of our friend the bad man we shall find that he does not care two straws for the axioms or deductions, but he does want to know what the [courts] will do in fact." Oliver Wendell Holmes, "The Path of the Law," *Harvard Law Review* 10 (1897), 457–478, *at* 460–461.

60. As noted in Thomas C. Grey, "Holmes and Legal Pragmatism," *Stanford Law Review* 41 (1989), 787–870, *at* 793–794.

61. See Laura Kalman, *Legal Realism at Yale, 1927–1960* (Chapel Hill: University of North Carolina Press, 1986); Brian Leiter, *Naturalizing Jurisprudence: Essays on Legal Realism and Naturalism in Legal Philosophy* (New York: Oxford University Press, 2007); William Twining, *Karl Llewellyn and the Realist Movement*, 2d ed. (New York: Cambridge University Press, 2012); Frederick Schauer, *Thinking Like a Lawyer: A New Introduction to Legal Reasoning* (Cambridge, MA: Harvard University Press, 2009), 124–147.

62. Karl N. Llewellyn, *The Theory of Rules* (Frederick Schauer, ed., Chicago: University of Chicago Press, 2011) (1937–1938), 11–23; Karl N. Llewellyn "A Realistic Jurisprudence: The Next Step," *Columbia Law Review* 30 (1930), 431–465. See also Frederick Schauer, "Legal Realism Untamed," *Texas Law Review* 91 (2013), 749–780.

63. Hans Kelsen, *General Theory of Law and State,* Anders Wedberg, trans. (Cambridge, MA: Harvard University Press, 1945), 15–45.

64. Hans Kelsen, "The Pure Theory of Law and Analytical Jurisprudence," *Harvard Law Review* 55 (1941), 44–70, *at* 57–58.

65. Kelsen, *General Theory of Law and State,* 29.

66. Max Rheinstein, ed., *Max Weber on Law in Economy and Society* (Cambridge, MA: Harvard University Press, 1954), 13.

67. Among French writers who explicitly accepted the centrality of coercion, see Henri Lévy-Ullman, *La Définition du Droit* (Paris: Larose, 1917), 146, 165;

Ernest Roguin, *La Science Juridique Pure,* vol. 1 (Paris: Librairie Générale de Droit et de Jurisprudence, 1923), 122. Roscoe Pound referred to their views as the "threat theory" of law. Roscoe Pound, "Book Review," *Texas Law Review* 23 (1945), 411–418, *at* 413.

68. Blaise Pascal, *Pensées,* William F. Trotter, trans. (New York: E. P. Dutton, 1941), §5, 298.

69. As quoted in the *Wall Street Journal,* November 13, 1962.

70. James A. Garfield, Speech to 38th Congress as Member of Congress from Ohio, *in* Russell Herman Conwell, *The Life, Speeches, and Public Services of James A. Garfield* (Portland, ME: George Stinson & Co., 1881), 199.

3. The Possibility and Probability of Noncoercive Law

1. Thus, Bentham wrote, in a passage that did not make it into the final edition of his work on law, that an essential task was "distinguishing a law from a piece of exhortation or advice." Jeremy Bentham, *Of the Limits of the Penal Branch of Jurisprudence* (Philip Schofield, ed., Oxford: Clarendon Press, 2010), 25 (editor's note, quoting from a fragment of the unpublished manuscript). Earlier, Hobbes had observed that "law in general, is not Counsell, but Command." Thomas Hobbes, *Leviathan,* Richard Tuck, ed. (Cambridge, UK: Cambridge University Press, 1991) (1651), 183. And as Jules Coleman and Brian Leiter describe Austin's basic position, "[w]ithout sanctions, commands would really be no more than requests." Jules Coleman & Brian Leiter, "Legal Positivism," *in* Dennis Patterson, ed., *A Companion to Philosophy of Law and Legal Theory* (Oxford: Blackwell, 1996), 241–260, *at* 244.

2. Roscoe Pound, "Book Review," *Texas Law Review* 23 (1945), 411–418, *at* 415.

3. The phrase "second-order rules" comes from Joseph Raz, *Practical Reason and Norms,* 2d ed. (Princeton, NJ: Princeton University Press, 1990), but Hart's earlier characterization of them as "rules about rules" captures the basic idea. H. L. A. Hart, *The Concept of Law,* 3d ed., Penelope A. Bulloch, Joseph Raz, & Leslie Green, eds. (Oxford: Oxford University Press, 2012), 94–99.

4. Famously, Ronald Dworkin distinguishes rules from principles in *Taking Rights Seriously* (London: Duckworth, 1977), but his distinction is questionable. Frederick Schauer, *Playing by the Rules: A Philosophical Examination of Rule-Based Decision-Making in Law and in Life* (Oxford: Clarendon Press, 1991), 12–14; Joseph Raz, "Legal Principles and the Limits of Law," *in* Marshall Cohen, ed., *Ronald Dworkin and Contemporary Jurisprudence* (London: Routledge, 1984), 73–87, *at* p. 82. For present purposes, however, nothing turns on Dworkin's or anyone else's distinction between rules and other kinds of prescriptions.

5. *River Wear Commissioners v. Adamson* [1877] 2 A.C. 743 (Q.B.); *Grey v. Pearson* (1857) 10 Eng. Rep. 1216, 1234 (H.L.). It has long been claimed, espe-

cially in the United States, that the canons of interpretation are largely noncon-straining, primarily because most of the canons, including the Golden Rule, can be avoided by recourse to still other canons mandating the contrary approach. See especially Karl N. Llewellyn, "Remarks on the Theory of Appellate Decision, and the Rules or Canons about How Statutes Are to Be Construed," *Vanderbilt Law Review* 3 (1950), 395–406 . Whether this skeptical claim is in fact true can be debated (see Michael Sinclair, " 'Only a Sith Thinks Like That': Llewellyn's 'Dueling Canons,' One to Seven," *New York Law School Law Review* 50 (2006), 919–992), but that debate would take us too far away from the basic point in the text.

6. Pound, "Book Review," 415.

7. Ibid., 416.

8. Ibid., 417.

9. Frederic Harrison, "The English School of Jurisprudence: Part II—Bentham's and Austin's Analysis of Law," *Fortnightly Review* 24 (1878), 682–703. And see the detailed analysis of Harrison's views in Wilfrid E. Rumble, *Doing Austin Justice: The Reception of John Austin's Philosophy of Law in Nineteenth Century England* (London: Continuum, 2005).

10. A valuable analytic survey of these developments is Gerald J. Postema, "Analytic Jurisprudence Established," *in* Gerald J. Postema, *A Treatise of Legal Philosophy and General Jurisprudence* (Dordrecht, Netherlands: Springer, 2011), 3–42. See also Rumble, *Doing Austin Justice,* 178–241; Neil Duxbury, "English Jurisprudence between Austin and Hart," *Virginia Law Review* 91 (2005), 1–91.

11. Carleton Kemp Allen, "Legal Duties," *Yale Law Journal* 40 (1931), 331–380, *at* 346.

12. Ibid., 351, See also, and even earlier, Edwin M. Borchard, "Book Review," *Yale Law Journal* 28 (1919), 840–843, *at* 842, lamenting that Austin's conception of law excludes many legal rules that are not made by the sovereign, and John C. Gray, "Some Definitions and Questions in Jurisprudence," *Harvard Law Review* 6 (1892), 21–35, *at* 26, noting that much that is clearly law is not subject to sanctions at all.

13. Austin explicitly acknowledged that many of the laws excluded by his narrow definition would normally be understood to be part of law more broadly. John Austin, *The Province of Jurisprudence Determined,* Wilfrid E. Rumble, ed. (Cambridge, UK: Cambridge University Press, 1995) (1832), 31–37. And on Austin's recognition of permissive laws, see David A. Gerber, Book Review, *Archiv für Rechts- und Sozialphilosophie* 61 (1975), 450–451.

14. Thus, Bentham recognized a set of procedural and other secondary rules, which he labeled "corroborative appendages" and "remedial appendages." Jeremy Bentham, *Of the Limits of the Penal Branch,* 41. Bentham's recognition of the role of constitutive or permissive laws is thoroughly examined in David Lyons, *In the Interest of the Governed: A Study in Bentham's Philosophy of*

Utility and Law, rev. ed. (Oxford: Clarendon Press, 1991), xviii, 108, 112–116, 125–137.

15. See Lyons, *In the Interest of the Governed,* 134–136.

16. John Austin, *Lectures on Jurisprudence,* vol. II, Lecture XXIII (London: John Murray, 1862), 141.

17. The claim that nullity can be a sanction is more fully developed by Hart than by Austin himself (Hart, *The Concept of Law,* 33–35), but Hart then proceeds to argue against it. A useful elaboration on and partial critique of Hart's critique is Richard Stith, Punishment, Invalidation, and Nonvalidation: What H. L. A. Hart Did Not Explain," *Legal Theory,* vol. 14 (2008), 219–232.

18. Hart, *The Concept of Law,* 33–35.

19. A less benign side effect has been that generations of students and scholars have learned their Austin from Hart rather than from Austin's own texts. This is particularly unfortunate because Hart explicitly acknowledged that his reconstruction of Austin's views was intended to set out a clear target that may not accurately have captured the depth and nuance of Austin's own writings (Hart, *The Concept of Law,* 18), and because Hart, for all his justified influence, was not known as a careful or sympathetic reader of the works of other authors. See Nicola Lacey, *A Life of H. L. A. Hart: The Nightmare and the Noble Dream* (Oxford: Oxford University Press, 2004), 301; Frederick Schauer, "The Best Laid Plans," *Yale Law Journal* 120 (2010), 586–621, *at* 594, note 29.

20. H. L. A. Hart, "Definition and Theory in Jurisprudence," *in* H. L. A. Hart, *Essays in Jurisprudence and Philosophy* (Oxford: Clarendon Press, 1984), 21–48.

21. John R. Searle, *Speech Acts: An Essay in the Philosophy of Language* (Cambridge, UK: Cambridge University Press, 1969), 33–42. Similar ideas are in Max Black, "The Analysis of Rules," *in* Max Black, *Models and Metaphors* (Ithaca, NY: Cornell University Press, 1962), 95–139, *at* 123–125; B. J. Diggs, "Rules and Utilitarianism," *American Philosophical Quarterly* 1 (1964), 32–44; and John Rawls, "Two Concepts of Rules," *Philosophical Review* 64 (1955), 3–32. For critiques, albeit directed more to the wisdom of labeling constitutive act descriptions as "rules" than to the basic idea, see Joseph Raz, *Practical Reason and Norms,* 2d ed. (Princeton, NJ: Princeton University Press, 1990), 108–113; Frederick Schauer, *Playing by the Rules,* 7, note 13.

22. At least not in the conceptual sense. I put aside the contingent empirical possibility that neither cars nor roads would exist without the laws that make constructing roads and manufacturing cars possible.

23. Thus, although the idea of "negligence" may exist within and be defined by law, a surgeon may with no law at all neglect to remove a sponge from the patient's body cavity after completing an operation.

24. The relationship between the legal idea of contract and the moral idea of promise has generated a huge literature. See Charles Fried, *Contract as Promise*

(Cambridge, MA: Harvard University Press, 1981); Jody Kraus, "The Correspondence of Contract and Promise," *Columbia Law Review* 109 (2009), 1603–1649; Joseph Raz, "Promises in Morality and Law," *Harvard Law Review* 95 (1982), 916–938; T. M. Scanlon, "Promises and Contracts," *in* T. M. Scanlon, *The Difficulty of Tolerance* (Cambridge, UK: Cambridge University Press, 2003), 234–269; Seana Valentine Shiffrin, "Is a Contract a Promise?" *in* Andrei Marmor, ed., *The Routledge Companion to Philosophy of Law* (New York: Routledge, 2012), 241–257.

25. Leslie Green offers a similar argument about same-sex marriage. He recognizes that no one is required to marry or to marry someone of the opposite sex. But when law authorizes one form of marriage but not another, and thus gives options to some but not to others, its very drawing of the distinction operates as an exercise of coercion. Leslie Green, "The Concept of Law Revisited," *Michigan Law Review* 94 (1996), 1687–1717, *at* 1703–1704.

26. Ibid., 1702. Other attempts to rehabilitate the idea that nullity can function as a genuine sanction include Theodore M. Benditt, *Law as Rule and Principle* (Sussex, UK: Harvester Press, 1978), 142–157; Philip Mullock, "Nullity and Sanction," *Mind* 83 (1974), 439–441; Richard Stith, "Punishment, Invalidation, and Nonvalidation: What H. L. A. Hart Did Not Explain," *Legal Theory* 14 (2008), 219–232; Richard H.S. Tur, "Variety or Uniformity," *in* Luís Duarte d'Almeida, James Edwards, & Andrea Dolcetti, eds., *Reading HLA Hart's* The Concept of Law (Oxford: Hart Publishing, 2013), 37–58, at 47–50.

27. Hart, *The Concept of Law,* 34.

28. Ibid.

29. Ibid.

30. Ibid.

31. See Hans Oberdiek, "The Role of Sanctions and Coercion in Understanding Law and Legal Systems," *American Journal of Jurisprudence* 71 (1976), 71–94.

32. A. L. Goodhart, *The English Law and the Moral Law* (London: Stevens & Sons, 1953), 17.

33. *Longpre v. Diaz,* 237 U.S. 512, 528 (1915).

34. *California Department of Social Services v. Leavitt,* 523 F.3d 1025, 1035 (9th Cir. 2008).

35. On the relationship among moral, legal, and self-interested desires, preferences, reasons, and motivations, an important recent contribution, and one whose account of motivation is in some tension with the one that pervades this book, is Veronica Rodriguez-Blanco, *Law and Authority Under the Guise of the Good* (Oxford: Hart Publishing, 2014).

36. This is not a book of theology. Nevertheless, it is worth noting that threats of divine retribution or burning in eternal damnation are hardly universal to religious belief and religious understanding. In some religious traditions, the

commands of God are to be followed just because they are the commands of God, and they are to be followed even though neither thunderbolts nor the fires of Hell are there to be feared.

37. See, for example, Stefano Bertea & George Pavlakos, eds., *New Essays on the Normativity of Law* (Oxford: Hart Publishing, 2011); Scott J. Shapiro, *Legality* (Cambridge, MA: Harvard University Press, 2011), 181–188; Jules L. Coleman, "The Architecture of Jurisprudence," *Yale Law Journal* 121 (2011), 2–80; Christopher Essert, "From Raz's Nexus to Legal Normativity," *Canadian Journal of Law & Jurisprudence* 25 (2012), 465–482; John Gardner, "Nearly Natural Law," *American Journal of Jurisprudence* 52 (2007), 1–23; Andrei Marmor, "The Nature of Law: An Introduction," *in* Marmor, *The Routledge Companion*, 3–15, at 4, 11–12; Stephen Perry, "Hart on Social Rules and the Foundations of Law: Liberating the Internal Point of View," *Fordham Law Review* 75 (2006), 1171–1209; Veronica Rodriguez-Blanco, "Peter Winch and H. L. A. Hart: Two Concepts of the Internal Point of View," *Canadian Journal of Law & Jurisprudence* 20 (2007), 453–473.

38. See John Gardner, "How Law Claims, What Law Claims," *in* Matthias Klatt, ed., *Institutionalized Reason: The Jurisprudence of Robert Alexy* (Oxford: Oxford University Press, 2012), 29–44.

39. Joseph Raz, *Practical Reason and Norms,* 2d ed. (Oxford: Oxford University Press, 1999).

40. On the latter, see especially Kurt Baier, *The Moral Point of View* (Ithaca, NY: Cornell University Press, 1958).

41. See especially David Enoch, "Reason-Giving and the Law," *Oxford Studies in the Philosophy of Law,* vol. 1 (Leslie Green & Brian Leiter, eds.) (Oxford: Oxford University Press, 2011), 1–38. To the same effect, and also valuable, is Torben Spaak, "Plans, Conventions, and Legal Normativity," *Jurisprudence* 3 (2012), 509–521, and Brian Bix, Book Review, *Ethics* 122 (2012), 444–448, *at* 447–448. A contrary view is defended by Veronica Rodriguez-Blanco in a series of articles, including "The Moral Puzzle of Legal Authority," *in* Bertea & Pavlakos, *New Essays,* 86–106; "If You Cannot Help Being Committed to It, then It Exists: A Defense of Robust Normative Realism," *Oxford Journal of Legal Studies* 32 (2012), 823–841; "Reasons in Action v. Triggering Reasons: A Reply to Enoch on Reason-Giving and Legal Normativity," *Problema* 7 (2013), *at* http://biblio.juridicas.unam.mx/revista/FilosofiaDerecho/.

42. For the state of Hawaii's understandable desire to provide protectionist support for a pineapple wine industry that would likely struggle if left to compete on the intrinsic merits of the product itself, see *Bacchus Imports, Ltd. v. Dias,* 468 U.S. 263 (1984).

43. Joseph Raz, *The Authority of Law: Essays on Law and Morality* (Oxford: Clarendon Press, 1979), 104–105. In more recent expositions, Raz reiterates that an account of the nature of law "consists of propositions about the law

which are necessarily true" (Joseph Raz, "Can There Be a Theory of Law?," *in* Martin P. Golding & William P. Edmundson, eds., *The Blackwell Guide to the Philosophy of Law and Legal Theory* (Oxford: Basil Blackwell, 2005), 324), and that the theses of a general theory of law claim to be about "necessary truths" (Joseph Raz, "On the Nature of Law," *Archiv für Rechts- und Sozialphilosophie* 82 (1996), 1–25, *at* 2). To the same effect are Andrei Marmor, *Interpretation and Legal Theory*, 2d ed. (Oxford: Clarendon Press, 2005), 27, and R. H. S. Tur, "What Is Jurisprudence," *Philosophical Quarterly* 28 (1978), 149–161, *at* 155. Critical commentary includes Brian Bix, "Raz on Necessity," *Law and Philosophy* 22 (2003), 537–559, *at* 546–549, and Danny Priel, "Jurisprudence and Necessity," *Canadian Journal of Law and Jurisprudence* 20 (2007), 173–200. As the quotation in the text indicates, Raz may simply be offering a view about the differentiation of academic disciplines and not about what is, in the final analysis, worth knowing. But I suspect that he and others are interested not only in marking the boundaries between philosophy and other disciplines— boundaries that are themselves far more contested than they acknowledge—but also in claiming the independent importance of an essentialist inquiry, an importance that this and the ensuing sections seek to challenge.

44. Scott J. Shapiro, *Legality* (Cambridge, MA: Harvard University Press, 2011), 13–22.

45. H. L. A. Hart, "Definition and Theory," 407. This includes legal systems that extraterrestrials might have. John Austin, *Lectures*, 406–407.

46. Julie Dickson, *Evaluation and Legal Theory* (Oxford: Hart Publishing, 2001), 17.

47. I do not want (yet) to make too much of the concept of a concept. For present purposes, we can agree with Kenneth Ehrenburg that "[t]alking about a concept of law is really just a shorthand way of talking about the nature of legal practices." Kenneth M. Ehrenburg, "Law Is Not (Best Considered) an Essentially Contested Concept," *International Journal of Law in Context* 7 (2011), 209–232, *at* 210.

48. For the related claim that coercion and force "are not part of the concept of the state," see Christopher W. Morris, "State Coercion and Force," *Social Philosophy and Policy* 29 (2012), 28–49.

49. A valuable survey of these issues is Brian Bix, "Conceptual Questions and Jurisprudence," *Legal Theory* 1 (1995), 465–479. For a skeptical view of some of the main methodological lines of contemporary jurisprudential conceptual analysis, see Brian Leiter, "Realism, Hard Positivism, and Conceptual Analysis," *Legal Theory* 4 (1998), 533–547, *at* 544–547.

50. See *Lozman v. City of Riviera Beach, Florida*, 133 S. Ct. 735 (2013).

51. See James A. Hampton, "Thinking Intuitively: The Rich (and at Times Illogical) World of Concepts," *Current Directions in Psychological Science* 21 (2012), 398–402, *at* 399. Related research to the same end includes James

A. Hampton, "Typicality, Graded Membership, and Vagueness," *Cognitive Science* 31 (2007), 355–383; Steven A. Sloman, "Feature-Based Induction," *Cognitive Psychology* 25 (1993), 231–280; Ling-ling Wu & Lawrence W. Barsalou, "Perceptual Simulation in Conceptual Combination: Evidence from Property Generation," *Acta Psychologica* 132 (2009), 173–189.

52. Ludwig Wittgenstein, *Philosophical Investigations,* 4th ed., G. E. M. Anscombe, P.M.S. Hacker, & Joachim Schulte, trans. (Oxford: Basil Blackwell, 2009), 66–67.

53. Bernard Suits, *The Grasshopper: Games, Life and Utopia* (Peterborough, Ontario: Broadview Press, 2005) (1978). To the same effect, and more recently, see Colin McGinn, *Truth by Analysis: Games, Names, and Philosophy* (Oxford: Oxford University Press, 2012). Suits offers a more complete definition: "To play a game is to engage in activity designed to bring about a specific state of affairs, using only means permitted by specific rules, where the means permitted by the rules are more limited in scope than they would be in the absence of such rules, and where the sole reason for accepting the rules is to make possible such activity." Suits, *The Grasshopper,* 48–49. See also Bernard Suits, "What Is a Game?" *Philosophy of Science* 34 (1967), 148–156.

54. Max Black, *Problems of Analysis: Philosophical Essays* (Ithaca, NY: Cornell University Press, 1954), 28; John Searle, *Speech Acts: An Essay in the Philosophy of Language* (Cambridge, UK: Cambridge University Press, 1969), 162–174. See also Hilary Putnam, "The Analytic and the Synthetic," *in* Herbert Feigl & Grover Maxwell, eds., *Scientific Explanation, Space, and Time,* vol. III. Minnesota Studies in the Philosophy of Science. (Minneapolis: University of Minnesota Press, 1962), 358–397, *at* 378. On Kripke's response to Searle and Searle's rejoinder, see Karen Green, "Was Searle's Descriptivism Refuted?" *Teorema* 17 (1998), 109–113.

55. The principal cognitive science source for prototype theory is the work of Eleanor Rosch. See Eleanor Rosch, "Principles of Categorization," *in* Eleanor Rosch & Barbara B. Lloyds, eds., *Cognition and Categorization* (Hillsdale, NJ: Lawrence Erlbaum Associates, 1978), 27–48; Eleanor Rosch & Carolyn B. Mervis, "Family Resemblances: Studies in the Internal Structure of Categories," *Cognitive Psychology* 7 (1975), 573–605. See also Hans Kamp & Barbara Partee, "Prototype Theory of Compositionality," *Cognition* 57 (1995), 129–191; Gregory L. Murphy & Douglas L. Medin, "The Role of Theories in Conceptual Coherence," *Psychological Review* 92 (1985), 289–316. Philosophical adaptations include Dirk Geeraerts, "On Necessary and Sufficient Conditions," *Journal of Semantics* 5 (1986), 275–291; Sally Haslanger, "Gender and Race: (What) Are They? (What) Do We Want Them to Be?" *Noûs* 34 (2000), 131–155; William Ramsey, "Prototypes and Conceptual Analysis," *Topoi* 11 (1992), 59–70. Prototype theory and objections to it are described in Eric Margolis & Stephen Lawrence, "Concepts," *Stanford Encyclopedia of Philosophy,* at http://plato.stanford.edu/entries/concepts/ (2011).

56. See especially Mark Johnston & Sarah-Jane Leslie, "Concepts, Analysis, Generics and the Canberra Plan," *Philosophical Perspectives* 26 (2012), 113–171; Sarah-Jane Leslie, "Generics: Cognition and Acquisition," *Philosophical Review* 117 (2008), 1–47; Sarah-Jane Leslie, "Generics and the Structure of the Mind," *Philosophical Perspectives* 21 (2007), 375–403. It is noteworthy that the recent scholarship has often and usefully combined philosophical analysis with experimental cognitive psychology. See, for example, Sarah-Jane Leslie, Sangeet Khemlani, & Sam Glucksberg, "All Ducks Lay Eggs: The Generic Over-generalization Effect," *Journal of Memory and Language* 65 (2011), 15–31.

57. Among the prominent defenses of conceptual analysis and the classical definition of concepts are Frank Jackson, *From Ethics to Metaphysics: A Defense of Conceptual Analysis* (Oxford: Clarendon Press, 1998), and McGinn, *Truth by Analysis*. At the opposite extreme are those who reject classical essentialism even for natural kinds and mathematical entities. See Joseph Almog, "Nature without Essence," *Journal of Philosophy* 107 (2010), 360–383.

58. Or even that we need concepts at all. See Edouard Machery, *Doing without Concepts* (New York: Oxford University Press, 2009).

59. Or, relatedly, whether there might be in a society "multiple and conflicting concepts" of the same phenomenon, including law. Bix, "Raz on Necessity," 556.

60. For a similar conclusion, albeit reached by a different route, see Brian Leiter, "The Demarcation Problem in Jurisprudence: A New Case for Skepticism," *Oxford Journal of Legal Studies* 31 (2011), 663–677. See also the anti-essentialist arguments in Brian Leiter, "Why Legal Positivism (Again)?," *at* http:ssrn.com/abstract=2323013.

61. H. L. A. Hart, "Positivism and the Separation of Law and Morals," *Harvard Law Review* 71 (1958), 593–629, *at* 606–615. The example is reprised in Hart, *The Concept of Law*, 125–127.

62. For textual support of this claim, see Frederick Schauer, "Hart's Anti-Essentialism," *in* Andrea Dolcetti, Luis Duarte d'Almeida, & James Edwards, *Reading H. L. A. Hart's* The Concept of Law (Oxford: Hart Publishing, 2013), 237–246.

63. And thus Brian Bix rightly and skeptically asks whether, even if law has essential properties and even if we can identify them by conceptual analysis, the "achievements" of such an enterprise "are substantial." Brian Bix, "Joseph Raz and Conceptual Analysis," *APA Newsletter on Philosophy of Law* 6/2 (2007), 1–7, *at* 5.

64. See Richard A. Posner, "What Do Judges Maximize? (The Same Thing Everybody Else Does)," *Supreme Court Economic Review* 3 (1993), 1–41; Frederick Schauer, "Incentives, Reputation, and the Inglorious Determinants of Judicial Behavior," *University of Cincinnati Law Review* 68 (2000), 615–636.

65. For exploration of how an entire government (and, *mutatis mutandis,* and entire legal system) could be grounded on officials acting in a "net of fear" of one another or of a single despot, see Gregory S. Kavka, *Hobbesian Moral*

and Political Theory (Princeton, NJ: Princeton University Press, 1986), 254–257. See also Matthew H. Kramer, *In Defense of Legal Positivism: Law without Trimmings* (New York: Oxford University Press, 1994), 94; Sean Coyle, "Practices and the Rule of Recognition," *Law & Philosophy* 25 (2006), 417–452, *at* 497.

66. I have not forgotten about Hitler or Stalin. But neither they nor the regimes they dominated were motivated by greed, or even greed for power, as much as by a grotesque moral vision, but a moral vision nonetheless. That may not be so for the modern and not so modern kleptocracies whose officials, especially at the top, create legal systems as part of a regime whose only goal may be the accumulation of wealth or, sometimes, power for its own sake.

67. Entire books have been written about the relationship between law and the "rule of law." This is not one of those books. Nevertheless, I subscribe to the view that the rule of law entails certain values of morality or efficiency that may not be satisfied by all legal systems. As long as the rule of law is not a redundancy, then we can imagine—and indeed observe—law without the rule of law.

68. On the intriguing possibility that law is less about the state's use of coercion than about limiting and regulating that use, see Patricia Mindus, "Austin and Scandinavian Realism," *in* Michael Freeman & Patricia Mindus, eds., *The Legacy of John Austin's Jurisprudence* (Dordrecht, Netherlands: Springer, 2013), 73–106, *at* 99–106.

69. Oliver Wendell Holmes Jr., "The Path of the Law," *Harvard Law Review* 10 (1897), 457–478, *at* 459.

70. Hart, *The Concept of Law,* 39.

71. Ibid., 78.

72. Scott J. Shapiro, *Legality* (Cambridge, MA: Harvard University Press, 2011).

73. Ibid., 69–73.

4. In Search of the Puzzled Man

1. See Chapter 3.

2. The literature on the rise of the administrative state and administrative regulation is vast. Useful contributions include Susan Rose-Ackerman & Peter L. Lindseth, eds., *Comparative Administrative Law* (Cheltenham, UK: Edward Elgar, 2010); James M. Landis, *The Administrative Process* (New Haven, CT: Yale University Press, 1938); Paul L. Joskow & Roger G. Noll, "Regulation in Theory and Practice," *in* Gary Fromm, ed., *Studies in Public Regulation* (Cambridge, MA: Harvard University Press, 1981), 1–78; Giandomenico Majone, "The Rise of the Regulatory State in Europe," *West European Politics* 17 (1994), 77–101; David H. Rosenbloom, "The Judicial Response to the Rise of the American Administrative State," *American Review of Public Administration* 15 (1981), 29–51.

3. See, for example, Julie Dickson, *Evaluation and Legal Theory* (Oxford: Hart Publishing, 2001); Joseph Raz, "The Problem about the Nature of Law," in *Ethics in the Public Domain: Essays in the Morality of Law and Politics* (Oxford: Clarendon Press, 1994), 195–209; Leslie Green, "Positivism and the Inseparability of Law and Morals," *New York University Law Review* 83 (2008), 1035–1058, *at* 1043 ("not all necessary truths are important truths").

4. See Danny Priel, "Jurisprudence and Necessity," *Canadian Journal of Law and Jurisprudence* 20 (2007), 173–200, *at* 184–186.

5. H. L. A. Hart, *The Concept of Law*, 3d ed., Penelope A. Bulloch, Joseph Raz, & Leslie Green, eds. (Oxford: Clarendon Press, 2012), 39–40.

6. See Chapter 3, especially section 3.3.

7. "Why should not law be equally if not more concerned with the 'puzzled man' or 'ignorant man' who is willing to do what is required, if only he can be told what it is?" Hart, *The Concept of Law,* 40.

8. The statement in the text is slightly too quick. Law might be causally efficacious in indicating to the uninformed or the unsure what their law-independent responsibilities are, as is argued persuasively in Donald H. Regan, "Reasons, Authority, and the Meaning of 'Obey': Further Thoughts on Raz and Obedience to Law," *Canadian Journal of Law and Jurisprudence* 3 (1990), 3–28. See also Donald H. Regan, "Authority and Value: Reflections on Raz's *Morality of Freedom*," *Southern California Law Review* 62 (1989), 995–1095; Donald H. Regan, "Law's Halo," *Social Philosophy and Policy* 4 (1986), 15–30. To much the same effect is David Enoch, "Reason-Giving and the Law," *Oxford Studies in the Philosophy of Law*, vol. 1 (Brian Leiter & Leslie Green, eds.) (2011), 1–38, noting the possibility that law's reason-giving capacity may be strictly "epistemic."

9. See, in the context of criminal law theory, Michael Plaxton, "The Challenge of the Puzzled Man," *McGill Law Journal* 58 (2012), 451–480.

10. Scott Shapiro, *Legality* (Cambridge, MA: Harvard University Press, 2011), is even more empirically and quantitatively explicit, emphasizing his assumption that there are "many" "Good Citizens" who "accept that the duties imposed by [legal] rules are separate and independent moral reasons to act" (69–70). And to the same effect is Christopher Essert, "Legal Obligation and Reasons," *Legal Theory* 19 (2013), 63–88, *at* 64–66.

11. Hart, *The Concept of Law*, 80, 91. See also ibid., 79 ("[T]he simple model of law as the sovereign's coercive orders failed to reproduce some of the salient features of a legal system"). But for the view that Hart and his successors have similarly failed to reproduce some of the salient features of a legal system, albeit different salient features, see Brian Bix, "John Austin and Constructing Theories of Law," *in* Michael Freeman & Patricia Mindus, eds., *The Legacy of John Austin's Jurisprudence* (Dordrecht, Netherlands: Springer, 2013), 1–13; and Brian Bix, Book Review, *Ethics* 122 (2012), 444–448, *at* 447.

12. "If you want to know the law and nothing else, you must look at it as a bad man, who cares only for the material consequences which such knowledge enables him to predict, not as a good one, who finds his reasons for conduct, whether inside the law or outside, in the vaguer sanctions of conscience." Oliver Wendell Holmes Jr., "The Path of the Law," *Harvard Law Review* 10 (1897), 457–478, at 459.

13. Robert H. Mnookin & Lewis Kornhauser, "Bargaining in the Shadow of the Law: The Case of Divorce," *Yale Law Journal* 88 (1979), 950–997.

14. Jeremy Bentham, *Of the Limits of the Penal Branch of Jurisprudence*, Philip Schofield, ed. (Oxford: Clarendon Press, 2010), 6, 91, 142–160.

15. See Plaxton, "The Challenge," 456–458. "[It is] quite problematic [for Hart] to claim, as a descriptive matter, that we can have legal obligations in the absence of at least a threat of sanctions. Hart produced no empirical evidence in support of such a claim" (457). And see also Stephen R. Perry, "Hart's Methodological Positivism," *Legal Theory* 4 (1998), 427–467.

16. See Plaxton, "The Challenge."

17. Hart, *The Concept of Law*, 91.

18. Although my understanding of what it is to "obey" does not rely on ordinary usage, it is nevertheless conventional. See Joseph Raz, "The Obligation to Obey: Revision and Tradition," *Notre Dame Journal of Law, Ethics & Public Policy* 1 (1984), 139–155; Regan, "Reasons, Authority, and the Meaning of 'Obey'."

19. Or, for that matter, even if I said, "Don't eat!"

20. There is an interesting question about the extent to which, if at all, law plays a role in creating moral beliefs or in informing people about moral requirements of which they might otherwise be unaware. The Scandinavian Realists, who were ethical noncognitivists and thus denied the existence of a moral reality, are important figures here because they believed the moral beliefs people held were substantially created or influenced by the commands of the law. See especially Axel Hägerström, *Inquiries into the Nature of Law and Morals*, Karl Olivecrona, ed., C. D. Broad, trans. (Stockholm: Almqvist & Wiksell, 1953); Anders Vilhelm Lundstedt, *Legal Thinking Revised: My Views on Law* (Stockholm: Almqvist & Wiksell, 1956). And for valuable analysis and commentary, see Patricia Mindus, *A Real Mind: The Life and Work of Axel Hägerström* (Dordrecht, Netherlands: Springer, 2012). The question of the causal effect of positive law on the moral beliefs of the citizenry is an empirical one, as to which there are both supporters and skeptics. A valuable review of the literature, which has a positive but qualified conclusion about the ability of law to affect moral beliefs, is Kenworthy Bilz & Janice Nadler, "Law, Psychology, and Morality," *in* Daniel Bartels et al., eds., *Moral Judgment and Decision Making* (*Psychology of Learning and Motivation*, vol. 50) (San Diego, CA: Academic Press,

2009), 101–131. Examples of greater skepticism about the causal powers of law on moral beliefs include Gerald N. Rosenberg, *The Hollow Hope: Can Courts Bring about Social Change?* (Chicago, IL: University of Chicago Press, 1991); Nigel Walker & Michael Argyle, "Does the Law Affect Moral Judgments?," *British Journal of Criminology* 4 (1964), 570–581. For present purposes I assume not only that there really are law-independent moral requirements but that positive law typically plays something other than the principal role in inculcating knowledge of and belief in those requirements.

21. The literature on the ability of people to behave morally and altruistically, even without the threat of sanctions, is vast. Useful exemplars include Daniel M. Bartels, "Principled Moral Judgment and the Flexibility of Moral Judgment and Decision Making," *Cognition* 108 (2008), 381–417; Gert Cornelissen et al., "Rules or Consequences? The Role of Ethical Mind-Sets in Moral Dynamics," *Psychological Science* 24 (2013), 482–488; Ernst Fehr & Urs Fischbacher, "The Nature of Human Altruism," *Nature* 425 (2003), 785–791; Shaun Nichols, "Norms with Feeling: Towards a Psychological Account of Moral Judgment," *Cognition* 84 (2002), 221–236; Jamil Zaki & Jason P. Mitchell, "Intuitive Prosociality," *Current Directions in Psychological Science* 22 (2013), 466–470.

22. Reza Banakar, "Can Legal Sociology Account for the Normativity of Law?," *in* Matthias Baier, , ed., *Social and Legal Norms* (Farnham, Surrey, UK: Ashgate Publishing, 2013), ch. 2.

23. Joseph Raz, *Practical Reason and Norms,* 2d ed. (Oxford: Oxford University Press, 1999).

24. The standard citation is H. L. A. Hart, "Commands and Authoritative Legal Reasons," *in* H. L. A. Hart, *Essays on Bentham: Jurisprudence and Political Theory* (Oxford: Oxford University Press, 1982), 243–268, *at* 262–266. See also Kenneth Einar Himma, "H. L. A. Hart and the Practical Difference Thesis," *Legal Theory* 6 (2000), 1–43, *at* 26–27; Frederick Schauer, "Authority and Authorities," *Virginia Law Review* 94 (2008), 1931–1961. A skeptical challenge to the idea that authority is content-independent is P. Markwick, "Independent of Content," *Legal Theory* 9 (2003), 43–61. And a different skeptical challenge, focusing on the relation between content-independence and political authority, is George Klosko, "Are Political Obligations Content Independent?," *Political Theory* 39 (2011), 498–523.

25. The *locus classicus* is W. D. Ross, *The Right and the Good* (Oxford: Clarendon Press, 1930), 19–47. Ross uses the language of "prima facie" rights and duties, but more common nowadays is to express the same idea with the term "pro tanto." See also Alan Gewirth, "Are There Any Absolute Rights?," *Philosophical Quarterly* 31 (1981), 1–16; Robert Nozick, "Moral Complications and Moral Structures," *Natural Law Forum* 13 (1968), 1–50; Frederick Schauer, "A Comment on the Structure of Rights," *Georgia Law Review* 27

(1993), 415–434; John R. Searle, "*Prima Facie* Obligations," *in* Joseph Raz, ed., *Practical Reasoning* (Oxford: Oxford University Press, 1978), 81–90; Judith Thomson, "Some Ruminations on Rights," *Arizona Law Review* 19 (1977), 45–60.

26. Letter to Congressman Hill, July 6, 1935, in *The Public Papers and Addresses of Franklin D. Roosevelt,* vol. 4 (Washington, DC: Government Printing Office, 1938), 297–298.

27. See Kenneth Einar Himma, "H. L. A. Hart and the Practical Difference Thesis," *Legal Theory* 6 (2000), 1–43; Scott J. Shapiro, "Law, Morality, and the Guidance of Conduct," *Legal Theory* 6 (2000), 127–170.

28. Socrates's arguments are recounted by Plato in the *Crito,* and the surrounding events are also set out in *Euthyphro, Apology,* and *Phaedo.* A particularly valuable analysis is Thomas C. Brickhouse & Nicholas D. Smith, *Socrates on Trial* (Princeton, NJ: Princeton University Press, 1989).

29. Thomas Hobbes, *Leviathan,* Richard Tuck, ed. (Cambridge, UK: Cambridge University Press, 1991) (1651); John Locke, *Two Treatises on Government,* Peter Laslett, ed. (Cambridge, UK: Cambridge University Press, 1988) (1690).

30. John Rawls, "Legal Obligation and the Duty of Fair Play," *in* Sidney Hook, ed., *Law and Philosophy* (New York: New York University Press, 1964), 3–18. See also Jonathan Hecht, "Fair Play—Resolving the Crito—Apology Problem," *History of Political Thought* 32 (2011), 543–564.

31. See Mark C. Murphy, "Surrender of Judgment and the Consent Theory of Political Authority," *Law and Philosophy* 16 (1997), 115–143.

32. See Eerik Lagerspetz, *The Opposite Mirrors: An Essay on the Conventionalist Theory of Institutions* (Dordrecht, Netherlands: Kluwer Academic, 1999); Chaim Gans, "The Normativity of Law and Its Co-ordinative Function," *Israel Law Review* 16 (1981), 333–349; Gerald J. Postema, "Coordination and Convention at the Foundations of Law," *Journal of Legal Studies* 11 (1982), 165–203; Noel Reynolds, "Law as Convention," *Ratio Juris* 2 (1989), 105–120.

33. See Thomas Christiano, *The Constitution of Equality: Democratic Authority and Its Limits* (New York: Oxford University Press, 2008).

34. See Joseph Raz, "The Obligation to Obey: Revision and Tradition," *Notre Dame Journal of Law, Ethics & Public Policy* 1 (1984), 139–162; M. B. E. Smith, "Is There a Prima Facie Obligation to Obey the Law?," *Yale Law Journal* 82 (1973), 950–976. Two valuable overviews are William Edmundson, "State of the Art: The Duty to Obey the Law," *Legal Theory* 10 (2004), 215–259; and George Klosko, "The Moral Obligation to Obey the Law," *in* Andrei Marmor, *The Routledge Companion to Philosophy of Law* (New York: Routledge, 2012), 511–526.

35. The leading modern work is A. John Simmons, *Moral Principles and Political Obligations* (Princeton, NJ: Princeton University Press, 1979). More or less in the same vein, but with important variations, are Leslie Green, *The Au-*

thority of the State (Oxford: Clarendon Press, 1988); Robert Paul Wolff, *In Defense of Anarchism* (Berkeley, CA: University of California Press, 1970).

36. Hart, *The Concept of Law,* 198.

5. Do People Obey the Law?

1. Tom R. Tyler, *Why People Obey the Law,* 2d ed. (Princeton, NJ: Princeton University Press, 2006).

2. H. L. A. Hart, *The Concept of Law,* 3d ed., Penelope A. Bulloch, Joseph Raz, & Leslie Green, eds. (Oxford: Oxford University Press, 2012), 39.

3. See Scott J. Shapiro, *Legality* (Cambridge, MA: Harvard University Press, 2011), 69–70, describing the "many" "Good Citizens" who comply with the law *qua* law even without the threat of punishment.

4. Tom R. Tyler, "Compliance with Intellectual Property Laws: A Psychological Perspective," *NYU Journal of International Law and Politics* 29 (1997), 213–236, *at* 224. Similarly, "the research suggests that people's behavior is *more* strongly influenced by their sense of what is morally appropriate than by their concerns over being punished for rule breaking." Tom R. Tyler, "Beyond Self-Interest: Why People Obey Laws and Accept Judicial Decisions," *The Responsive Community,* Fall (1998), 44–52, *at* 45.

5. Tyler, "Beyond Self-Interest," 45.

6. See www.psych.nyu/edu/tyler/lab.

7. Indeed, Tyler himself, more recently, acknowledges the role that law-independent cooperation may play. Tom Tyler, "The Psychology of Cooperation," *in* Eldar Shafir, ed., *The Behavioral Foundations of Public Policy* (Princeton, NJ: Princeton University Press, 2013), 77–90.

8. See, for example, C. Daniel Batson & Laura L. Shaw, "Evidence for Altruism: Toward a Pluralism of Prosocial Motives," *Psychological Inquiry* 2 (1991), 107–122; Augusto Blasi, "Moral Cognition and Moral Action: A Theoretical Perspective," *Developmental Review* 3 (1983), 178–210; Robert Hogan, "Moral Conduct and Moral Character: A Psychological Perspective," *Psychological Bulletin* 79 (1973), 217–232; John A. King et al., "Doing the Right Thing: A Common Neural Circuit for Appropriate Violent or Compassionate Behavior," *NeuroImage* 30 (2006), 1069–1076; Louis A. Penner et al., "Prosocial Behavior: Multilevel Perspectives," *Annual Review of Psychology* 56 (2005), 365–392; Jane Allyn Piliavin & Hong-Wen Charng, "Altruism: A Review of Recent Theory and Research," *American Review of Sociology* 16 (1990), 27–65; Lauren J. Wispé, "Positive Forms of Social Behavior: An Overview," *Journal of Social Issues* 28 (1972), 1–19. Other valuable contributions are collected in Walter Sinnott-Armstrong, ed., *Moral Psychology* (Cambridge, MA: MIT Press, 2008). There are continuing debates about whether seemingly altruistic behavior is at some deeper level produced by self-interest, as with the good feelings that such

behavior fosters in the altruist (see Martin L. Hoffman, "Is Empathy Altruistic?," *Psychological Inquiry* 2 (1991), 131–133), but for our purposes this debate is beside the point. Both those who see deep altruism and those who see altruism as based on deep egoism would agree on the widespread occurrence of law-independent and sanction-independent non-self-serving behavior.

9. See Roy F. Baumeister, Todd F. Heatherton, & Dianne M. Tice, *Losing Control: How and Why People Fail at Self-Regulation* (San Diego, CA: Academic Press, 1994); Roy F. Baumeister, Kathleen D. Vohs, & Dianne M. Tice, "The Strength Model of Self-Control," *Current Directions in Psychological Science* 16 (2007), 351–355.

10. See Linda J. Skitka, "The Psychology of Moral Conviction," *Social and Personality Psychology Compass* 4 (2010), 267–281.

11. In addition to Tyler's work, see Mike Hough, Jonathan Jackson, & Ben Bradford, "Legitimacy, Trust and Compliance: An Empirical Test of Procedural Justice Theory Using the European Social Survey," *at* http://ssrn.com/abstract =2234339.

12. Tyler qualifies his findings by making plain that they apply largely when the probability of punishment is low. Tyler, *Why People Obey the Law,* 22. But the qualification assumes that people's subjective probability of punishment tracks the objective probability, which may not be true. Especially when the penalties are severe, people may systematically have subjective probabilities of punishment that are higher than the objective probabilities. And to the extent that this is so, the assumption that people are not responding to the possibility of punishment when the objective probabilities are low is a potentially pervasive error.

13. Tyler, *Why People Obey the Law,* 19–68. Hough et al., "Legitimacy, Trust and Compliance," using a different data set and looking at Europe instead of the United States, reached a different conclusion, finding that legitimacy, although a statistically significant determinant of compliance with the law, is less of a determinant than are both consistency with the agent's moral beliefs and the agent's perceived risk of sanctions.

14. Tyler, *Why People Obey the Law,* 41–43, 187–190.

15. See Elizabeth Mullen & Janice Nadler, "Moral Spillovers: The Effect of Moral Violations on Deviant Behavior," *Journal of Experimental Social Psychology* 44 (2008), 1239–1245; Linda J. Skitka, Christopher W. Bayman, & Brad L. Lytle, "The Limits of Legitimacy: Moral and Religious Convictions as Constraints on Deference to Authority," *Journal of Personality and Social Psychology* 97 (2009), 567–578; Linda J. Skitka & Elizabeth Mullen, "Moral Convictions Often Override Concerns about Procedural Fairness: A Reply to Napier and Tyler," *Social Justice Research* 21 (2008), 529–546.

16. Tyler's predominant methodology is the survey rather than the experiment. Surveys are frequently valuable but may be less so when people are

asked to respond about their inclination to engage in behaviors they believe are socially valued, such as obedience to law. In such cases, professed willingness to comply may be, as discussed below, an unreliable indicator of actual compliance.

17. Tyler, *Why People Obey the Law,* Table 4.4 (46).

18. Ibid., 45–46.

19. See also Jonathan Jackson et al., "Why Do People Comply with the Law? Legitimacy and the Influence of Legal Institutions," *British Journal of Criminology* 52 (2012), 1051–1071.

20. For a similar conclusion, see Leslie Green, "Who Believes in Political Obligation?," *in* John T. Sanders & Jan Narveson, eds., *For and against the State: New Philosophical Readings* (Lanham, MD: Rowman & Littlefield, 1996), 1–17, *at* 10–14.

21. Tyler, "Beyond Self-Interest," 45.

22. See, for example, Ernest Q. Campbell, "The Internalization of Moral Norms," *Sociometry* 27 (1964), 391–412; Ernst Fehr & Urs Fischbacher, "The Nature of Human Altruism," *Nature* 425 (2003), 785–791; Ernst Fehr & Urs Fischbacher, "Social Norms and Human Cooperation," *Trends in Cognitive Sciences* 8 (2004), 185–190. A comprehensive collection of perspectives is in Walter Sinnott-Armstrong, ed., *Moral Psychology* (Cambridge, MA: MIT Press, 2007).

23. Spike Lee (producer, writer, and director), *Do the Right Thing* (Universal Pictures, 1989).

24. See Robert M. Axelrod, *The Evolution of Cooperation* (New York: Basic Books, 1984); Elinor Ostrom, "Collective Action and the Evolution of Social Norms," *Journal of Economic Perspectives* 14 (2000), 137–158. See also James Andreoni, William T. Harbaugh, & Lise Vesterlund, "The Carrot or the Stick: Rewards, Punishments, and Cooperation," *American Economic Review* 93 (2003), 893–902.

25. Fiery Cushman, Liane Young, & Marc Hauser, "The Role of Conscious Reasoning and Intuition in Moral Judgments: Testing Three Principles of Harm," *Psychological Science* 17 (2006), 1082–1089.

26. See Alan Page Fiske & Philip E. Tetlock, "Taboo Trade-offs: Reactions to Transactions that Transgress the Spheres of Justice," *Political Psychology* 18 (1997), 255–297.

27. See Karl Aquino & Americus Reed II, "The Self-Importance of Moral Identity," *Journal of Personality and Social Psychology* 83 (2002), 1423–1440.

28. For example, Campbell, "The Internalization of Moral Norms."

29. See W. D. Hamilton, "The Genetical Evolution of Social Behavior," *Journal of Theoretical Biology* 7 (1964), 1–52; Kalle Parvinen, "Joint Evolution of Altruistic Cooperation in a Metapopulation of Small Local Populations," *Theoretical Population Biology* 85 (2013), 12–19.

30. See Joshua D. Greene et al., "An fMRI Investigation of Emotional Engagement in Moral Judgment," *Science* 293 (2001), 2105–2108; Joshua D. Greene et al., "The Neural Bases of Cognitive Conflict and Control in Moral Judgment," *Neuron* 44 (2004), 389–400; Dominique J.-F. de Quervain et al., "The Neural Basis of Altruistic Punishment," *Science* 305 (2004), 1254–1258.

31. Failure to attend to this distinction bedevils much of the literature on compliance with international law, which often fails to distinguish national acts consistent with international law from national acts caused, at least in part, by international law. The point is discussed in George W. Downs, David M. Rocke, & Peter N. Barsoom, "Is the Good News about Compliance Good News about Cooperation?," *International Organization* 50 (1996), 379–406.

32. See, for example, Donald H. Regan, "Law's Halo," *in* Jules Coleman & Ellen Frankel Paul, eds., *Philosophy and Law* (Oxford: Basil Blackwell, 1987), 15–30.

33. Law is necessarily general, and by virtue of its generality will inevitably generate erroneous results on occasion. Aristotle first captured the idea and argued that equity was the necessary method of "rectification" of the mistakes occasioned by the intrinsic imprecision of general rules and general law. Aristotle, *Nicomachean Ethics,* trans. J. A. K. Thomson (Harmondsworth, UK: Penguin, 1977), ¶1137a-b. See also Aristotle, *The "Art" of Rhetoric,* trans. John Henry Freese (Cambridge, MA: Harvard University Press, 1947), ¶1374a, where Aristotle says that "equity, although just, and better than a kind of justice, is not better than absolute justice—only than the error due to generalization." For a historical, exegetical, and legal analysis of Aristotle on equity, see John Triantaphyllopoulos, "Aristotle's Equity," *in* Alfredom Mordechai Rabello, *Aequitas and Equity: Equity in Civil Law and Mixed Jurisdictions* (Jerusalem: The Hebrew University of Jerusalem, 1997), 12–22. On the problem of rule-generated error, see Frederick Schauer, *Profiles, Probabilities, and Stereotypes* (Cambridge, MA: Harvard University Press, 2003), 27–54; Frederick Schauer, *Playing by the Rules: A Philosophical Examination of Rule-Based Decision-Making in Law and in Life* (Oxford: Clarendon Press, 1991), *passim.*

34. N. J. Schweitzer et al., "The Effect of Legal Training on Judgments of Rule of Law Violations," paper presented to the American Psychology-Law Association, March 5, 2008, *at* http://www.allacademic.com/meta/p229442_index.html. To much the same effect is N. J. Schweitzer, Douglas J. Sylvester, & Michael J. Saks, "Rule Violations and the Rule of Law: A Factorial Survey of Public Attitudes," *DePaul Law Review* 56 (2007), 615–636.

35. Joshua R. Furgeson, Linda Babcock, & Peter M. Shane, "Behind the Mask of Method: Political Orientation and Constitutional Interpretive Preferences," *Law & Human Behavior* 32 (2008), 502–510; Joshua R. Furgeson, Linda Babcock, & Peter M. Shane, "Do a Law's Policy Implications Affect Beliefs about

Its Constitutionality? An Experimental Test," *Law & Human Behavior* 32 (2008), 219–227.

36. Ziva Kunda, "The Case for Motivated Reasoning," *Psychological Bulletin* 108 (1990), 489–498. A prominent legal application is Dan M. Kahan, "Foreword: Neutral Principles, Motivated Cognition, and Some Problems for Constitutional Law," *Harvard Law Review* 126 (2011), 1–77. A good discussion of motivated reasoning can also be found in Peter H. Ditto, David A. Pizarro, & David Tannenbaum, "Motivated Moral Reasoning," *Psychology of Learning and Motivation* 50 (2009), 307–338.

37. See Keith E. Stanovich & Richard F. West, "On the Failure of Intelligence to Predict Myside Bias and One-Side Bias," *Thinking & Reasoning* 14 (2008), 129–167; Keith E. Stanovich & Richard F. West, "Natural Myside Bias Is Independent of Cognitive Ability," *Thinking & Reasoning* 13 (2007), 225–247; Keith E. Stanovich, Richard F. West, & Maggie E. Toplak, "Myside Bias, Rational Thinking, and Intelligence," *Current Directions in Psychological Science* 22 (2013), 259–264.

38. See Eileen Braman, *Law, Politics, and Perception: How Policy Preferences Influence Legal Reasoning* (Charlottesville, VA: University of Virginia Press, 2009); Linda Babcock and Joshua Furgeson, "Legal Interpretations and Intuitions of Public Policy," *in* Jon Hanson, ed., *Ideology, Psychology, and Law* (New York: Oxford University Press, 2012), 684–704; Linda Babcock & Joshua Furgeson, "Experimental Research on the Psychology of Disputes," *in* Jennifer Arlen, ed., *Research Handbook on the Economics of Torts* (Cheltenham, UK: Edward Elgar, 2014), 360–82. The same phenomenon appears to exist with respect to non-legal norms. Cristina Bicchieri & Alex K. Chavez, "Norm Manipulation, Norm Evasion: Experimental Evidence," *Economics and Philosophy*, 29 (2013), 175–198.

39. Legal Realism has many dimensions, but the focus on judicial opinions and justifications as law-based rationalizations for decisions reached on nonlegal grounds is most associated with, inter alia, Jerome Frank, *Law and the Modern Mind* (New York: Brentano's, 1930); Joseph C. Hutcheson Jr., "The Judgment Intuitive: The Function of the 'Hunch' in Judicial Decision," *Cornell Law Quarterly* 14 (1929), 274–288; Herman Oliphant, "A Return to Stare Decisis," *American Bar Association Journal* 14 (1928), 71–076, 107, 159–162. This understanding of Legal Realism is shared by Brian Leiter, who analyzes it and relates it to contemporary jurisprudential debates in Brian Leiter, *Naturalizing Jurisprudence: Essays on American Legal Realism and Naturalism in Legal Philosophy* (New York: Oxford University Press, 2007). See also Frederick Schauer, *Thinking Like a Lawyer: A New Introduction to Legal Reasoning* (Cambridge, MA: Harvard University Press, 2009), 124–147; Frederick Schauer, "Editor's Introduction," *in* Karl N. Llewellyn, *The Theory of Rules,* Frederick

Schauer, ed. (Chicago, IL: University of Chicago Press, 2011), 1–28; Frederick Schauer, "Legal Realism Untamed," *Texas Law Review* 91 (2013), 749–780.

40. See Duncan Kennedy, "Freedom and Constraint in Adjudication: A Critical Phenomenology," *Journal of Legal Studies* 36 (1986), 518–562.

41. See Saul M. Kassin & Samuel R. Sommers, "Inadmissible Testimony, Instructions to Disregard, and the Jury: Substantive Versus Procedural Considerations," *Personality & Social Psychology Bulletin* 25 (1997), 1046–1054.

42. Much of the research has been conducted in the context of the use of epistemically relevant but legally inadmissible evidence. A useful overview is Nancy Steblay, Harmon N. Hosch, Scott E. Culhane, & Adam McWethy, "The Impact on Juror Verdicts of Judicial Instruction to Disregard Inadmissible Evidence," *Law & Human Behavior* 30 (2006), 469–492.

43. Associated Press Story, December 5, 1967, as published in numerous newspapers, including the *Kentucky New Era*.

44. Associated Press Story (by Joann Loviglio), August 11, 2001, as published in numerous newspapers, including the *Topeka Capital-Journal*.

45. *San Francisco Chronicle,* May 9, 2007.

46. See Hearing of the New York City Council Health Committee on a Bill to Increase the Dog Licensing Surcharge Fee, December 17, 2010, *at* www .shelterreform.org/2010DecHealthMetting.html; Report of the Manhattan Borough President, www.mbpo.org/re;ease_details.asp?id=2029 (2006).

47. See Lior Jacob Stahilevitz, "How Changes in Property Regimes Influence Social Norms: Commodifying California's Carpool Lanes," *Indiana Law Journal* 75 (2000), 1231–1294, *at* 1242, note 52.

48. When Los Angeles County, for example, attempted to operate its subway system without active enforcement of the law requiring payment of the fare, a majority of people did not pay, causing the transit authority to give up the "experiment" and install turnstiles. See "LA Subway Installs First Turnstiles," *Boston Globe,* May 4, 2013, A2. See also Ronald V. Clarke, Stephane Contre, & Gohar Petrossian, "Deterrence and Fare Evasion: Results of a Natural Experiment," *Security Journal* 23 (2010), 5–17.

49. www.pulitzercenter.org/reporting/roads-kill-worldwide-quick-facts-fatal ity-driver-automobile-accident-intoxicant-enforcement.

50. Ming-yue Kan & Maggie Lau, "Tobacco Compliance in Hong Kong," *Nicotine and Tobacco Research* 10 (2008), 337–340; Ming-yue Kan & Maggie Lau, "Minor Access Control in Hong Kong under the Framework Convention on Tobacco Control," *Health Policy* 95 (2010), 204–210.

51. Adam Nagourney & Rick Lyman, "Few Problems with Cannabis for California," *New York Times,* October 27, 2013, 1.

52. The misleading nature of the word "voluntary" in the tax context is noted in Leandra Lederman, "Tax Compliance and the Reformed IRS," *Kansas Law Review* 51 (2003), 971–1011.

53. Much of what follows comes from Internal Revenue Service Release IR-2012-4 (January 6, 2012) ("IRS Releases New Tax Gap Estimates"); Internal Revenue Service Report GAO/T-66D-97-35 (1997) ("Taxpayer Compliance: Analyzing the Nature of the Income Tax Gap"); Maurice Allingham & Agnar Sandmo, "Income Tax Evasion: A Theoretical Analysis," *Journal of Public Economics* 1 (1972), 323–338; Internal Revenue Service, "Reducing the Federal Tax Gap: A Report on Improving Voluntary Compliance" (2007); James Andreoni, Brian Erard, & Jonathan Feinstein, "Tax Compliance," *Journal of Economic Literature* 36 (1998), 818–860; Charles Clotfelter, "Tax Evasion and Tax Rates: An Analysis of Individual Returns," *Review of Economics and Statistics* 65 (1983), 363–373; Lederman, "Tax Compliance."

54. See James Alm, "Tax Compliance and Administration," in *Handbook on Taxation* (New York: Marcel Dekker, 1999); John L. Mikesell & Liucija Birksyte, "The Tax Compliance Puzzle: Evidence from Theory and Practice," *International Journal of Public Administration* 30 (2007), 1045–1081.

55. Stanley Milgram, *Obedience to Authority: An Experimental View* (New York: Harper & Row, 1974); Stanley Milgram, "Some Conditions of Obedience and Disobedience to Authority," *Human Relations* 18 (1965), 57–76; Stanley Milgram, "Behavioral Study of Obedience," *Journal of Abnormal and Social Psychology* 67 (1963), 371–378. The notoriety is based partly on the substance of the studies, partly on the implications of the studies for understanding the Holocaust, and partly on the trauma imposed on the subjects, the last explaining why it is hard to imagine the experiments being approved today by an institutional review board. Indeed, the Milgram experiments were at least part of the reason for the creation of institutional review boards themselves.

56. For discussion, see, for example, Neil Lutsky, "When Is 'Obedience' Obedience? Conceptual and Historical Commentary," *Journal of Social Issues* 51 (1995), 55–65; David R. Mandel, "The Obedience Alibi: Milgram's Account of the Holocaust Reconsidered," *Analyse & Kritik* 20 (1998), 74–94. See also Herbert C. Kelman & V. Lee Hamilton, *Crimes of Obedience: Toward a Social Psychology of Authority and Responsibility* (New Haven, CT: Yale University Press, 1989).

57. When understood as a claim of authority and not the actual existence of justified authority, the description in the text captures some of the highly influential work of Joseph Raz. See, for example, Joseph Raz, *Ethics in the Public Domain: Essays in the Morality of Law and Politics* (Oxford: Clarendon Press, 1994), 325–338; Joseph Raz, *The Morality of Freedom* (Oxford: Clarendon Press, 1988); Joseph Raz, *The Authority of Law: Essays on Law and Morality* (Oxford: Clarendon Press, 1979), 233–249.

58. The commentary is voluminous. See Arthur G. Miller, *The Obedience Experiments: A Case Study of Controversy in Social Science* (New York: Praeger, 1986); Thomas Blass, *The Man Who Shocked the World: The Life and Legacy*

of Stanley Milgram (New York: Basic Books, 2004); Thomas Blass, "Understanding Behavior in the Milgram Obedience Experiment," *Journal of Personality and Social Psychology* 60 (1991), 398–413; Jerry Burger, "Replicating Milgram: Would People Still Obey Today?," *American Psychologist* 64 (2009), 1–11; Steven J. Gilbert, "Another Look at the Milgram Obedience Studies: The Role of the Gradated Series of Shocks," *Personality and Social Psychology Bulletin* 7 (1981), 690–695; Moti Nassani, "A Cognitive Reinterpretation of Stanley Milgram's Observations on Obedience to Authority," *American Psychologist* 45 (1990), 1384–1385; Stephen D. Reicher, S. Alexander Haslam, & Joanne R. Smith, "Working toward the Experimenter: Reconceptualizing Obedience within the Milgram Paradigm as Identification-Based Followership," *Perspectives on Psychological Science* 7 (2012), 315–324; Philip G. Zimbardo, "On 'Obedience to Authority,' " *American Psychologist* 239 (1974), 566–567.

59. See especially Reicher et al., "Working toward the Experimenter."

60. Much of the research is summarized in Robert B. Cialdini & Noah J. Goldstein, "Social Influence: Compliance and Conformity," *Annual Review of Psychology* 55 (2004), 591–621. As this article exemplifies, however, the tilt of much of the research, perhaps still influenced by the Milgram experiments and the belief that the Holocaust was more the product of excess obedience than of willing conformity, has been on excess rather than insufficient obedience. This is curious, for it is hardly clear that the harms from excess obedience, in the aggregate, are greater than those of insufficient obedience. Plainly this conclusion will vary with context, but, still, it appears to be a background and largely acontextual assumption in much of the research that excess obedience is a greater problem than insufficient obedience.

61. Ronald Dworkin, *Justice in Robes* (Cambridge, MA: Belknap/Harvard University Press, 2008); Ronald Dworkin, *Law's Empire* (Cambridge, MA: Harvard University Press, 1986); Ronald Dworkin, *Taking Rights Seriously* (Cambridge, MA: Harvard University Press, 1977).

62. Ruth Gavison, "Legal Theory and the Role of Rules," *Harvard Journal of Law & Public Policy* 14 (1991), 727–770, at 740–741. Similar language is in Ruth Gavison, "Comment," *in* Ruth Gavison, ed., *Issues in Contemporary Legal Philosophy: The Influence of H. L. A. Hart* (Oxford: Clarendon Press, 1987), 21–32, at 29–32.

63. See N. W. Barber, "Legal Realism, Pluralism and Their Challengers," *in* Ulla Neergaard & Ruth Nielsen, eds., *European Legal Method—Towards a New European Legal Realism* (Copenhagen: DJOEF Publishing, forthcoming 2013).

64. See Frederick Schauer, "Official Obedience and the Politics of Defining 'Law,' " *Southern California Law Review* 86 (forthcoming 2013).

65. For references, see above, Chapter Four, note 13.

66. See Kenworthey Bilz & Janice Nadler, "Law, Psychology, and Morality," *in* Daniel Bartels et al., eds., *Moral Judgment and Decision Making (Psychology*

of Learning and Motivation, Volume 50) (San Diego, CA: Academic Press, 2009), 101–131.

67. Nigel Walker & Michael Argyle, "Does the Law Affect Moral Judgements?," *British Journal of Criminology* 4 (1964), 570–581.

68. Leonard Berkowitz & Nigel Walker, "Laws and Moral Judgments," *Sociometry* 30 (1967), 410–422. For the critique, see Bilz & Nadler, "Law, Psychology, and Morality."

69. See Michael Klarman, *From the Closet to the Altar: Courts, Backlash, and the Struggle for Same-Sex Marriage* (New York: Oxford University Press, 2012); Marieka M. Klawitter & Victor Flatt, "The Effects of State and Local Antidiscrimination Policies on Earnings by Gays and Lesbians," *Journal of Policy Analysis and Management* 17 (1998), 658–686.

70. 347 U.S. 483 (1954).

71. Gerald N. Rosenberg, *The Hollow Hope: The Courts and Social Change* (Chicago, IL: University of Chicago Press, 1991).

72. William K. Muir Jr., *Law and Attitude Change: Prayer in the Public Schools* (Chicago, IL: University of Chicago Press, 1973).

73. V. Lee Hamilton & Joseph Sanders, "Crimes of Obedience and Conformity in the Workplace: Surveys of Americans, Russians, and Japanese," *Journal of Social Issues* 51 (1995), 67–88.

74. See Hearing of the New York City Council Health Committee.

75. See Raymond Fisman & Edward Miguel, "Corruption, Norms, and Legal Enforcement: Evidence from Diplomatic Parking Tickets," *Journal of Political Economy* 115 (2007), 1020–1048.

6. Are Officials above the Law?

1. The best-known modern version of the story is found in Stephen W. Hawking, *A Brief History of Time: From the Big Bang to Black Holes* (New York: Bantam Books, 1988), 1. Justice Antonin Scalia of the U.S. Supreme Court uses a different version in *Rapanos v. United States,* 547 U.S, 715, 754 (2006).

2. Indeed, this much is conceded even by those for whom sanctions are part of neither the concept of law nor of legal obligation. See Joseph Raz, *Between Authority and Interpretation: On the Theory of Law and Practical Reason* (Oxford: Oxford University Press, 2009), 158–159; Joseph Raz, *The Concept of a Legal System: An Introduction to the Theory of Legal System,* 2d. ed. (Oxford: Clarendon Press, 1980), 150–151, 185–186.

3. H. L. A. Hart, *The Concept of Law,* 3d ed., Penelope A. Bulloch, Joseph Raz, & Leslie Green, eds. (Oxford: Oxford University Press, 2012), 26–44. And, earlier, see James Bryce, *Studies in History and Jurisprudence* (Oxford: Oxford University Press, 1901), 538; Albert Venn Dicey, *Introduction to the Study of the Law of the Constitution* (London: Macmillan, 1915) (1885), 26–27.

4. And thus, Austin created the picture of a sovereign to whom the subjects gave habitual obedience but who gave habitual obedience to no one. John Austin, *The Province of Jurisprudence Determined,* Wilfred E. Rumble, ed. (Cambridge, UK: Cambridge University Press, 1986), Lecture VI.

5. "In Hobbes's political theory, the power of the sovereign has no legal limits." Perez Zagorin, "Hobbes as a Theorist of Natural Law," *Intellectual History Review* 17 (2007), 239–255, *at* 253.

6. Judges might, for example, be promoted to higher courts based, in part, on the frequency with which their judgments are upheld on appeal. Or they may discover that their assignments and other working conditions were dependent on pleasing their superiors. Those superiors might base their evaluative judgments on the extent of legal compliance, or instead on other and nonlegal criteria, but for present purposes, the point is only that even judges often operate in a hierarchical environment in which rewards and punishments are not irrelevant. For an example of this phenomenon in the context of Japan, see J. Mark Ramseyer & Eric B. Rasmussen, "Why Are Japanese Judges So Conservative in Politically Charged Cases," *American Political Science Review* 95 (2001), 331–344.

7. Indeed, the problem of the infinite regress—the turtle problem—pervades the questions about the foundations of mathematics and language, among others, with Gödel and Wittgenstein being two of the thinkers who have spawned many of the debates. See Ludwig Wittgenstein, *Philosophical Investigations,* G. E. M. trans., 3d ed. (New York: Macmillan, 1958); Ludwig Wittgenstein, *Remarks on the Foundations of Mathematics,* G. H. von Wright, R. Rhees, & G. E. M. Anscombe, eds., rev. ed. (Cambridge, MA: MIT Press, 1978); Jean van Heijenoort, ed., *From Frege to Gödel: A Source Book on Mathematical Logic, 1879–1931* (Cambridge, MA: Harvard University Press, 1967) (containing a translation of Gödel's paper, along with commentary). See also G. P. Baker & P. M. S. Hacker, *Skepticism, Rules, and Language* (Oxford: Blackwell, 1986); Saul Kripke, *Wittgenstein on Rules and Private Language* (Cambridge, MA: Harvard University Press, 1982); Colin McGinn, *Wittgenstein on Meaning: An Interpretation and Evaluation* (Oxford: Blackwell, 1984).

8. See Peter Suber, *The Paradox of Self-Amendment: A Study of Law, Logic, Omnipotence, and Change* (New York: Pater Lang Publishing, 1990).

9. Hart, *The Concept of Law,* 94–110.

10. "One violates a *legal* norm by going faster than 65 mph on most highways, while one violates a norm of *etiquette* by talking with one's mouth full at the table." Brian Leiter, "Positivism, Formalism, Realism," *Columbia Law Review* 99 (1999), 1138–1164, *at* 1141.

11. 29 C.F.R. 1910.96 (2012).

12. 5 U.S.C. §§701–706 (2010).

13. Occupational Safety and Health Act of 1970, Pub. L. No. 91–596, 84 Stat. 1590 (1970), *codified as amended,* 29 U.S.C. §§651–678 (2010).

14. Various aspects of this phenomenon are explored in Matthew Adler & Kenneth Einar Himma, eds., *The Rule of Recognition and the U.S. Constitution* (New York: Oxford University Press, 2009).

15. Note that it is a mistake, albeit a common one, to understand the Constitution, which might be the master operative rule within the legal system, as the ultimate rule of recognition. The ultimate rule of recognition is not the Constitution but, rather, that which makes the Constitution the master operative rule in the first place.

16. This example is developed at (perhaps excess) length in Frederick Schauer, "Amending the Presuppositions of a Constitution," *in* Sanford Levinson, ed., *Responding to Imperfection: The Theory and Practice of Constitutional Amendment* (Princeton, NJ: Princeton University Press, 1995), 145–161.

17. Hart maintained that acceptance by officials, and especially by judges (see Hanoch Sheinman, "The Priority of Courts in the General Theory of Law," *American Journal of Jurisprudence* 52 (2007), 229–258, *at* 237–238), was the key to the existence of a legal system. Hart, *The Concept of Law,* 112–117. Hart has been challenged on this score, however, especially by those who argue that acceptance by some segment of the population at large is either necessary or sufficient for a legal system to exist. See, for example, F. Patrick Hubbard, "Power to the People: The Takings Clause, Hart's Rule of Recognition, and Populist Law-Making," *University of Louisville Law Review* 50 (2011), 87–130, *at* 92–95; Jeremy Waldron, "Can There Be a Democratic Jurisprudence?," *Emory Law Journal* 58 (2009), 675–712, *at* 694–697. But we might (and will below) also ask whether the army has a role to play, as the ultimate existence of a legal system may depend on acceptance by the ultimate source of power in a society.

18. There are important connections between Hart's account and the hierarchy-of-norms picture of law famously offered by Hans Kelsen. Hans Kelsen, *Introduction to the Problems of Legal Theory: A Translation of the First Edition of Reine Rechtslehre or Pure Theory of Law,* Bonnie Litschewski Paulson & Stanley L. Paulson, trans. (Oxford: Clarendon Press, 1992); Hans Kelsen, *The Pure Theory of Law,* Max Knight, trans. (Berkeley, CA: University of California Press, 1967); Hans Kelsen, *General Theory of Law and State,* Anders Wedberg, trans. (Cambridge, MA: Harvard University Press, 1945). But whereas for Kelsen the comprehension of the legal structure rested on the presupposition (or transcendental understanding, in the Kantian sense) he called the *Grundnorm* ("basic norm"), Hart's ultimate rule of recognition was not a mental construct of the theorist but instead a foundational fact about the actual existence of legal systems.

19. A fact that was brought home by the way in which courts confronting the issue actually used the Kelsenian term *Grundnorm.* The controversy inspired important and jurisprudentially informed commentary. See F. M. Brookfield, "The Courts, Kelsen, and the Rhodesian Revolution," *University of Toronto*

Law Journal 19 (1969), 326–352; J. M. Eekelaar, "Rhodesia: The Abdication of Constitutionalism," *Modern Law Review* 32 (1969), 115–118; J. M. Eekelaar, "Principles of Revolutionary Legality," *in* A. W. B. Simpson, ed., *Oxford Essays in Jurisprudence (Second Series)* (Oxford: Oxford University Press, 1973), 22–43; J. M. Eekelaar, "Splitting the Grundnorm," *Modern Law Review* 30 (1967), 156–175; J. M. Finnis, "Revolutions and Continuity of Law," *in* Simpson, *Oxford Essays in Jurisprudence*, 44–76; J. W. Harris, "When and Why Does the *Grundnorm* Change?," *Cambridge Law Journal* 29 (1971), 103–133; A. M. Honoré, "Reflections on Revolution," *Irish Jurist*, vol. 2 (1967), 268–278; T. C. Hopton, "Grundnorm and Constitution: The Legitimacy of Politics," *McGill Law Journal* 24 (1978), 72–91.

20. On Kelsen, see note 18.

21. Thomas C. Schelling, *The Strategy of Conflict* (Cambridge, MA: Harvard University Press, 1960).

22. Elinor Ostrom, *Governing the Commons: The Evolution of Institutions for Collective Action* (Cambridge, UK: Cambridge University Press, 1990).

23. Robert C. Ellickson, *Order without Law: How Neighbors Settle Disputes* (Cambridge, MA: Harvard University Press, 1994).

24. Robert Axelrod, *The Evolution of Cooperation,* revised edition (New York: Basic Books, 2006).

25. David Lewis, *Convention: A Philosophical Study* (Cambridge, MA: Harvard University Press, 1969).

26. Edna Ullman-Margalit, *The Emergence of Norms* (Oxford: Clarendon Press, 1977).

27. Thomas Hobbes, *Leviathan,* Richard Tuck, ed. (Cambridge, UK: Cambridge University Press, 1991) (1651).

28. See Gillian K. Hadfield & Barry R. Weingast, "What Is Law? A Coordination Model of the Characteristics of Legal Order," *Journal of Legal Analysis* (2012), 471–514. For a case study of the operation of the process, see Avner Greif, *Institutions and the Path to the Modern Economy: Lessons from Medieval Trade* (New York: Cambridge University Press, 2006); Avner Greif, Paul Milgrom, & Barry R. Weingast, "Coordination, Commitment, and Enforcement: The Case of the Merchant Guild," *Journal of Political Economy* 102 (1994), 745–776.

29. Ronald Dworkin, *Law's Empire* (Cambridge, MA: Harvard University Press, 1986), 35. Whether Dworkin was factually correct implicates the acrimonious debate over the existence and extent of the fear-independent proclivities and sympathies of those below the pinnacle of the Nazi hierarchy. Compare Daniel Jonah Goldhagen, *Hitler's Willing Executioners: Ordinary Germans and the Holocaust* (New York: Vintage Books, 1996), with Norman G. Finkelstein & Ruth Bettina Birn, *A Nation on Trial: The Goldhagen Thesis and Historical Truth* (New York: Henry Holt & Co., 1998). In other words, the question is whether, as Dworkin contends, most Nazi officials behaved as they did for rea-

sons of fear of those above them in the Nazi hierarchy, or whether, as Goldhagen and others maintain, these officials are more accurately seen as willing participants than as frightened underlings. But whether the example is a good or bad one, it does highlight at least the possibility of a legal system resting on the fear-inducing and thus coercive capacities of one or a very small number of people at the top.

30. This might include a belief on the part of the population that the despot had a special call on the punitive powers of a deity. If you believe that the king is king because of divine right, and if you also believe that God has the power to condemn you to eternal hellfire for disobeying God's agent on earth, then it is straightforward to conceptualize the foundation of the king's legal system as resting on the threat of sanctions.

31. Hart, *The Concept of Law*, 95.

32. Ibid., 98.

33. See Joel Parker, *Lectures Delivered in the Law School of Harvard College* (New York: Hurd & Houghton, 1869), 66–71; Joseph E. Fallon. "Power, Legitimacy, and the Fourteenth Amendment," *Chronicles Magazine*, March (2002), 42–43.

34. See Bruce Ackerman, *We the People. Volume 2: Transformations* (Cambridge, MA: Harvard University Press, 2000).

35. Thus, the Supreme Court observed that "fundamental issues over the extent of federal supremacy [under the Constitution have] been resolved by war." *Testa v. Katt*, 330 U.S. 386, 390 (1947).

36. See Arthur Ripstein, "Self-Certification and the Moral Aims of the Law," *Canadian Journal of Law and Jurisprudence* 25 (2012), 201–217.

37. Hobbes, *Leviathan*, ch. 15.

38. See Jason Briggeman, "Governance as a Strategy in State-of-Nature Games," *Public Choice*, vol. 141 (2009), 481–491.

39. See Hart, *The Concept of Law*, 50–78.

40. A valuable analytic overview of the American regime, which can and often does subject police officers and other relatively low-level officials to civil liability for knowingly unconstitutional acts, is John C. Jeffries Jr., "The Liability Rule for Constitutional Torts," *Virginia Law Review* 99 (2013), 207–270.

41. This may or may not operate as a sanction, as discussed in Chapter 3.

42. That the judges of so-called apex courts are subject to no legal sanctions for erroneous decisions does not entail that their conclusions are uninfluenced by incentives. Good judges may indeed desire to do nothing other than what the law requires, but real judges operate in a world in which their decisions shape their external reputations and the esteem in which they are held by judicial colleagues, lawyers, the press, the public, and history. The degree of influence of such factors will plainly vary from judge to judge, but it seems folly to assume

that for all or even most judges such considerations are entirely irrelevant. See Richard A. Posner, "What Do Judges Maximize? (The Same Thing Everybody Else Does)," *Supreme Court Economic Review* 3 (1993), 1–41; Frederick Schauer, "Incentives, Reputation, and the Inglorious Determinants of Judicial Behavior," *University of Cincinnati Law Review* 68 (2000), 615–636.

43. Ibid.

44. See Jeffries, "The Liability Rule." See also Sheldon H. Nahmod, *Civil Rights and Civil Liberties Litigation: The Law of Section 1983,* 4th ed. (St. Paul, MN: West Group, 2008).

45. See Frederick Schauer, "The Political Risks (If Any) of Breaking the Law," *Journal of Legal Analysis* 4 (2012), 83–101.

46. A good overview of various different accounts and components of the Rule of Law is Richard H. Fallon Jr., " 'The Rule of Law' as a Concept in Constitutional Discourse," *Columbia Law Review* 97 (197), 1–56.

47. See Ronald A. Cass, *The Rule of Law in America* (Baltimore, MD: John Hopkins University Press, 2003), 34–45; Joseph Raz, *The Authority of Law: Essays on Law and Morality* (Oxford: Clarendon Press, 1979), 212; Geoffrey de Q. Walker, *The Rule of Law: Foundation of Constitutional Democracy* (Melbourne, Australia: Melbourne University Press, 1988), 31–32.

48. Pub. L. No. 93–148, 87 Stat. 55 (1973), codified at 50 U.S.C. §§1541–1548 (2010). The Resolution was first enacted as a response to the congressionally unauthorized incursion into Cambodia during the presidency of Richard Nixon. For one view of the history, see Thomas F. Eagleton, *War and Presidential Power: A Chronicle of Congressional Surrender* (New York: Liveright, 1974).

49. See Harold Hongju Koh (Legal Advisor, U.S. Department of State), "Statement Regarding the Use of Force in Libya," March 26, 2011, *at* http://www.state.gov/s/releases/remarks/159201.htm.

50. See, for example, Trevor W. Morrison, " 'Hostilities,' " *Journal of Law* 1 (Public Law Miscellaneous) (2011), 233–236; Trevor W. Morrison, "Libya, 'Hostilities,' the Office of Legal Counsel, and the Process of Executive Branch Interpretation," *Harvard Law Review Forum* 124 (2011), 62–74. See also Louis Fisher, "Military Operations in Libya—No War? No Hostilities?," *Presidential Studies Quarterly* 42 (2012), 176–189; Robert J. Spitzer, "Comparing the Constitutional Presidencies of George W. Bush and Barack Obama: War Powers, Signing Statements, Vetoes," *White House Studies* 12 (2013), 125–146.

51. See Jennifer Medina, "Charges Dropped against Mayor Who Performed Gay Weddings," *New York Times,* July 13, 2005, B5; Dean E. Murphy, "California Supreme Court Considers Gay Marriage Licenses," *New York Times,* May 26, 2004, A14.

52. 18 U.S.C. §1385 (2010).

53. See Interview with Ray Nagin, mayor of New Orleans, in *When the Levees Broke: A Requiem in Four Acts* (HBO Documentary Films, 2006).

54. For other examples, see Frederick Schauer, "When and How (If at All) Does Law Constrain Official Action?," *Georgia Law Review* 44 (2010), 769–801; Frederick Schauer, "Ambivalence about the Law," *Arizona Law Review* 49 (2007), 11–28.

55. See Schauer, "The Political Risks."

56. David Hume, *The History of England, from the Invasion of Julius Caesar to the Revolution of 1688,* vol. 6 (Indianapolis, IN: Liberty Fund, 1983) (1778), 482. I am grateful to Jon Elster for the reference.

57. See Eric A. Posner & Adrian Vermeule, *The Executive Unbound: After the Madisonian Republic* (New York: Oxford University Press, 2010), 15; Frederick Schauer, "The Political Risks."

58. See P. S. Atiyah & R. S. Summers, *Form and Substance in Anglo-American Law: A Comparative Study in Legal Reasoning, Legal Theory and Legal Institutions* (Oxford: Clarendon Press, 1987), maintaining that American legal culture is less formal and thus less concerned with law *qua* law when law conflicts with substance than is the legal culture in the United Kingdom.

7. Coercing Obedience

1. See especially Scott J. Shapiro, *Legality* (Cambridge, MA: Harvard University Press, 2011), 169–170, and Shapiro's engaging analysis of a fictional Cooking Club, which then transforms itself into an even more fictional Cooks Island. See also Joseph Raz, *Practical Reason and Norms,* 2d ed. (Oxford: Oxford University Press, 1999), 159–160; Hans Oberdiek, "The Role of Sanctions and Coercion in Understanding Law and Legal Systems," *American Journal of Jurisprudence* 21 (1976), 71–94, at 73.

2. Thus, even Shapiro, who is among the most prominent proponents of the view that coercion is not essential for law, and who maintains that coercion's nonessentiality is jurisprudentially important, acknowledges in Hobbesian language that "[i]t is indeed likely that life would be poor, nasty, brutish, and short without legal systems maintaining order through threats of coercion." Shapiro, *Legality,* 175. And so too for Joseph Raz. See Joseph Raz, *Between Authority and Interpretation: On the Theory of Law and Practical Reason* (Oxford: Oxford University Press, 2009), 158–159; Joseph Raz, *The Concept of a Legal System: An Introduction to the Theory of Legal System,* 2d ed. (Oxford: Clarendon Press, 1980), 150–151, 185–186.

3. H. L. A. Hart, *The Concept of Law,* 3d ed., Penelope A. Bulloch, Joseph Raz, & Leslie Green, eds. (Oxford: Oxford University Press, 2012), 199. See also Kenneth Einar Himma, "Law's Claim of Legitimate Authority," *in* Jules Coleman, ed., *Hart's Postscript: Essays on the Postscript to "The Concept of Law"* (Oxford: Oxford University Press, 2001), 271–309, *at* 307–309.

4. Raz, *Practical Reason and Norms,* 159–160.

5. Lest there be any doubt about the nature of Austin's claims about the status of coercion, the claims against which Hart and his predecessors are arguing, it is worth emphasizing that Austin's sanction-dependent command theory of law was in pursuit of "the essence or nature which is common to all laws that are laws properly so called." John Austin, *The Province of Jurisprudence Determined*, Wilfrid E. Rumble, ed. (Cambridge, UK: Cambridge University Press, 1995) (1832), 12.

6. See Frederick Schauer, "Hart's Anti-Essentialism," *in* Andrea Dolcetti, Luis Duarte d'Almeida, & James Edwards, eds., *Reading H. L. A. Hart's "The Concept of Law"* (Oxford: Hart Publishing, forthcoming 2013).

7. The "puzzled man" is introduced by Hart, *The Concept of Law,* 40. And Hart later comments on the "number and strength" of those who would engage in "mutual forbearance" of self-interest in favor of compliance with the law (197–198).

8. Indeed, even some theorists who believe that coercion is jurisprudentially important suppose that uncoerced obedience to law just because it is law is widespread. Note the "some" in the following: "Most of us, at one time or another, have complied with a law due to the risk of being caught and penalized. And some more recalcitrant people, we suspect, would persistently ignore their legal duties were it not for the spur of enforcement." Grant Lamond, "The Coerciveness of Law," *Oxford Journal of Legal Studies* 20 (2000), 39–62.

9. See Hart, *The Concept of Law,* 79–99.

10. Ibid., 79, 96–97.

11. This is the characterization offered, without endorsement, in Mark Greenberg, "The Standard Picture and Its Discontents," *Oxford Studies in the Philosophy of Law,* vol. 1, Leslie Green & Brian Leiter, eds. (2011), 39–106, *at* 91. The Razian texts that Greenberg accurately summarizes include Joseph Raz, *The Morality of Freedom* (Oxford: Oxford University Press, 1986); Joseph Raz, *Practical Reason and Norms,* 2d ed. (Oxford: Oxford University Press, 1999); Joseph Raz, *The Authority of Law: Essays on Law and Morality* (Oxford: Clarendon Press, 1979).

12. Scott Shapiro, *Legality* (Cambridge, MA: Harvard University Press, 2011), 391–392.

13. Although their leaders sometimes justify their power in the name of the moral goals of anticolonialism.

14. A good analysis of the view that law necessarily claims (but does not necessarily have) legitimate authority is in Brian Bix, "Robert Alexy, Radbruch's Formula, and the Nature of Legal Theory," *Rechtstheorie* 37 (2006), 139–149, *at* 146–148.

15. Greenberg ("The Standard Picture," 103) would argue that such systems represent defective law, and he would not resist his position being distinguished from that of Bentham, Austin, and some branches of the subsequent positivist tradition. But then the issue is joined about what it is that an account of law is

designed to accomplish. If, following Bentham and Austin, a theoretical account of law is designed to be descriptive with as few traces of moral evaluation as possible, then it needs to be able to describe and explain *as law* the systems noted in the text, something that an account requiring a system to claim legitimate authority seems unable to do.

16. To repeat, the word "bad," first used by Holmes in this context and then employed by Hart with Holmes as his foil, should be understood in a technical and nonpejorative way. The "bad" person is someone whose initial decisions about what to do are uninfluenced by the law but may well be influenced by morality. The bad person then obeys the law only because of the threat of sanctions, even though she may well have based her initial decision on sanction-independent moral values and motivations.

17. Tom R. Tyler, *Why People Obey the Law,* 2d ed. (Princeton, NJ: Princeton University Press, 2006), discussed above, Chapter 5.

18. *The Federalist,* No. 10 (1787–1788).

19. See Chapter 4. See also Elliot Sober & David Sloan Wilson, *Unto Others: The Evolution and Psychology of Unselfish Behavior* (Cambridge, MA: Harvard University Press, 1998); Karl Aquino & Americus I. Reed, "The Self-Importance of Moral Identity," *Journal of Personality and Social Psychology* 83 (2002), 1423–1440; Daniel M. Bartels, "Principled Moral Sentiment and the Flexibility of Moral Judgment and Decision Making," *Cognition* 108 (2008), 381–417; Daniel M. Bartels & Douglas L. Medin, "Are Morally Motivated Decision Makers Insensitive to the Consequences of Their Choices?," *Psychological Science* 18 (2007), 24–28; Ernest Q. Campbell, "The Internalization of Moral Norms," *Sociometry* 27 (1964), 391–412; John Darley, "Research on Morality: Possible Approaches, Actual Approaches," *Psychological Science* 4 (1993), 353–357; Ernst Fehr & Urs Fischbacher, "Social Norms and Human Cooperation," *Trends in Cognitive Sciences* 8 (2004), 185–190; Jonathan Haidt, "The Emotional Dog and Its Rational Tail: A Social Intuitionist Approach to Moral Judgment," *Psychological Review* 108 (2001), 814–834; Dennis L. Krebs, "Morality: An Evolutionary Account," *Perspectives on Psychological Science* 3 (2008), 149–172.

20. Christopher W. Morris, "State Coercion and Force," *Social Philosophy and Policy* 29 (2012), 28–49.

21. Note that rejecting an essentialist view of the nature of law is not a necessary condition for appreciating the importance of law's typical but not conceptually necessary properties. One can believe that our concept of law does have necessary or essential properties but that law's nonessential but empirically pervasive properties both characterize the experience of legality as we know it and are worthy of philosophical examination.

22. The rule actually prohibits bringing such items into the examination room, but the impetus behind the rule is the antecedent if puzzling desire of

Oxford undergraduates to throw food at one another upon completing their examinations.

23. To the same effect, an article in the April 2010 issue of *Sport Diver* magazine was entitled "Don't Pet the Sharks." Frankly, and even though I engage in scuba diving myself, it had never occurred to me to do so. But the title of the article informs me that perhaps I am unusual.

24. "No Soldier shall, in time of peace be quartered in any house, without the consent of the Owner, nor in time of war, but in a manner to be prescribed by law."

25. Such laws rarely mention cannibalism as such but typically couch their prohibitions in terms of desecration of dead bodies.

26. John Searle, *Speech Acts: An Essay in the Philosophy of Language* (Cambridge, UK: Cambridge University Press, 1969). See also Herman Tennessen, "What Is Remarkable in Psychology," *in* Joseph R. Royce & Leendert Mos, eds., *Annals of Theoretical Psychology,* vol. 2 (1984), 273–278.

27. The originator of the term is the philosopher Paul Grice, a major figure in the theory of speech acts. H. P. Grice, *Studies in the Way of Words* (Cambridge, MA: Harvard University Press, 1989), 269–282.

28. Larry Alexander & Emily Sherwin, *The Rule of Rules: Morality, Rules, and the Dilemmas of Law* (Durham, NC: Duke University Press, 2001). And here I also draw to some extent on earlier writing coauthored with Larry Alexander, although he is in no way responsible for my current understanding of the issue or the way in which it is presented here. See Larry Alexander & Frederick Schauer, "Law's Limited Domain Meets Morality's Unlimited Empire," *William and Mary Law Review* 48 (2007), 1579–1603; Larry Alexander & Frederick Schauer, "Defending Judicial Supremacy: A Reply," *Constitutional Commentary* 17 (2001), 455–482; Larry Alexander & Frederick Schauer, "On Extrajudicial Constitutional Interpretation," *Harvard Law Review* 110 (1997), 1359–1387.

29. The idea of a focal point for coordination is so commonly (and properly) attributed to Thomas Schelling (especially Thomas Schelling, *The Strategy of Conflict* (Cambridge, MA: Harvard University Press, 2006)) that such focal points are often called "Schelling points." See generally Ken Binmore & Larry Samuelson, "The Evolution of Focal Points," *Games & Economic Behavior* 55 (2006), 21–42.

30. See David M. DeJoy, "The Optimism Bias and Traffic Accident Risk Perception," *Accident Analysis and Risk Prevention* 21 (1989), 333–340; Ola Svenson, Baruch Fischhoff, & Donald MacGregor, "Perceived Driving Safety and Seatbelt Usage," *Accident Analysis and Risk Prevention* 17 (1985), 119–133. See, more generally, Mark D. Alicke & Olesya Govorun, "The Better-Than-Average Effect," *in* Mark D. Alicke, David A. Dunning, & Joachim Krueger, eds., *The Self in Social Judgment* (New York: Psychology Press, 2005), 85–107.

31. See Robert Burton, *On Being Certain: Believing You Are Right Even When You're Not* (New York: St. Martin's Press, 2008).

32. The literature is vast, and many of the most important articles are collected in Daniel Kahneman & Amos Tversky, *Choices, Values, and Frames* (Cambridge, UK: Cambridge University Press, 2000); and also in Daniel Kahneman, Amos Tversky, & Paul Slovic, eds., *Judgment Under Uncertainty: Heuristics and Biases* (Cambridge, UK: Cambridge University Press, 1979).

33. See Mary C. Kern & Dolly Chugh, "Bounded Ethicality: The Perils of Loss Framing," *Psychological Science* 20 (2009), 378–384. And on other possible causes of moral error, see Lynne C. Vincent, Kyle J. Emich, & Jack A. Goncalo, "Stretching the Moral Gray Zone: Positive Affect, Moral Disengagement, and Dishonesty," *Psychological Science* 24 (2012), 595–599.

34. The simple reference to "officials" in the text may be too simple. It would be plausible to hypothesize, for example, that those who aspire to and hold elective office may well be especially deficient in decisional modesty, while those who operate in the relative job security of the civil service may, conversely, be particularly and perhaps even excessively modest about their decision-making capacities.

35. See, for example, Philip K. Howard, *The Death of Common Sense* (New York: Random House, 1992).

36. See, for example, Albert E. Mannes & Don A. Moore, "A Behavioral Demonstration of Overconfidence in Judgment," *Psychological Science* 20 (2013), 1–8, and references therein.

37. Where the objection to state protectionism tends to fall under the heading of the so-called dormant or negative commerce clause.

38. *Bacchus Imports, Ltd. v. Dias,* 468 U.S. 263 (1984).

39. See Cass R. Sunstein & Edna Ullman-Margalit, "Second-Order Decisions," *Ethics* 110 (1999), 5–31.

8. Of Carrots and Sticks

1. Most of the efforts to explain altruism in terms of self-interest are either based on evolutionary theories (for example, Richard Dawkins, *The Selfish Gene,* anniversary edition (New York: Oxford University Press, 2006)) or are located within traditional economic paradigms. See, for example, James Andreoni, "Impure Altruism and Donations to Public Goods: A Theory of Warm-Glow Giving," *Economic Journal* 100 (1990), 464–477; Georg Kirchsteiger, Luca Rigotti, & Aldo Rustichini, "Your Morals Might Be Your Moods," *Journal of Economic Behavior and Organization* 59 (2006), 155–172. See also the discussion and analysis in Neera K. Badhwar, "Altruism vs Self-Interest: Sometimes a False Dichotomy," *Social Philosophy & Policy* 10 (1993), 90–117. This book is not the place to examine the full debate about the possibility of deep altruism, in large part because the basic claims here about the nature and effect of law are unaffected by the possibility that apparent altruism is merely shallow and reflective

of deep self-interest. As long as people can engage in seemingly altruistic behavior without legal compulsion, as much of the literature noted earlier has established, the possibility that such behavior is driven by indirect self-interest is largely irrelevant to questions about the effect of law.

2. Jeremy Bentham, *Of the Limits of the Penal Branch of Jurisprudence,* Philip Schofield, ed., (Oxford: Clarendon Press, 2010) (1789), 5–6. As David Lyons explains, it is an error, at least in Bentham's case, to conflate egoism and hedonism. A person whose decisions are based on maximizing the pleasure and minimizing the pain of *others,* as Bentham urged, might well be a hedonist in terms of understanding the interests of other people but not an egoist in terms of putting his or her own interests above those of others. David Lyons, *In the Interest of the Governed: A Study in Bentham's Philosophy of Utility and Law,* rev. ed. (Oxford: Clarendon Press, 1991), 69–74. Bentham's insistence that everyone should count for one and no more than one entails, and certainly did for Bentham, that the actor's own pleasure and pain counted for no more than the pleasure and pain of anyone else.

3. Bentham, *Of the Limits of the Penal Branch of Jurisprudence,* 6, 14–15.

4. See Chapter 5 and the references there.

5. Bentham, *Of the Limits,* 59–62.

6. See William A. Fischel, "The Political Economy of Just Compensation: Lessons from the Military Draft for the Takings Issue," *Harvard Journal of Law and Public Policy* 20 (1996), 23–63.

7. Some of the relevant research is summarized in Edward R. Christopherson & Susan L. Mortweet, *Parenting that Works: Building Skills that Last a Lifetime* (Chicago: American Psychological Association, 2003), 31–45, 65–66.

8. B. F. Skinner, *Science and Human Behavior* (New York: Macmillan, 1953).

9. For a sample of the literature, see Abram Ansel, "The Role of Frustrative Nonreward in Noncontinuous Reward Structures," *Psychological Bulletin* 55 (1958), 102–119; William M. Baum, "Rethinking Reinforcement: Allocation, Induction, and Contingency," *Journal of Experimental Analysis of Behavior* 97 (2012), 101–124.

10. With respect to human beings and not rats, and where the tasks are more complex with multiple iterations, there is some experimental evidence indicating that punishment is more effective in inducing the initial move away from complete self-interest but that further cooperation thereafter is better facilitated with rewards than with additional punishment or threats thereof. James Andreoni, William Harbaugh, and Lise Vesterlund, "The Carrot or the Stick: Rewards, Punishments, and Cooperation," *American Economic Review* 93 (2003), 893–902.

11. Bentham's insistence on including nonhuman sentient creatures within the utilitarian calculus—"the question is not, Can they reason? nor Can they talk? but Can they suffer?" (*Principles of Morals and Legislation,* chapter XVII)—suggests, however, that he was not uninterested in rats or their welfare.

12. Bentham did, albeit grudgingly, acknowledge that laws backed only by rewards could still be laws, but he proposed a separate label for such laws—"an *invitative* or *praemiary* law; or it might be stiled a *legislative invitation* or a bounty"—so as not to confuse them with what he took to be the more standard type of laws supported by punishment or other negative sanctions. Bentham, *Of the Limits,* 146. See also Lyons, *In the Interest,* 134–137.

13. Bentham, *Of the Limits,* 7, note a.

14. Ibid., 142.

15. Ibid., 144, note a.

16. Ibid., 143.

17. Ibid.

18. Bentham also appeared to believe that rewards were less coercive than punishments. See H. L. A. Hart, "Legal Powers," *in* H. L. A. Hart, *Essays on Bentham: Jurisprudence and Political Theory* (Oxford: Clarendon Press, 1982), 194–219. In Bentham's world, one in which punishment was usually harsh and rewards rare, this was undoubtedly true. Whether it is still true now is a more debatable question, at least in a context in which punishments may more often be minor and so-called rewards more often essential. So when Bentham (*Of the Limits,* 144, note a) noted that "the scale of pleasure . . . is very short and limited: the scale of pain is in comparison unlimited," he likely could not have imagined a world in which a lottery winner could win nearly $600 million on a $1 ticket, nor one in which there were some prisons with no bars but with tennis courts and libraries.

19. John Austin, *The Province of Jurisprudence Determined* (Wilfrid E. Rumble ed., Cambridge, UK: Cambridge University Press, 1995) (originally published 1832), 23.

20. Ibid., 23–24.

21. Ibid.

22. W. L. Morison, John Austin (Stanford, CA: Stanford University Press, 1982), 44. See also 65–67.

23. Putting aside the decreasing marginal value of money.

24. See, for example, Andreoni et al., "The Carrot or the Stick"; David L. Dickinson, "The Carrot vs. the Stick in Work Team Motivation," *Experimental Economics* 4 (2001), 107–124; Avery Wiener Katz, "The Option Element in Contracting," *Virginia Law Review* 90 (2004), 2187–2244, *at* 2201–2202; Shmuel Leshem & Abraham Tabbach, "Solving the Volunteers's Dilemma: The Efficiency of Rewards and Punishments," *at* http://ssrn/com.abstract=2264521; Donald Wittman, "Liability for Harm or Restitution for Benefit?" *Journal of Legal Studies* 13 (1984), 57–80.

25. See Daniel Kahneman & Amos Tversky, "Prospect Theory: An Analysis of Decision under Risk," *Econometrica* 47 (1979), 263–292; Amos Tversky & Daniel Kahneman, "The Framing of Decisions and the Psychology of Choice,"

Science 211 (1981), 453–458. See also Alfie Kohn, *Punished by Rewards: The Trouble with Gold Stars, Incentive Plans, A's, Praise, and Other Bribes* (New York: Houghton Mifflin, 1993); Daniel Balliet, Laetitia B. Mulder, & Paul A. M. Van Lange, "Reward, Punishment, and Cooperation: A Meta-Analysis," *Psychological Bulletin* 137 (2011), 594–615; Laetitia B. Mulder, "The Difference between Punishment and Rewards in Fostering Moral Consensus in Social Decision Making," *Journal of Experimental Social Psychology* 44 (2008), 1436–1443; Karl Sigmund, Christoph Hauert, & Martin A. Nowak, "Reward and Punishment," *Proceedings of the National Academy of Sciences* 98 (2001), 10757–10762.

26. See Gerrit De Geest & Giuseppe Dari-Mattiacci, "The Rise of Carrots and the Decline of Sticks," *University of Chicago Law Review* 80 (2013), 341–392; Giuseppe Dari-Mattiacci & Gerrit De Geest, "Carrots, Sticks, and the Multiplication Effect," *Journal of Law, Economics, and Organization* 26 (2010), 365–384.

27. In reality, the issue is more complex than this. Once we appreciate the implications of the fact that people who do not die from smoking-related illnesses will die from something else, questions arise about whether, for example, the medical costs of smoking-related illnesses are greater or less than those of other terminal illnesses, whether the gains from cigarette taxes are greater than the taxes lost from premature death, and whether any health care costs are offset by the pension savings from people dying earlier than later. On these and related issues, the conclusions are less clear than casual observations about the costs of smoking might suggest. Compare World Health Organization, *Assessment of the Economic Costs of Smoking* (Geneva: WHO Press, 2011); and Frank A. Sloan et al., *The Price of Smoking* (Cambridge, MA: MIT Press, 2004), with Jari Tiihonen et al., "The Net Effect of Smoking on Healthcare and Welfare Costs. A Cohort Study," *BMJ Open* 2, e001678 doi:10.1136/bmjopen-2012–110678, and W. Kip Viscusi, *Smoke-Filled Rooms: A Postmortem on the Tobacco Deal* (Chicago, IL: University of Chicago Press, 2002).

28. On the use of such conditional spending to induce (or coerce) the states into prohibiting purchase or use of alcohol by anyone under the age of twenty-one, see *South Dakota v. Dole*, 483 U.S. 203 (1987).

29. For discussion of the constitutional issues, see, for example, Lynn A. Baker, "Conditional Spending after *Lopez*, *Columbia Law Review* 95 (1995), 1911–1989; Mitchell N. Berman, "Coercion without Baselines: Unconstitutional Conditions in Three Dimensions," *Georgetown Law Journal* 90 (2001), 1–112.

30. See Sarah Conly, *Against Autonomy: Justifying Coercive Paternalism* (Cambridge, UK: Cambridge University Press, 2012), 3–4.

31. That rewards are particularly ineffective in the context of prison regulations (including the requirement of not attempting to escape) should cause little surprise once we appreciate that the target population is a group disproportionately likely to make bad decisions, disproportionately likely to irrationally un-

derestimate the likelihood of apprehension and punishment, and disproportionately unlikely to perceive the value of nonimmediate rewards. Much of the research is summarized in Paul H. Robinson & John M. Darley, "Does Criminal Law Deter? A Behavioural Science Investigation," *Oxford Journal of Legal Studies* 24 (2004), 173–205.

32. From experimental economics, see Ernst Fehr & Simon Gächter, "Fairness and Retaliation: The Economics of Reciprocity," *Journal of Economic Perspectives* 14 (2000, 159–181; Theo Offerman, "Hurting Hurts More than Helping Helps," *European Economic Review* 46 (2002), 1423–1437. And from social psychology, see Roy F. Baumeister, Ellen Bratslavsly, Catrin Finkenauer, & Kathleen D. Vohs, "Bad Is Stronger than Good," *Review of General Psychology* 5 (2001), 323–370; Susan T. Fiske, "Attention and Weight in Person Perception: The Impact of Negative and Extreme Behavior," *Journal of Experimental Research in Personality* 22 (1980), 889–906; Paul Rozin & Edward B. Royzman, "Negativity Bias, Negativity Dominance, and Contagion," *Personality and Social Psychology Review* 5 (2001), 296–320.

33. Bentham, *Of the Limits,* 146.

34. Accessible explanations of the issue are in Burkhard Bilger, "Raw Faith: The Nun and the Cheese Underground," *New Yorker,* August 19, 2002, 150–162; U.S. Food and Drug Administration, "The Dangers of Raw Milk," *at* www.fda.gov/Food/ResourcesForYou/consumers/ucm07951.htm; Harry G. West, "Food Fears and Raw-Milk Cheese," *Appetite* 51 (2008), 25–29. See also Frederick Schauer, *Profiles, Probabilities, and Stereotypes* (Cambridge, MA: Harvard University Press, 2003), 278–291.

35. The device—a proprietary product called SawStop—received a safety commendation from the U.S. Consumer Product Safety Commission in July 2001, thus raising the question whether government awards—the governmental equivalent of the teacher's gold star—can provide sufficient incentives for socially beneficial behavior. In this case, despite the ability to use receipt of the award for marketing purposes, it appears otherwise. On the issue in general, see Jeff Plugis, "Consumer Safety: A Fight over Table Saws," *Bloomberg Business Weeks Magazine,* June 9, 2011, *at* www.businessweek.com/magazine/content /11_25/b423303271256.htm. Also relevant is the role of private law—tort law in particular—in enforcing and creating legal standards, a topic that will be addressed in Chapter 9. In this particular context, see *Osario v. One World Technologies, Inc.,* 716 F. Supp. 2d 155 (D. Mass. 2010), *aff'd,* 659 F.3d 81 (1st Cir. 2011), finding liability against a table saw manufacturer who had failed to install such a device on the saws it sold.

36. This is not a book on aesthetics, in no small part because the author is stunningly unqualified to write one. Nevertheless, the suggestion in the text is in the neighborhood of theories generally known as "institutionalist" and associated most prominently with George Dickie. See George Dickie, *Art and Value* (Oxford:

Blackwell, 2001); George Dickie, *The Art Culture* (New Haven, CT: Yale University Press, 1984). See also Lydia Goehr, *The Imaginary Museum of Musical Works* (Oxford: Oxford University Press, 1994); Larry Shiner, *The Invention of Art* (Chicago, IL: University of Chicago Press, 2001); Derek Matravers, "The Institutional Theory: A Protean Culture," *British Journal of Aesthetics* 40 (2000), 242–250.

37. See Ronald Dworkin, "A Reply by Ronald Dworkin," *in* Marshall Cohen, ed., *Ronald Dworkin and Contemporary Jurisprudence* (Totowa, NJ: Rowman & Littlefield, 1984), 247–300, at 259, 261–263.

38. It is appropriate here to nod in the direction of Niklas Luhmann, *Law as a Social System,* Klaus A. Zeigert, trans. (Oxford: Oxford University Press, 2004), whose understanding of law and many other social institutions was largely a sociological rather than a conceptual one. See also Hugh Baxter, "Autopoiesis and the 'Relative Autonomy' of Law," *Cardozo Law Review* 19 (1987), 1987–2090.

9. Coercion's Arsenal

1. There is a vast literature on the mechanisms of deterrence, but for present purposes all we need accept is that under conditions of both high penalty (at least relative to the potential gains from the offense) and high probably of enforcement, the deterrent aspect of law is relatively uncontroversially effective. There is, however, debate about the extent to which *low*-probability but high-penalty prohibitions are effective as deterrents. For the view that expected penalty is all or most of what matters, and that low-probability, high-penalty punishment is a roughly equivalent deterrent to high-probability, low-penalty punishment, the classic is Gary Becker, "Crime and Punishment: An Economic Analysis," *Journal of Political Economy* 76 (1968), 169–217. See also Daniel Kessler & Steven D. Levitt, "Using Sentence Enhancements to Distinguish between Deterrence and Incarceration," *Journal of Law and Economics* 42 (1999), 343–363. And for the view that sentence size has little effect on deterrence at low levels of enforcement, see Tom R. Tyler, *Why People Obey the Law,* 2d ed. (Princeton, NJ: Princeton University Press, 2006); John M. Darley, "On the Unlikely Prospect of Reducing Crime Rates by Increasing the Severity of Prison Sentences," *Journal of Law & Policy* 13 (2005), 181–247; Paul H. Robinson & John M. Darley, "Does Criminal Law Deter? A Behavioural Science Investigation," *Oxford Journal of Legal Studies* 24 (2004), 173–205.

2. See Jan C. van Oirs & Ben Vollard, "The Engine Immobilizer: A Non-Starter for Car Thieves," Tilburg Law and Economics Center (TILEC) Discussion Paper 2013–001 (January 14, 2013), *at* http://ssrn.com/abstract=2202165.

3. On force as being a form of and not distinguished from coercion, see Benjamin Sachs, "Why Coercion Is Wrong When It's Wrong," *Australasian Journal of Philosophy* 91 (2013), 63–82, *at* 63.

4. See Mitchell Berman, "The Normative Function of Coercion Claims," *Legal Theory* 8 (2002), 45–89; William A. Edmundson, "Coercion," *in* Andrei Marmor, ed., *Routledge Companion to the Philosophy of Law* (New York: Routledge, 2012), 451–466.

5. See E. Allan Farnsworth, "Coercion in Contract Law," *University of Arkansas Little Rock Law Journal* 5 (1982), 329–343.

6. See Patricia J. Falk, "Rape by Fraud and Rape by Coercion," *Brooklyn Law Review* 64 (1998), 39–180.

7. In the United States, see, for example, *Ashcraft v. Tennessee,* 322 U.S. 143 (1936); *Brown v. Mississippi,* 297 U.S. 278 (1936).

8. A valuable collection of various perspectives is Roland Pennock & John W. Chapman, eds., *Coercion: Nomos XIV* (Chicago, IL: Atherton, 1972).

9. The statement in the text is an oversimplification of the basic theme of Robert Nozick, "Coercion," *in* Sidney Morgenbesser, Patrick Suppes, & Morton White, eds., *Philosophy, Science, and Method: Essays in Honor of Ernest Nagel* (New York: St. Martin's Press, 1969), 440–472.

10. The most important defense of a moralized conception of coercion is Alan Wertheimer, *Coercion* (Princeton, NJ: Princeton University Press, 1989). See also Scott Anderson, "Coercion," *Stanford Encyclopedia of Philosophy,* at http://plato.stanford.edu/entries/coercion (2011); Martin Gunderson, "Threats and Coercion," *Canadian Journal of Philosophy* 9 (1979), 247–259; Hans Oberdiek, "The Role of Sanctions and Coercion in Understanding Law and Legal Systems," *American Journal of Jurisprudence* 21 (1976), 71–94, *at* 80–81.

11. The incompleteness of Austin's discussion of the actual nature of sanctions is discussed and partly remedied in Matthew H. Kramer, "John Austin on Punishment," University of Cambridge Legal Studies Research Paper 45/2011 (September 2011), *at* http://ssrn.com/abstract=1934750.

12. See Chapter 11.

13. P. G. Wodehouse, "The Truth about George," in *Meet Mr. Mulliner* (1927).

14. "The duty to keep a contract at common law means a prediction that you must pay damages if you do not keep it, and nothing else." Oliver Wendell Holmes Jr., "The Path of the Law," *Harvard Law Review* 10 (1897), 457–478, *at* 462.

15. This is more or less implicit in the pure economic theory of the criminal law. See Becker, "Crime and Punishment."

16. The existence of a private remedy in which victims, especially in class actions, can recoup all of their losses (as well as substantial additional payments to lawyers for the class) makes insider trading (see section 9.5) far less lucrative than it would be were the extent of exposure limited to a criminal fine of a set amount.

17. I say "almost" because there are crimes that do not fit this mold. Speeding is a crime, but it would be a mistake to think that all municipalities would prefer no speeding to much speeding and a large amount of revenue from speeding

fines. Moreover, some unlawful activities, including speeding, may have economic benefits, and thus it is not clear that the optimal amount of speeding is zero. Indeed, it may not be only speeding that can be characterized in this way. Insofar as lawful behavior is undertaken under conditions of uncertainty about whether it is or will be found unlawful, and insofar as the lawful behavior is beneficial, eliminating the unlawful behavior will eliminate some lawful and beneficial behavior. And thus setting the optimal amount of unlawful behavior is far more complex than just attempting to make it as low as possible.

18. On philosophical anarchism, including the view that there is no moral obligation to obey the law just because it is the law, see A. John Simmons, *Moral Principles and Political Obligations* (Princeton, NJ: Princeton University Press, 1979), and also Chapter 4.

19. Note the difference between discouraging and eliminating. In many domains it is not clear that the optimum level of crime is zero. Zero is almost certainly the optimal rate of murder and rape, but in other areas, excess fear of punishment may not only produce very little crime but also too little of a more beneficial activity. If the penalties for insider trading were set at the point where the level of that activity were reduced to zero, would there be too little serious research about securities or too little investment by corporate insiders in the companies for which they are responsible? If the optimal level of speeding were zero, would the rate of traffic flow be inefficiently low? When the penalties for patent or copyright infringement are too high, is there too little innovation?

20. *New York Times,* June 6, 1985, A22.

21. *New York Times,* January 6, 1997.

22. See, for example, Stephen P. Garvey, "Can Shaming Punishments Educate?," *University of Chicago Law Review* 65 (1998), 733–794; Dan M. Kahan, "What's Really Wrong with Shaming Sanctions," *Texas Law Review* 84 (2006), 2075–2095; Dan M. Kahan, "What Do Alternative Sanctions Mean?," *University of Chicago Law Review* 63 (1996), 591–653, at 630–653; David R. Karp, "The Judicial and Judicious Use of Shaming Penalties," *Crime & Delinquency* 44 (1998), 277–294; Dan Markel, "Are Shaming Punishments Beautifully Retributive? Retributivism and the Implications for the Alternative Sanctions Debate," *Vanderbilt Law Review* 54 (2001), 2157–2242; James Q. Whitman, "What Is Wrong with Inflicting Shame Sanctions?," *Yale Law Journal* 107 (1998), 1055–1092; Toni M. Massaro, "Shame, Culture, and American Criminal Law," *Michigan Law Review* 89 (1991), 1880–1944; David A. Skeel Jr., "Shaming in Corporate Law," *University of Pennsylvania Law Review* 149 (2001), 1811–1868.

23. Much of which is marvelously and gruesomely recounted in Marcus Clarke's 1836 novel *For His Natural Life.*

24. Oona Hathaway & Scott Shapiro, "Outcasting: Enforcement in Domestic and International Law," *Yale Law Journal* 121 (2011), 252–349.

25. See Roger Cotterrell, *Law's Community: Legal Ideas in Sociological Perspective* (Oxford: Clarendon Press, 1995). Leslie Green objects, claiming that the inability to distinguish those institutions that *are* law from those that are analogous to law has produced a great deal of "bad jurisprudence." Leslie Green, "The Morality in Law," Oxford Legal Studies Research Paper 12/2013 (February 24, 2013), *at* http://ssrn.com/abstract=2223760. Green attributes the problem to a puzzling inability of some theorists to grasp the difference between "counts as" and "is analogous to," but one of many more charitable readings would say that some theorists simply disagree with Green's view that law "properly so called," to use Austin's term, excludes special-purpose norm systems such as those of clubs and associations and that "regulat[ing] all kinds of things" is not an essential property of law. Moreover, once we recognize that various forms of religious law purport to regulate "all kinds of things" and that international trade law, like the WTO, is rather special purpose, Green's distinction becomes more problematic. He may yet be correct, and we will return to these issues in Chapter 11, but at the very least we ought not to accept too quickly that those who see law in various locations other than the nation-state and who see law even when it is being specialized are simply confused.

26. See note 25.

10. Awash in a Sea of Norms

1. See, for example, Michael Hechter & Karl-Dieter, eds., *Social Norms* (New York: Russell Sage, 2005); Cristina Bicchieri & Ryan Muldoon, "Social Norms," *Stanford Encyclopedia of Philosophy, at* www.plato.stanford.edu/entries/social -norms/; Jon Elster, "Social Norms and Economic Theory," *Journal of Economic Perspectives* 3 (1999), 99–117; Ernst Fehr & Urs Fischbacher, "Social Norms and Human Cooperation," *Trends in Cognitive Sciences* 8 (2004), 185–190; Elinor Ostrom, "Collective Action and the Evolution of Social Norms," *Journal of Economic Perspectives* 4 (2000), 137–158; Barak D. Richman, "Norms and Law: Putting the Horse before the Cart," *Duke Law Journal* 62 (2012), 739–766; H. Peyton Young, "Social Norms and Economic Welfare," *European Economic Review* 42 (1998), 821–830.

2. See Jon Elster, "Norms of Revenge," *Ethics* 100 (1990), 862–885.

3. See Richard McAdams, "The Origin, Development, and Regulation of Norms," *Michigan Law Review* 96 (1997), 338–433.

4. At least for legal theorists, the iconic distinction between behavioral regularities and rule-governed behavior is H. L. A. Hart, *The Concept of Law,* 3d ed., Penelope A. Bulloch, Joseph Raz, & Leslie Green, eds. (Oxford: Clarendon Press, 2012), 9–12, 55–60. Hart unfortunately jumbled together the sound distinction between habit and rule-governed behavior on the one hand and the equally sound distinction between internal and external points of view on the

other. Both distinctions are sound, but because it is possible to identify rule-governed behavior from the outside, as it were, it is a mistake to assume that the error of neglecting the internal point of view is caused by, the cause of, or even correlated with failing to adopt the internal point of view. Understanding rule-governed behavior requires appreciating that those whose behavior is rule-governed have an internal point of view regarding the rules, but this appreciation, as Joseph Raz has argued, can be identified entirely descriptively and from the outside. Joseph Raz, *The Authority of Law: Essays on Law and Morality* (Oxford: Clarendon Press, 1979), 153–157.

5. As opposed to putting on one sock and then one shoe and then the other sock and finally the second shoe. The example comes from an episode of the American television series *All in the Family*.

6. Robert Ellickson, *Order without Law: How Neighbors Settle Disputes* (Cambridge, MA: Harvard University Press, 1991).

7. Lisa Bernstein, "Private Commercial Law in the Cotton Industry: Creating Cooperation through Rules, Norms, and Institutions," *Michigan Law Review* 90 (2001), 1724–1788; Lisa Bernstein, "Merchant Law in a Merchant Court: Rethinking the Code's Search for Immanent Business Norms," *University of Pennsylvania Law Review* 144 (1996), 1765–1820; Lisa Bernstein, "Opting out of the Legal System: Extralegal Contractual Relations in the Diamond Industry," *Journal of Legal Studies* 21 (1992), 115–157. For reasons that will become apparent later in this chapter and then in Chapter 11, the cotton and diamond examples are more complex because, unlike the whaling norms and the norms of the ranchers in Shasta County, the cotton and diamond industries, as Bernstein has explained, inscribed some of their norms in canonical rule books and also developed tribunals for the resolution of disputes and the enforcement of the norms. And thus, once this degree of formality became entrenched, we might just want to call the formally enforced norm systems of the cotton and diamond industries law, albeit not the law of the political state.

8. See Dan M. Kahan, "Privatizing Criminal Law: Strategies for Private Norm Enforcement in the Inner City," *UCLA Law Review* 46 (1999), 1859–1872, *at* 1863–1864. And on the many norms of gang culture more generally, see Jeffrey Fagan, "The Social Organization of Drug Use and Drug Dealing among Urban Gangs," *Criminology* 27 (1989), 633–670.

9. See Aaron K. Perzanowski, "Tattoos and IP Norms," *Minnesota Law Review* 98 (2013), 511–591.

10. See Dotan Oliar & Christopher Sprigman, "There's No Free Laugh (Anymore): The Emergence of Intellectual Property Norms and the Transformation of Stand-up Comedy," *Virginia Law Review* 94 (2008), 1787–1867.

11. See, for example, Cristina Bicchieri, *The Grammar of Society: The Nature and Dynamics of Social Norms* (New York: Cambridge University Press, 2006); Jon Elster, *The Cement of Society: A Study of Social Order* (Cambridge, UK:

Cambridge University Press, 1989); Edna Ullman-Margalit, *The Emergence of Norms* (Oxford: Clarendon Press, 1977). And see also Eric Posner, *Law and Social Norms* (Cambridge, MA: Harvard University Press, 2000); Robert Axelrod, "An Evolutionary Approach to Norms," *American Political Science Review* 80 (1986), 1095–1011.

12. See Fehr & Fischbacher, "Social Norms"; Toshio Yamagishi, "The Provision of a Sanctioning System as a Public Good," *Journal of Personality and Social Psychology* 51 (1986), 110–116; Toshio Yamagishi, "Serious of Social Dilemmas and the Provision of a Sanctioning System," *Social Psychology Quarterly* 51 (1988), 32–42.

13. *Contra* Hobbes, it may not be necessary for the sanctions to be externally imposed, and members of cooperative groups may develop and impose their own sanctions on potential defectors in order to allow the group norms to persist. See Elinor Ostrom, James Walker, & Roy Gardner, "Covenants with and without the Sword—Self-Governance Is Possible," *American Political Science Review* 86 (1992), 404–417.

14. See *Alfred F. Beckett, Ltd. v. Lyons*, [1967] Ch. 449. 1 All. Eng.L.R. 833; *Mills v. Colchester Corp.* [1867] L.R. 2 C.P. 476; Rupert Cross, *Precedent in Engish Law*, 3d ed. (Oxford: Clarendon Press, 1977), 160; David J. Bederman, "The Curious Resurrection of Custom: Beach Access and Judicial Takings," *Columbia Law Review* 96 (1996), 1375–1455, *at* 1391–1392.

15. *Mercer v. Denne* [1904] 2 Ch. 534, *aff'd* [1905] 2 Ch. 538 (C.A.). For a more detailed description and an analysis of the larger issue of incorporation of custom into common law, see Andrew C. Loux, "The Persistence of the Ancient Regime: Custom, Utility, and the Common Law in the Nineteenth Century," *Cornell Law Review* 79 (1993), 183–218. See also David J. Bederman, *Custom as a Source of Law* (Cambridge, UK: Cambridge University Press, 2010); E. K. Braybrooke, "Custom as a Source of English Law," *Michigan Law Review* 50 (1951), 71–94; Frederick Schauer, "The Jurisprudence of Custom," *Texas Journal of International Law* 48 (2013), 523–534.

16. The category of those with great faith in the normative power of law seems disproportionately occupied by lawyers, judges, law professors, and law students. But perhaps we should not be surprised, no more than we are surprised by the commitment of Texans and Saudis to the economic and security importance of oil exploration and drilling.

17. An important recent analysis and overview of the relationship between law and attitudinal (and behavioral) change is Kenworthey Bilz & Janice Nadler, "Law, Moral Attitudes, and Behavioral Change," *in* Eyal Zamir & Doron Teichman, eds., *Oxford Handbook of Behavioral Economics and the Law* (New York: Oxford University Press, forthcoming 2014). See also Dan M. Kahan, "Social Influence, Social Meaning, and Deterrence," *Virginia Law Review* 83 (1997), 349–395.

18. See Lior Jacob Strahilevitz, "How Changes in Property Regimes Influence Social Norms: Commodifying California's Carpool Lanes," *Indiana Law Journal* 75 (2000), 1232–1294, *at* 1232–1234, 1984–1290.

19. See Lawerence Lessig, "The Regulation of Social Meaning," *University of Chicago Law Review* 62 (1995), 943–1045, *at* 1029. On social norms and smoking, see Edna Ullman-Margalit, "Revision of Norms," *Ethics* 100 (1990), 756–767.

20. See Matthew Iglesias, "Buenos Aires' Dog Poo Problem," *Slate*, October 15, 2012, *at* www.slate.com/blogs/moneybox/2012/10/15/buenos_aires_dog_doo _Argentina's_capital_has_a_lot_of_pet_excrement.html.

21. That is, assuming they are morally inclined but are not always aware of the specific behavior that will trigger their extant moral inclinations. On the distinction between genuine reasons and the facts that will trigger already present genuine reasons—triggering reasons—see David Enoch, "Reason-Giving and the Law," *in* Leslie Green & Brian Leiter, eds., *Oxford Studies in the Philosophy of Law,* vol. 1 (Oxford: Oxford University Press, 2011), 1–38.

22. Ibid.

23. The important distinction between indicative and intrinsic reasons is introduced and developed in Donald H. Regan, "Law's Halo," *in* Jules Coleman & Ellen Frankel Paul, eds., *Philosophy and Law* (Oxford: Basil Blackwell, 1987), 15–30; Donald H. Regan, "Authority and Value: Reflections on Raz's *Morality of Freedom*," *Southern California Law Review* 62 (1989), 995–1095; and, in greatest depth, Donald H. Regan, "Reasons, Authority, and the Meaning of 'Obey': Further Thoughts on Raz and Obedience to Law," *Canadian Journal of Law and Jurisprudence* 3 (1990), 3–28.

24. See *Cooper v. Aaron*, 358 U.S. 1 (1958).

25. The causal effect of the law, or the causal effect of the highly salient U.S. Supreme Court decision in *Brown v. Board of Education*, 347 U.S. 483 (1954), on racial attitudes is widely assumed, but an influential challenge to the conventional wisdom is Gerald N. Rosenberg, *The Hollow Hope: Can Courts Bring About Social Change?* (Chicago, IL: University of Chicago Press, 1991).

26. The classics include Leon Festinger & James M. Carlsmith, "Cognitive Consequences of Forced Compliance," *Journal of Abnormal & Social Psychology* 58 (1959), 203–210; and Herbert C. Kelman, "Attitude Change as a Function of Response Restriction," *Human Relations* 6 (1953), 185–214. A good summary of subsequent psychological research is in Travis Proulx, Michael Inzlicht, & Eddie Harmon-Jones, "Understanding All Inconsistency Accommodation as a Palliative Response to Violated Expectations," *Trends in Cognitive Sciences* 16 (2012), 285–291. A contemporary application to legal and policy issues is Ann P. Kinzig et al., "Social Norms and Global Environmental Challenges: The Complex Interaction of Behaviors, Values, and Policy," *BioScience* 63 (2013), 164–175. And the relationship between social norms and sanctions is valuably analyzed in Cédric Paternotte & Jonathan Grose, "Social Norms

and Game Theory: Harmony or Discord,?" *British Journal of the Philosophy of Science*, 64 (2013), 551–587, especially 564–566.

27. Typical is this undocumented assertion: "[M]ost people tend to regard the law as having moral force, rather than solely as a cost that they must take into account in weighing the benefits and disadvantages of alternative courses of action. . . ." Milton C. Regan Jr., "How Does Law Matter?," *The Green Bag 2d*, vol. 1 (1998), 265–275.

28. The possibility that law provides nonprudential but still not moral reasons provided by the law underlies the claims of those who believe in law's so-called normativity and are at pains to try to explain it. See, for example, Jules Coleman, *The Practice of Principle: In Defence of a Pragmatist Approach to Legal Theory* (New York: Oxford University Press, 2003), chapter 7; Scott J. Shapiro, *Legality* (Cambridge, MA: Harvard University Press, 2011), 181–188; Andrei Marmor, "The Nature of Law," *The Stanford Encyclopedia of Philosophy*, at http://plato.stanford.edu/archives/fall2008/entrues/law phil-nature/ (2008); Gerald J. Postema, "Coordination and Convention at the Foundation of Law," *Journal of Legal Studies* 11 (1982), 165–203, *at* 165. Not everyone agrees that law's normativity is a problem, however, with some theorists subscribing instead to the view that whatever prudence-independent or sanction-independent normative power law *qua* law has is solely a function of the existence (or not) of a moral reason to obey the law just because it is the law. See Enoch, "Reason-Giving"; Frederick Schauer, "Positivism Through Thick and Thin," *in* Brian Bix, ed., *Analyzing Law: New Essays in Legal Theory* (New York: Oxford University Press, 1998), 65–78; Torben Spaak, "Legal Positivism, Law's Normativity, and the Normative Force of Legal Justification," *Ratio Juris* 16 (2003), 469–485.

29. H. L. A. Hart, *The Concept of Law*, 3d ed., Penelope A. Bulloch, Leslie Green, & Joseph Raz, eds. (Oxford: Clarendon Press, 2012), 40, discussed at length in Chapter 4.

30. Ellickson, *Order without Law*, 177; Lewis A. Kornhauser, "Are There Cracks in the Foundations of Spontaneous Order?," *N. Y. U. Law Review* 67 (1992), 647–673, *at* 652; Carol M. Rose, "The Several Futures of Property: Of Cyberspace and Folk Tales, Emission Trades and Ecosystems," *Minnesota Law Review* 83 (1998), 129–182, *at* 157.

31. John Stuart Mill, *On Liberty* (London: John W. Parker and Son, 1859).

32. Merchants who significantly cut their prices in order to gain an advantage over their competitors, for example, are far more likely to be condemned by their fellow merchants than lauded, suggesting that the norm in some classes of merchants may be a norm of soft price-fixing rather than a norm condemning the practice.

33. Which is, to repeat a running theme of this book, not the same as there being a moral reason to obey the law requiring the payment of taxes. This correct distinction is rarely explicitly noted in the literature on tax compliance, but

it is occasionally implicit, as in Yair Listokin & David M. Schizer, "I Like to Pay Taxes: Taxpayer Support for Government Spending and the Efficiency of the Tax System," *Tax Law Review* 66 (2013), 179–216, *at* 179.

34. See Joshua D. Blank & Daniel Z. Levin, "When Is Tax Enforcement Publicized?," *Virginia Tax Review* 30 (2010), 1–37.

35. Hart, *The Concept of Law,* 55–61, 79–91.

36. On whether and how such a norm might be inculcated, see Ian MacMullen, "Educating Children to Comply with Laws," *Journal of Political Philosophy* 21 (2013), 106–124.

37. Henry David Thoreau, "On the Duty of Civil Disobedience," in *Walden and "Civil Disobedience"* (New York: Signet, 1980) (1849), 228.

38. Nor, of course, are the pedestrians of Manhattan or Harvard Square, who may represent the opposite extreme.

11. The Differentiation of Law

1. And so it is, too, these days with online legal and nonlegal databases.

2. On the view that an account of law must explain how law can make a practical difference in our deliberations, see Jules L. Coleman, "Incorporationism, Conventionality, and the Practical Difference Thesis," *Legal Theory* 4 (1998), 381–425, *at* 383; Scott J. Shapiro, "Law, Morality, and the Guidance of Conduct," *Legal Theory* 6 (2000), 127–170.

3. There are many reasons to distinguish the law from the legal system, but one of the most important is that legal decision makers, paradigmatically judges, are plainly part of the legal system but equally plainly draw on inputs (the rules of grammar, the meaning of nontechnical terms, and the principles of arithmetic, for example) that are not themselves law. How much of what judges and other legal actors use in reaching decisions should be considered as law remains contested. Hans Kelsen insisted that "every law-applying act is only partly determined by law." (Hans Kelsen, *Pure Theory of Law,* 2d ed., Max Knight, trans. (Berkeley, CA: University of California Press, 1967). And to much the same effect, Joseph Raz has distinguished law from the legal reasoning of lawyers and judges, maintaining that the latter does and must inevitably draw on a large number of nonlegal inputs, including but not limited to morality. Joseph Raz, "Postema on Law's Authority and Public Practical Reason: A Critical Comment," in *Between Authority and Interpretation: On the Theory of Law and Practical Reason* (Oxford: Oxford University Press, 2009), 373–396. By contrast, Ronald Dworkin implicitly adopts a capacious conception of law that understands most of what judges do and use as law. Ronald Dworkin, *Justice in Robes* (Cambridge, MA: Harvard University Press, 2008); Ronald Dworkin, *Law's Empire* (Cambridge, MA: Harvard University Press, 1986); Ronald Dworkin, *Taking Rights Seriously* (London: Duckworth, 1977). (In this respect,

Dworkin's understanding of law as being largely dependent on what lawyers and judges do and use is similar to institutional theories of art that define "art" largely in terms of what artists and other members of the institutional art culture take to be art. See George Dickie, *The Art Circle: A Theory of Art* (New Haven, CT: Yale University Press, 1984). See also Stephen Davies, *Definitions of Art* (Ithaca, NY: Cornell University Press, 1991), 78–114.) And still others believe that law is nothing other than the social decision as to what judges may and may not use, thus allowing both very broad and very narrow conceptions of the legitimate inputs into legal arguments and decisions to count as law. W. J. Waluchow, *Inclusive Legal Positivism* (Oxford: Clarendon Press, 1994); Coleman, "Incorporationism"; Kenneth Einar Himma, "Inclusive Legal Positivism," *in* Jules L. Coleman & Scott J. Shapiro, *Oxford Handbook of Jurisprudence and Philosophy of Law* (New York: Oxford University Press, 2002), 125–165. The debates among those who hold these positions have been carried on for decades, with no clear view about their victor or even about their value, but for present purposes all we need accept is the crude notion that there is at least some difference between the idea of law and the full set of rules, actors, and institutions that together comprise the legal system.

4. Niklas Luhmann, *The Differentiation of Society,* Stephen Holmes & Charles Larmore, trans. (New York: Columbia University Press, 1984). On the differentiation of law in particular, see Niklas Luhmann, *Law as a Social System,* Klaus Ziegert, trans., Fatima Kastner & Richard Nobles, eds. (New York: Oxford University Press, 2008); Niklas Luhmann, *A Sociological Theory of Law,* Martin Albrow & Elizabeth King-Utz, trans. (London: Routledge & Kegan Paul, 1985); Niklas Luhmann, *Ausdifferenzierung des Rechts: Beiträge zur Rechtssoziologie und Rechtstheorie* (Frankfurt am Main: Suhrkamp Verlag, 1981).

5. The technical term for this phenomenon of progressively increasing differentiation, and a term adapted from biology, is, at least for Luhmann and his followers, *autopoiesis.* See Gunther Teubner, *Autopoietic Law: A New Approach to Law and Society* (Berlin: Walter de Gruyter, 1988).

6. On the way in which, especially in the United States, important and policy-consequential scientific debates are resolved through a litigation process in which the principal advocates are not themselves scientists, see Sheila Jasanoff, *Science at the Bar: Law, Science and Technology in America* (Cambridge, MA: Harvard University Press, 1997).

7. *Prohibitions del Roy* (1607) 12 Co. Rep. 63. See also Edward Coke, *The First Part of the Institutes of the Laws of England; or A Commentary upon Littleton,* Charles Butler, ed. (London: E. Brooke, 1809) (1628). For commentary, see, for example, Jerome Bickenbach, "The 'Artificial Reason' of the Law," *Informal Logic* 12 (1990), 23–32; Charles Fried, "The Artificial Reason of the Law or: What Lawyers Know," *Texas Law Review* 60 (1981), 35–58; John Underwood Lewis, "Sir Edward Coke (1552–1633): His Theory of 'Artificial

Reason' as a Context for Modern Basic Legal Theory," *Law Quarterly Review* 84 (1968), 330–342.

8. See Gerald J. Postema, *Bentham and the Common Law Tradition* (Oxford: Clarendon Press, 1986), 4–13, 19–27; Anthony J. Sebok, *Legal Positivism in American Jurisprudence* (New York: Cambridge University Press, 1998), 23–32.

9. See Frederick Schauer, *Thinking Like a Lawyer: A New Introduction to Legal Reasoning* (Cambridge, MA: Harvard University Press, 2009).

10. Challenges to the claims about the distinct, or even the somewhat differentiated, nature of legal reasoning have come from different quarters, including some of the Legal Realists (see, for example, Jerome Frank, "Are Judges Human? Part One: The Effect on Legal Thinking of the Assumption that Judges Behave Like Human Beings," *University of Pennsylvania Law Review* 80 (1931), 17–53); some branches of the Critical Legal Studies movement (see, for example, Roberto Mangabeira Unger, *The Critical Legal Studies Movement* (Cambridge, MA: Harvard University Press, 1983)); and some scholars with quite different jurisprudential commitments (for example, Larry Alexander & Emily Sherwin, *Demystifying Legal Reasoning* (New York: Cambridge University Press, 2008)).

11. Thus, Leslie Green, in describing the views of Joseph Raz, has observed that "[t]he law begins and ends with the *sources*—the statutes, cases, and conventions, insofar as their existence and content can be ascertained by reference to matters of social fact. . . ." Leslie Green, "Three Themes from Raz," *Oxford Journal of Legal Studies* 25 (2005), 503–523, at 504.

12. John Gardner, "Legal Positivism: 5½ Myths," *American Journal of Jurisprudence* 46 (2001), 199–227, at 199.

13. An emphasis on authority is explaining the nature of law is most strongly associated these days with the writings of Joseph Raz. See, for example, Joseph Raz, *Between Authority and Interpretation: On the Theory of Law and Practical Reason* (Oxford: Oxford University Press, 2009); Joseph Raz, *Ethics in the Public Domain: Essays in the Morality of Law and Politics* (Oxford: Oxford University Press, 1994); Joseph Raz, *Practical Reason and Norms*, 2d ed. (Oxford: Oxford University Press, 1999); Joseph Raz, *The Authority of Law: Essays in Law and Morality* (Oxford: Clarendon Press, 1979). Obviously there is much in this book that takes issue with Raz's methodological commitment to locating the properties that law necessarily possesses, and with the implications of Raz's restriction of jurisprudential inquiry to such essential properties, but these disagreements are not inconsistent with recognizing the special importance of authority to law and legal decision making, nor with acknowledging Raz's singular role in helping us to understand it.

14. See Scott Hershovitz, "The Authority of Law," *in* Andrei Marmor, *The Routledge Companion to Philosophy of Law* (New York: Routledge, 2012), 65–75; Scott Hershovitz, "The Role of Authority," *Philosopher's Imprint, at* www.philosophersimprint.org/011007 (March 2011); Frederick Schauer, "Au-

thority and Authorities," *Virginia Law Review* 95 (2008), 1931–1961; Scott J. Shapiro, "Authority," *in* Coleman & Shapiro, *Oxford Handbook*, 382–439.

15. See Frederick Schauer, "The Limited Domain of the Law," *Virginia Law Review* 90 (2004), 1909–1956. The degree to which the domain is limited—the extent to which sources otherwise usable in nonlegal decision making environments are not usable in law—is not only a matter of degree but is also subject to change over time. See Frederick Schauer & Virginia J. Wise, "Non-Legal Information and the Delegalization of Law," *Journal of Legal Studies* 29 (2000), 495–515.

16. One way of understanding Ronald Dworkin's influential challenge to Hart and to the modern legal positivist tradition is to see Dworkin as denying that judicial decision making is or can be restricted to a limited domain of sources identifiable by a rule of recognition. Ronald Dworkin, *Law's Empire* (Cambridge, MA: Harvard University Press, 1986); Ronald Dworkin, *Taking Rights Seriously* (London: Duckworth, 1977). For elaboration of this understanding of Dworkin, see Schauer, "The Limited Domain"; Frederick Schauer, "Constitutional Invocations," *Fordham Law Review* 47 (1997), 1295–1312.

17. H. L. A. Hart, *The Concept of Law*, 3d ed., Penelope A. Bulloch, Joseph Raz, and Leslie Green, eds., (Oxford: Clarendon Press, 2012), 6.

18. Ibid., 7, 82.

19. H. L. A. Hart, "Positivism and the Separation of Law and Morals," *Harvard Law Review* 71 (1958), 593–629, *at* 603.

20. Ibid., 6.

21. See Leslie Green, "The Morality in Law," Oxford Legal Studies Research Paper 12/2013, *at* https://paper.ssrn.com/sol3/papers.cfm?abstract-id+2223760.

22. Indeed, we can say much the same thing about the organizations that are branded these days as "terrorist." Even if we steer well clear of controversies over which organizations deserve the obviously pejorative label and which do not, it is plain that many terrorist organizations are complexly organized and highly rational and sophisticated in their decision making. See Jessica Stern, *Terror in the Name of God: Why Religious Militants Kill* (New York: HarperCollins, 2003). And thus we should not be surprised by the discovery that many terrorist organizations have primary and secondary rules, rules of recognition, and the internalization of an ultimate rule of recognition by leaders and followers alike.

23. Linguistic usage is curious here. We refer to "WTO law," "EU law," "canon law," and "tribal law," but only to the "rules" that govern the Marylebone Cricket Club and the employees of General Motors. Is it because in ordinary usage the word "law" is reserved for rules that are not only canonically inscribed but also exist within organizations purporting to exercise comprehensive and not limited jurisdiction? The Marylebone Cricket Club does not claim the power to regulate all aspects of the lives of its members, but the Seneca Nation, lying entirely

within the borders of the United States, does, and so too does the Catholic Church. But the WTO claims nothing of the kind, and we are left with the puzzle of just what kinds of claims and what kinds of connections with the nation-state are necessary for people to attach the word "law" to some but not all of the organizations that have primary and secondary rules, rules of recognition, and just the kind of internalization of the ultimate rule of recognition that for Hart was the most important determinant of the existence of law.

24. I put aside the occasionally important issues of extraterritorial jurisdiction, issues that may arise when a nation-state seeks to regulate the activities of its citizens abroad, or seeks to regulate activities of its own citizens (or its own corporations and associations) in ways that implicate and possibly tread on the laws of other nation-states.

25. John Austin, *The Province of Jurisprudence Determined*, Wilfrid E. Rumble, ed. (Cambridge, UK: Cambridge University Press, 1995) (1832), 164–293.

26. The frequent physical violence of hockey, and the tolerated presence of fighting within North American professional hockey, present interesting and related jurisprudential issues. The hockey player who punches another player may be penalized with a term in the penalty box, but the hockey player who punches another player five times and then kicks him when he is down may be penalized with a term in the Kingston Penitentiary. In this sense hockey's legal system is not entirely self-contained, and the intersection between the laws of hockey and the laws of the Province of Ontario presents a complex question going to the heart of many important question of legal theory.

27. Max Weber, "Politics as a Vocation" (1919), *in* H. H. Gerth & C. Wright Mills, eds., *From Max Weber: Essays in Sociology* (New York: Oxford University Press, 1946), 77–128. To the same effect, see John Rawls, *Political Liberalism* (New York: Columbia University Press, 1993), 136: "[Political] power is always coercive power backed up by the government's use of sanctions, for government alone has the authority to use force in upholding its laws."

28. Compare Brian Leiter, "The Demarcation Problem in Jurisprudence: A New Case for Skepticism," *Oxford Journal of Legal Studies* 32 (2011), 1–15. I am in agreement with Leiter about the impossibility of demarcation of law, but nevertheless believe that he moves far too quickly from the premise of the impossibility of demarcation to what seems to me to be a skeptical conclusion about the possibility of nondemarcating differentiation.

29. Bertrand Russell, "Vagueness," *Australasian Journal of Philosophy* 1 (1923), 84–92.

30. Arthur Ripstein wrestles with the same problem of differentiating between law and various other institutions—the Canadian Chess Federation is one of his examples—that appear to have primary and secondary rules, claims of authority over their members, and the power to enforce their rules in some way or another. For Ripstein, the key to differentiating law is in law's self-certifying nature and

the fact that law can use force to enforce its edicts without securing the permission of another body. Arthur Ripstein, "Self-Certification and the Moral Aims of the Law," *Canadian Journal of Law and Jurisprudence* 25 (2012), 201–217. Ripstein's analysis is perceptive, but it may be more Austinian than he cares to admit, insofar as the line between the power of self-certification and what Austin calls "sovereignty" is elusive. Moreover, Ripstein's efforts to distinguish a condominium board's power to use force to enforce its authority and an American state's power to do the same thing, given that both are subordinate to national authority, in terms of presumption of authority seems strained. Although American states may be presumed to have physical enforcement power absent an affirmative act of withdrawal by the federal government, the presumptions are different in systems less constitutionally federalized than the United States. More particularly, it may be that some subordinate institutions have pretentions of lawful comprehensive authority—the *departments* of France, for example—even though their relationship with national authority is such that there is far less of a presumption of enforcement authority.

31. Scott J. Shapiro, *Legality* (Cambridge, MA: Harvard University Press, 2011), 169–175.

32. See, as part of a large literature, Nigel Harvey, "Confidence in Judgment," *Trends in Cognitive Sciences*, vol. 1 (1997), 78–82; Pascal Mamassian, "Overconfidence in an Objective Anticipatory Motor Task," *Psychological Science* 19 (2008), 601–606; Albert E. Mannes & Don A. Moore, "A Behavioral Demonstration of Overconfidence in Judgment," *Psychological Science* 20 (2013), 1–8; Don A. Moore & Paul J. Healy, "The Trouble with Overconfidence," *Psychological Review* 115 (2008), 502–517. And for an important application of this basic idea to many pervasive aspects of modern life and modern policy, see Sarah Conly, *Against Autonomy: Justifying Coercive Paternalism* (Cambridge, UK: Cambridge University Press, 2012).

33. Indeed, for all of his incessantly favorable views about law, Lon Fuller remains one of the most important theorists of the idea that the nature of legal decision making is suited to some social tasks but not to others. Lon L. Fuller and Kenneth I. Winston, "The Forms and Limits of Adjudication," *Harvard Law Review* 92 (1978), 353–409.

INDEX

Simmons, A. John, 196n. 35
Skinner, B.F., 111
Social norms. *See* Norms
Socrates, 6, 55, 64, 196n. 28
Sovereignty, 77–78, 163, 206nn.4, 5
Spaak, Torben, 174n. 16, 188n. 41
Stephen, James Fitzjames, 10
Subsidies, 115–116
Suits, Bernard, 38, 172n. 10, 190n. 53
Summers, Robert 179n. 17

Thoreau, Henry David, 70, 152
Threats, 124–125
Tyler, Tom, 57–61, 63–64, 67, 73, 97

Ullman-Margalit, Edna, 81

Weber, Max, 22, 164
Wertheimer, Alan, 221n. 10
Wittgenstein, Ludwig, 38, 172n. 10
Wodehouse, P.G., 130